Praise for

A Midwife in Amish Country

"*A Midwife in Amish Country* is a moving book about accepting and growing into one's calling, including the highs and lows of homebirth midwifery and lots of terrific birth stories! Kim Osterholzer is an engaging writer, inviting the reader to follow her through her years of apprenticeship serving women and families as they bring new life into the world."

> —Rahima Baldwin Dancy, author of *Special Delivery*, childbirth activist, and midwife (retired)

"*A Midwife in Amish Country* is a captivating read. Kim Woodard Osterholzer keeps us spellbound with the intimate beauty and earthy tenderness of midwifery among the Amish, taking us where we've never been before and immersing us in the most sacred of moments."

> —Cindy Lambert, coauthor of *One Light Still Shines*

"Kim Osterholzer gives us a rare glimpse into the heart of the Amish community. Beautifully written. *A Midwife in Amish Country* is destined to become a classic for midwives and those who aspire to be."

> —Serena B. Miller, award-winning author of *More Than Happy: The Wisdom of Amish Parenting*, serenabmiller.com

"The beauty of midwifery care is that it serves 'Motherbaby' in all circumstances and belief systems. In *A Midwife in Amish Country*, Kim Osterholzer has written her story of becoming. May it inspire midwives of every persuasion to follow their calling as it comes from the core of who they are, because truly this is the key to competent service."

> —Elizabeth Davis, CPM, Co-Director of National Midwifery Institute, Inc., author of *Heart & Hands: A Midwife's Guide to Pregnancy and Birth*, and the international bestseller, *Orgasmic Birth: Your Guide to a Safe, Satisfying, and Pleasurable Birth Experience*, elizabethdavis.com

"With breathtaking beauty, Kim Osterholzer shares her journey into the heart of God and the homes of Amish families giving birth in *A Midwife in Amish Country*. Real-life insight into Amish homes gives this book a descriptive appeal to anyone wanting to learn more about an Amish community. Kim's personal journey weaves through her stories, bringing the love and redemption of Christ to each person reading these pages. You will be richer for walking through this journey with Kim!"

—Sara Daigle, author of *Women of Purpose* and *Dare to Love Your Husband Well*

"As a professional caring for women who wish to make a safe return to fitness, I am thrilled to know a midwife like Kim Osterholzer exists and is passionately working to minimize trauma on the frontlines of birth. These stories, these chapters full of encouragement, give me hope and inspire me to continue the work I do. I wish every midwife and fitness pro would get their hands on *A Midwife in Amish Country* and read it!"

—Beth Learn, founder of Fit2b.com

"*A Midwife in Amish Country* is a tale for hopeful teenage girls, for nostalgic menopausal women, for child-bearing and child-rearing mothers. It's a book of life—its first breath, its seasons, from its ordinary to its heart-stopping moments, and its endings. In it, Kim Osterholzer tells of the midwife's creed—to keep out of the way and let women and their families tend to the work of bringing forth new life. But she tells us, too, about her own life as one of these invisible helpers—her dreams of becoming a full-fledged midwife, free of the annoying and inconvenient tendency to nausea at the business of birthing, her fears of hurting a client through ineptness, her own sense of inadequacy for the many roles of her life and of her increasing dependence on the Creator of life. We follow her through her young romance, marriage, the homebirths of her own children, ministry to the church youth group; all the while we come along as she catches babies in a midwifery apprenticeship she describes is much like the birth experience itself—a refining fire."

—Eleanor Bertin, author of the novel *Lifelines*, and *Pall of Silence*, a memoir

"As you read *A Midwife in Amish Country*, you'll find you're not just observing the story, but participating. Kim Osterholzer draws you in through her vivid descriptions of the surroundings and her heart, and she shares her story in a powerfully vulnerable way—mothers find strength, babies are delivered, and she finds joy in the reality that she was born for this! Come along to experience the inspiration of new birth in Kim, her clients, and yourself!"

—Marie Monville, author of *One Light Still Shines*

A Midwife in Amish Country

a MIDWIFE *in* AMISH COUNTRY

CELEBRATING GOD'S GIFT OF LIFE

Kim Woodard Osterholzer

SALEM
BOOKS

Salem Books™ is a trademark of Salem Communications Holding Corporation

Regnery® is a registered trademark of Salem Communications Holding Corporation

Cataloging-in-Publication data on file with the Library of Congress

ISBN 978-1-62157-727-0
e-book ISBN 978-1-62157-755-3

Published in the United States by
Salem Books
An imprint of Regnery Publishing
A Division of Salem Media Group
300 New Jersey Ave NW
Washington, DC 20001
www.SalemBooks.com

Manufactured in the United States of America

10 9 8 7 6 5 4 3 2 1

Books are available in quantity for promotional or premium use. For information on discounts and terms, please visit our website: www.Regnery.com.

To Jesus Christ, the Reason and the Way I do everything.
"...Christ in (me) the Hope of Glory" (Colossians 1:27)
"...All things are possible with God." (Mark 10:27)

To my two husbands,
the late Brent Woodard and Steven Osterholzer.
To Brent, for encouraging me continually to become a midwife.
To Steven, for continually encouraging me to write this book.

To Hannah Simmons and Paul Woodard, my children.
Wasn't that one heck of a trip?
Thanks for hanging on for the ride.
There's no one like you two in all the world.

To Evangeline, Brent, and Elyse, my grandchildren,
and to the grandchildren yet to be born.
I love you more than I can hope to say.

CONTENTS

"I wanted to become a midwife because I AM a midwife."
—Clara Nolan, Granny Midwife, Mississippi, in Carla Hartley,
Helping Hands: The Apprentice Workbook

Chapter

ONE

THERE IT IS! OH, GOD, THANK YOU.

I found the stone farmhouse easily enough. It was the only one along that isolated stretch of gravel.

But it was the isolated stretch of gravel I had troubling finding in the gloom of the rain-splattered night. My nerves and stomach were coiled into a knot so tight I found it hard to think clearly, and then, just as I reached the intersection of what I thought ought to be Hacker and M-66, a semi-truck roared past me, rocking my minivan like a rowboat on rough waters and sending a spray of mud across my windshield, obliterating my view of the minuscule green sign marking the corner.

The paper scrap with scribbled directions I'd crushed against the steering wheel fluttered to the floor as I skimmed through the intersection, and my already-quickened pulse surged in my chest and thundered into my head.

Ah! Gosh! I know that's it. I gotta go back! But what if it isn't? Oh, Lord! Oh, Lord God! What am I doing out here? Please help me! Please help me get there! Please help me get there and please help me do a good job and please, please help me not faint or throw up!

I swung the vehicle around and roared back. I slowed when I approached the intersection again, squinting past the swish of wiper blades to read the sign.

Who makes these things so tiny? Hacker! Yes!

I skittered around the corner, then crunched and rumbled along the washboard of sandy dirt as rapidly as I felt I safely could.

I shrugged my shoulders, shook my head, and relaxed my grip on the steering wheel a mite, taking a measure of comfort in the fact I found the laboring mother's road, though only a very little comfort. The evening's foray into solo practice was thrust on me of a sudden. I'd attended but one birth alone through my nine years catching babies and I was still twenty-nine days from taking my midwifery examination.

The outline of a house rose from the darkness and sea of wet, windswept fields, interrupting the train of my thoughts. My heart tripled its pace, but as I rolled into the driveway, the four sturdy feet of a rusting windmill standing before the weather-beaten, whitewashed barn and long, low row of rickety fencing illumined by the sweeping fan of my headlights helped to smooth the disheveled edges of my soul. The place was new to me, but the landscape was as familiar as home, looking, as it did, like most Amish farms, like my own grandfather's farm—even like my lifetime.

I released the breath I'd been holding and glanced toward the house. The glimmering light beckoning to me from the borders of a window shade further eased my anxious spirit.

I climbed from the warmth of my van into an icy breeze laced with raindrops, gathered my bags, and picked my way among the puddles scattered between me and the front door.

I let myself into a narrow mudroom and my nostrils filled with the pungent crosshatching of odors singular to Amish entryways. The aroma of rich soil and that which springs from the soil. A whiff of grease, oils, and well-worn leather. The tang of harsh soaps. The musk of workhorse flanks, of udders bulging with warm milk, of guard dogs, of barn cats. The acridity of hens and the funk of swine. Scents that cling to boots and coats, fraying straw hats and bonnets lining the wall. Smells rubbed into the very floorboards and windowpanes and doorjambs of the room by generations of folk who'd spent their lives close to earth.

I tapped lightly at the kitchen door, but turned its knob without waiting for a response. Midwives never wait before the doors of the laboring.

"Hello?" I said, and I stepped inside.

Three smiles shone in the mellow light of an oil lamp as I squeezed myself into the room and, at once, I had work-worn hands moving to ease my bags from my shoulders and a rivulet of *Deutsch*-seasoned talk filling my ears.

"Come on in! Glad you're here! Thank you much for coming! How was the drive? How were the roads? Had you any trouble finding the place?"

Before I could even think to answer, a burly young man extended a massive hand my way. "David Ray," he said with a nod of his head. The hearty pump I received nearly yanked me from my feet. Once up, once down. *Pow*. One hundred percent Amish farm boy.

Two women followed David. They looked enough alike to be sisters. A set of plump figures clad in dark, unadorned dresses fastened up at the bodice with straight pins, two graying heads capped in white, four thick hands wrapped in blue veins, four mildly swollen ankles disappearing into blocky black shoes.

But one wore a pair of wire-rimmed spectacles and the other did not. "Elizabeth, Ruthann's mother," said the wearer of the spectacles as I received another solid pump of my hand. "My, but your little hand is so cold!"

"And I'm David Ray's mother," said the last woman with a smile and a pump. "Nora."

As I shed my coat and slipped off my boots, Nora and I realized we'd already met. Nine summertimes before, in the first year of my apprenticeship, I helped Jean Balm, Nora's midwife and my preceptor, care for her through her last pregnancy. The realization seemed to mollify the two mothers a bit, especially as Nora recalled that I, too, was pregnant then. They began to inquire after my family as I bent to fish my Doppler and blood pressure cuff from the depths of my bag, but stopped short when a soft moan reminded us why I was there.

I glanced at my wristwatch and straightened. "Now then, where's Ruthann?"

The three ushered me into the shadows of the next room where I could just make out a figure curled on a sofa. I knelt beside her. David settled himself at her feet.

"Hello, Ruthann."

The woman's hand found and squeezed my forearm in answer to my whispered greeting, but she drew in a long, deep breath in lieu of making a response.

I kept still as she breathed her way through a ferocious contraction. The fingers on my arm tightened, tightened, tightened, and then relaxed as she exhaled.

"Hello, Kim. Thank you for coming." I could feel the smile in her voice.

I paused. Would I ever cease to be surprised by the strength of these women, gracious and gentle and grateful, even in the throes of their labors?

I smiled, too. "How's it going? That contraction sounded good."

"I hope good! The pains have been comin' pretty regular since I called, and getting hard. I wanted to get into the bath once for some relief, but *Mamm* said I oughtn't till you said it'd be alright."

"Okay, good! Yes, you can get in the tub, I think. But may I listen quick to your baby first? I'd like to get your blood pressure, too."

"Oh, yes."

I glanced toward the figures silhouetted in the doorway. "Will one of you get a light for me, please? And will the other draw the bath?"

The ladies retreated in a murmur of voices. A moment later, the sound of running water issued from the bathroom, and Elizabeth returned to us with the lamp in hand. Its light danced across the twin surfaces of her eyeglasses and set her *kapp* aglow as the shadows streaked behind her.

Ruthann drew in another lungful of air and her fingers tightened again on my arm.

I could see her now. She was young and slender, all arms, legs, and belly sheathed in a hand-stitched nightgown with a headful of dark hair bound into a scarf she'd knotted beneath her chin. She covered her face with her free hand and she blew and breathed and writhed slightly as her womb again squeezed her in its muscular grasp.

Sixty-four seconds ticked by. She sighed and relaxed.

"Good, Ruthann. So good. May I listen to your baby now?"

Her black-brown eyes fluttered open, found mine and blinked, then she blushed and fumbled to expose the vast surface that was once her waist.

A ping of sympathy pricked my heart.

She's shy and, of course, I've embarrassed her. Poor thing. Here, after having grown accustomed to Jean, she has to have someone new.

Amish girls were always dreadfully shy—shy almost to the point of shame when it came to their bodies. I glanced away to squirt a dollop of gel onto the Doppler probe, wishing for a way to ease her anxieties—to tell her I was safe, to assure her I'd not be looking at her body, to promise I'd not notice or think of its details, to say all I wanted was to know the state of the child hidden within her. But I said nothing—what could I say? Trust is a thing only to be earned, and time is its currency.

I swept the probe over her taut flesh until the pattering refrain and rhythm of the unborn child's life-force filled the air.

Ruthann looked at me again and her face brightened with a wonderful smile and I thought she might be okay with me tending to her after all.

I returned her smile and counted the precious beats.

When I'd laid aside the Doppler and finished taking her blood pressure, Ruthann asked if she could get into the water. At my nod, she hoisted herself to her feet and fairly sprinted across the span of hardwood floors separating her from the bathroom, intent on making it into the tub before another contraction could catch her out of it.

I returned to the kitchen and rummaged around in my book bag for a scrap of paper and a pen, since I didn't have Ruthann's chart with me. I checked the time and jotted a few notes, then set the rest of my gear and Ruthann's supplies in order. Elizabeth and Nora pulled the hide-a-bed from the sofa and covered the old mattress with a layer of plastic and a sheet, while I found and arranged the packages of disposable under-pads, the roll of paper towels, the olive oil, the wash cloths, the baby blankets, and the trash bags.

When the three of us were finished with our tasks, we seated ourselves together at the kitchen table, but Ruthann called through the door to invite her mothers to join her in the bathroom.

I was surprised she wanted company, but, for all the signs of impending labor she'd experienced through the day, she kept herself home from a wedding she had her heart set on attending, and said she guessed she'd at least like to hear about it. The women grabbed up their chairs without hesitation and disappeared into the steamy room.

I remained at the table, content to warm my toes and fingertips by the fire crackling in the wood stove, and glad for the chance to think, pray, and gather my courage, but a moment later, the door swung open again. David Ray took up a third chair and motioned to me with a nod of his head. "She says you're to come in, too."

"I don't want you to feel left out," Ruthann called. "And surely you'd like to hear about the wedding?"

I followed David and the chair into the bathroom, and I had to stifle a laugh when I passed the tub, for there was Ruthann, reclining against a pillow in the water—fully clothed in her nightgown.

As the women talked, I began to unwind, one tense muscle, one twisted organ, one overwrought thought at a time, lulled by the hiss and glow of the crusty lamp swinging from its hook on the ceiling, by the lilt of the womanly Amish vernacular mingling with the wisps of steam rising in fine tendrils from the warm water, and by the long, slow breaths of the laboring woman.

In the timeless quiet, my mind began to drift from the talk until I saw where I was through the eyes of myself at a younger year.

I could scarcely believe I was really there in that tiny room with a family—strangers to me, and Amish at that—on the cusp of birthing a child. It was both heavy and heady to realize I was the one soul responsible for the outcome; I was the honest-to-goodness midwife. Jean was away from home, and I was called on to take her place. I smiled at that thought and shook my head as eighteen years' worth of memories spiraled through my mind like the reel of an old-time film.

I'd become aware of homebirth midwifery in my teens when I stumbled across a book about a midwife who'd served among the Amish in Pennsylvania. I had only just surrendered my life to God, but my surrender was powerful, and the catalyst was the unshakable sense I'd been born with a significant purpose to fulfill in life. It was then I found and consumed the beautiful little book and closed it knowing without a doubt the Lord created and called me to the very same profession.

From there, however, one obstacle after another loomed before me like great, craggy mountain peaks.

The challenges ranged from an inconvenient inclination toward squeamishness, to my tender age, to the dearth of apprenticeships available to aspiring midwives, to the strangeness of the only recently resurrected profession of homebirth midwifery, to the scarcity of Amish populations.

Eight years passed and I had all but yielded to the obduracy of those impediments when, soon after my marriage and the birth of my first child, the Lord struck them a blow, inspiring Jean to invite me to apprentice with her.

———

A splash and a groan recalled me to the present. I fetched my Doppler and knelt beside the woman in the tub, tucking a strand of damp hair that had escaped from her kerchief behind one of her ears and helping her to a sip of water before sending the music of her baby's vibrant life reverberating through the little room.

Smiles creased the four faces before me as I turned to record my findings. I settled back into my chair and my thoughts settled back into the groove they'd been running along.

My eyes soaked in my surroundings as my mind roamed.

A hand-painted saw blade covered the wall opposite me. It read, "David Ray and Ruthann Detweiler, together forever, August 2nd, 2000." A kelly-green window shade was drawn against the night, trimmed with a frill of batiste. A hand pump stood in place of a faucet at the antique sink and the bathtub was an impossibly outdated iron model standing on claw feet. It was fastened into the corner of the bathroom by a broad wooden shelf.

David lounged along the shelf and I saw him with fresh eyes. He wore an incongruously stained, pale pink shirt buttoned up to his collarbones and tucked into a pair of barn door trousers. The trousers would have ordinarily been held up with a set of suspenders, as belts are *fabodda*, or forbidden, but I noticed they'd been removed and flung over a hook on the back of the bathroom door. His shock of hair was dutifully trimmed into a bowl cut and his square jaw hidden beneath a wildly scraggly, moustache-less beard.

And then, of course, there were the women, looking every bit as ancient, as antique as the fixtures in the room. Soft-spoken, deferential, hardworking, mothers and grandmothers of many.

I'd become accustomed to all this as I worked alongside Jean and rarely noticed the differences between our worlds any longer, but in the first year of my service among the Amish, the differences were so stark they almost cost me my calling.

Ruthann breathed her way through her labor while her mothers regaled her with a recounting of the wedding particulars from table service to table servers, and I thought back to my beginnings as a midwife apprentice among the inimitable people.

Chapter

TWO

ONE OF THE FIRST BIRTHS I ATTENDED THROUGH
my apprenticeship was for an Amish family living at the extreme
northern edge of Indiana in late September, 1993. Jean called an
hour or so before dawn and sent me scampering into the day
with my hair flying and my heart pounding.

The mother-to-be, Salome Hochstetler, was an angelic creature, if there ever was one—tiny and graceful as they come. She
suffered a disorder of some sort. I failed to retain its name, but
remembered it affected the composition of her musculature and
left her limping. She'd also endured the loss of a child a few years
earlier, though what happened was never explained to me, and I
felt I shouldn't ask.

I thought of her pain and sorrows every time I saw her, ever
reminded by her awkward gait, and I was struck by the way she
refused to allow her trials to dampen her spirits or dim her faith.

She greeted us at her door, smiling and laughing as she always
did, and we knew we'd arrived too early, so we passed the morning

checking on a number of families in the area while we waited for Salome's labor to get more serious.

Things picked up gradually toward noon, but still only very gradually. Jean suggested we go for a ride in her car in hopes the bumps and jostles would strengthen her pains. The trip accomplished what we hoped but, by the time it did, Jean realized she'd lost her way in the labyrinth of rutted, back-woods roads. Salome, in spite of contractions washing one after the other over her diminutive frame with increasing intensity, gamely straightened in her seat, laughed her good-natured laugh, and guided us back to her home as she ran her hands round and round her swollen, surging belly.

My heart sank a mite as we pulled into her driveway. For as much as I enjoyed Salome and her husband, Nathan, I struggled mightily to bear their home. The young couple lived in a barn of sorts, a barn that doubled as one edge of a full to overflowing pigpen. Salome's living arrangements shocked me to silence at my first visit with her and that shock spilled over to vex my entire first year attending births.

When I began attending home visits with Jean, the disparity between my expectations of the Plain People and the actual condition of their lives proved a deterrent. Where I'd pictured the prim, pristine houses of Amish film and fiction, I found bluntly functional homes filled with a bustling, Spartan folk wearing patched and sweat-stained clothes. I was taken aback by the rough hands, the weather-battered faces, the round and weary shoulders, the bare and blackened feet, the grossly swollen ankles, and the legs strangled with bulging veins.

I blanched at the number of younger families living in barns, in sheds, and in the basements of partially-constructed homes. I reeled at the harsh realities of houses warmed only by wood or coal stoves and lit only by lanterns, serviced by pumps at kitchen sinks, by windmills that failed to draw water on still days, by tiny propane-fueled refrigerators and wringer washers, by wash boards, by yards and yards of clotheslines, by sad irons and push-reel lawn mowers, by chamber pots stashed in wooden boxes, and by dark, drafty, stinking outhouses.

I had to learn to regard with nonchalance the rolls of fly paper that dangled from the ceilings and snagged my braids when I leaned too close, the mice scampering under doors and along the edges of baseboards, the bicycle wheel drying racks suspended over stoves and trimmed with perfect circles of damp socks or beef jerky, the ropes strung with chicken feet and stretched between outbuildings, the carcasses of unrecognizable animals littered about the yards by naughty dogs, the boxes of chirping chicks or orphaned lambs in living rooms, the riotous pigsties, the milk cows loose along roadsides, and the giant draft horse we once found tied to a basement support pole to warm up after he'd crashed through a frozen pond.

I was forced to listen unperturbed and respectfully to the abundance of old wives' tales such as, if you reach your arms over your head to hang clothes on the line or to wash windows in the last trimester of pregnancy, your baby will turn breech; if you get a scare anytime at all while pregnant, your baby will be born with a birth mark; or if your baby isn't fed a sip of cold water soon after birth, it will tend toward belly ache.

I had to appear unfazed by the severity of their religion, a religion promising no guarantees in return for the strictest adherence to the sternest rules. No electricity, no telephones, no vehicles.

Nothing to ease the rigors of life. Life fraught with endless work and limitless opportunities to flounder and fail.

In the beginning, all of that so clogged my senses I could hardly see or hear the people I was called on to serve, and I began to suspect I wasn't made of the stuff of midwives after all.

———

Once we'd made it back inside the makeshift affair that was Salome's home, though it was an exceptionally warm afternoon, she closed all her windows and drew every last leaf-green shade in keeping with the modesty of her culture. Nathan lit a kerosene lamp and hung it from the ceiling to compensate for the gloom, and Salome crept up onto her bed.

As the hours of afternoon passed, the temperature in the tiny bedroom rose, and the air, thick already with the smell of the hogs, thickened with the fumes of the fuel and, increasingly, with the unmistakable odor of birth—an odor I hadn't quite come to terms with.

Before long, I found it almost impossible to breathe.

I excused myself for a quick trip to the—ah, boy—outhouse.

I'd hoped a brief respite from the stifling bedroom would forestall my deterioration, but, perched on a rough slab of wood nominally separating me from generations of waste while fat and odiferous pigs grunted and scratched their backs nearly at my feet, I found my insides churning and a telltale chilly sweat dampening my skin, warning me I was teetering at the far edge of consciousness.

Good gosh! What's the matter with me? Am I really this sensitive?

I begged God to help me as the roiling of my belly filled my mouth with brackish saliva. I staggered from the outhouse and went to the sink where I worked the pump handle as vigorously as I could in my compromised state. Finally, a stream of blessedly cool water trickled forth and I splashed it over my flushed cheeks and neck, then forced myself back to the bedroom.

Jean glanced at my face when I returned. "Kim," she whispered. "What's wrong? You look like death."

I smiled and nodded at her, then looked away, determined to pull myself together.

In the recesses of my mind, my prayers ran on a loop like a medieval chant.

God! Oh, my God! I know You've called me to this vocation! Please! Oh, please! Help! Help me! God! Oh, my God—

Salome was curled on her side, inhaling and exhaling through the profoundly powerful sensations generated by her slight body, her head resting on one of Nathan's thighs while Nathan's calloused hands ran the course of her back in a hypnotic rhythm of strokes.

I began to feel better by degrees as, little by little, Salome's breaths became groans—as, little by little, her groans became grunts—as, little by little by little, Salome began to push. Soon a small oval of scalp appeared—appeared and retreated, appeared and retreated—with each appearance revealing just a bit more oval.

The magic of the moment wound itself around me and I lost myself in the unfurling miracle. We doused the woman's bulging tissues with dribbles of oil, and I marveled at the way the head, covered in a mass of shimmering black curls and wrinkled with the overlapping plates of its skull, shifted forward and back, forward and back until, all at once, it shifted forward and expanded to its fullest diameter, filling entirely the space of its mother's womanhood, spreading her delicate but resilient tissues like the petals of a blossoming flower.

"Oooooooh!" Salome squirmed and sucked in a breath. "Oooh! It burns! It burns!"

"Easy, Salome." Jean crooned, and she laid her gentle hands firmly over the woman's burning skin, soothing it with oil and with her tender touch. "Easy now—just breathe…"

"Oh! Oh! I can't!"

"Yes, you can, Salome. Look at me. Look at my eyes."

Salome's eyes, wildly dilated, opened and fixed on Jean's.

"Breathe with me, Salome, breathe with me like this—" And the two women blew and panted together as Salome eased the smooth, round head with its glossy locks into the light.

"Aaaaaaaaahhhhhhhhhh—" Salome buried her face in her husband's lap, as he gazed transfixed at the sight of his child, streams of tears seeping into lines forged by his smile.

"You're almost finished, Mother, the baby's almost here."

Another contraction began to build as the baby's face turned toward Salome's thigh.

Jean whispered, "Catch it, Kim."

Salome groaned with effort, and the baby spun into my hands with a tremulous wail.

I froze for just a moment, mesmerized by the brand-new life before me, and then I passed the wee, slick thing into Salome's arms as Salome's and Nathan's and the child's cries rang in our ears.

I sat back, awestruck.

Awestruck, that is, until I felt a wave of warmth pool around my knees and looked down to see that it was a gush of blood.

I knew the blood was only from the separation of the placenta from Salome's uterus, but, as the blood soaked into the fabric of my jeans, the spell was broken and the suffocating heat and mephitic odors rushed upon me again and, again, I found myself on the brink of a swoon.

God! Oh, my God! Please! Oh, please! God! Oh, my God! Please—

I scrambled from the bed and stumbled for the door and melted into a puddle on Salome and Nathan's front stoop.

I stayed out there a long while—fretting, doubting, agonizing, praying, grieving—worrying and wondering whatever would become of my destiny.

But, for all the turmoil of my soul, the whispery breezes of evening began to cool the day and pacify my raw senses and the thrill of having witnessed the birth of another glorious life swelled and swept over me from my head to my heels.

At last, I rejoined the happy scene within. Jean's eyes held a question, but Salome and Nathan were blessedly oblivious to my plight, completely taken with the fresh baby suckling at Salome's breast.

Jean and I busied ourselves with feeding and tidying and checking and charting as daylight slid past the edge of the horizon. We opened the windows and lit candles and lamps, and the chirring of crickets rose to replace the goodnight chorus of the songbirds. One star after another winked into the darkness as it deepened, and Salome's parents walked over from the house next door to welcome the newest member of their family. Chairs were set about the bed, and a lively gurgling of *Deutsch* sprang up among the four.

I can still feel the enchantment of that night these many years distant.

I can feel still, too, the concern that hovered beneath the surface of my tenuous composure—the dismal suggestion I was unequal, on so many levels, to the call to midwifery.

But, if I could have seen how things would turn out, if I'd have understood, as I served, the sights and smells that so staggered me at first would begin to recede into the background, allowing individual souls to emerge in all their pricelessness and, with them, my respect for their straightforward way of life, I'd have been better able to wipe the tears from my eyes.

If I knew then I'd come to cherish the warmth and charm of lamp and lantern light, to treasure visions of intricate quilts stretched across hand-fashioned frames and the thrum of treadle sewing machines—if I knew one day I'd glory in the rows of magenta beets and golden peaches gleaming in glass jars on pantry shelves, the loaves of fresh bread cooling on racks, the great vats of fragrant grape juice bubbling away on stove tops, the metal pails of speckled eggs awaiting washing, the rank and file of tomatoes ripening on window sills, and the basketfuls of dappled apples smelling tartly sweet in doorways, I'd have been able to take a breath and blow my nose.

Had I realized one day I'd be at home with hardwood floors bedecked with rainbows of braided rugs; with grandfather clocks and saw blades and footstools painted and burned and etched with wedding announcements and the names and birthdates of babies; with dinner bells and weather vanes and lightning rods standing at odd angles from rooftops; with well-ordered gardens edged with beds of brilliant flowers; with stands of fruit-laden trees; with the delightful variety of family-run shops with "no Sunday sales" printed on their signs; with the wonderment of teams of six and eight Belgians led by barefooted school boys; with the clip-clop and clatter of horse-drawn buggies rattling down dusty roadways; with the distinctive cadence of Amish talk; with the melody of women breathing through their labors; and with the splutterings and wails of newly birthed babies, I would have stood and squared my trembling shoulders.

If I could have recognized, though I'd never come to envy the brutality of their lives, I'd become entirely captured by the hospitality, the frank earthiness, the generosity, the insatiable curiosity, and the appetite for fun marking these uncommon people—my clients, my teachers, my friends—I would have laughed outright. And, more than anything, had I been able to grasp then the way the Lord Almighty is able to take the trials of our lives and twist them into creations of unspeakable beauty and significance, why, I'd have spread my hands toward the star-washed sky and shouted my thanks and praise!

Indeed, to know then what I know now would have done much to ease my troubled mind that balmy autumnal night, but I didn't know—I couldn't know.

I just had to swallow my tears and whisper my prayers and press ever onward.

The second birth of my apprenticeship was intense.

The first birth of my apprenticeship was, too.

Chapter

THREE

RING!

The rude noise scattered my dreams and sent my pulse crashing into my ears. I jolted upright. What was that? I patted my hand over the bedside table, searching for the clock. Why had I set the alarm last night? Wasn't it Saturday morning?

Just as my fingertips brushed against it, a second jarring ring startled me, and I sent the glowing numbers clattering to the floor. I shifted closer to the edge of the bed and reached for the cord caught on the corner of the tabletop, grateful I wouldn't have to get out of bed to retrieve it.

Ring!

I blinked. *The phone! It's the phone!*

I dropped the clock and scrambled from the bed. "Hello?"

"Good morning, Kim," said a cheery voice in my ear. "How would you like to come to a birth with me?"

The hammering of my heart made me doubt what I'd heard. *Is this—*

"Ah, pardon? May I ask who—"

"Kim, it's Jean." She laughed lightly. "Would you like to come to a birth?"

A surge of adrenaline gushed down my legs and set them atremble. *Oh, my gosh. Oh, my gosh! It is Jean.*

It was my own midwife—now my preceptor—Jean Balm, summoning me to the bedside of a laboring woman. After eight years filled with hopes and dreams and one disappointment after another, here she was, inviting me to a homebirth with her as though it were just one of those things she did on Saturday mornings. Which, of course, it often was.

I flung my nightgown away and scrounged for my jeans in the predawn gloom. I glanced toward my husband. He hadn't stirred. Not surprising. He'd only just climbed into bed an hour or so ago after working a night shift.

Ah, poor guy. He works so hard. His job as a police officer made me nervous sometimes, and especially so when he had to do it on only a few hours' sleep. I felt a pang of concern. Now he'd have to get up with Hannah, our eighteen-month-old, when she woke.

I plunged a foot down a pant leg. "Brent?"

Nothing.

"Brent!"

Still nothing. *Good grief, where's my bra?*

"Brent! Honey!" He grunted.

I got my other foot into my jeans, then I jerked and jiggled them past my hips as I hopped over to my husband's side of the bed. "Honey!" I shook his shoulder, noticing the strap of my bra beneath the crack of the closet door. He groaned and moved to roll over, but I shook him again. "Brent! Hon! Babe! Wake up! I'm going to a birth!"

"Wha—"

I snatched the errant article of underclothing from its hiding place on the closet floor and snapped it into place. "Hon, I'm going to a birth with Jean Balm!"

He squinted at me. "Huh?"

"I'm going to a birth with Jean! I can't believe you didn't hear the phone ring."

He propped himself onto an elbow and swiped a big, freckled hand over his face. "Whoa—okay..." He rubbed a bit of the sleep from a brown eye. "Oh—no—wait a second..."

He paused, obviously struggling to gather his thoughts. I thrust my arms through the sleeves of the t-shirt I found dangling on the closet doorknob. My chin caught on the collar as I tried to pull it over my head. *Ah, geesh!* I tried again and got it on.

Brent sat up. "Okay. You're going to a birth? Wow. When?"

"Right now. Just as soon as Jean gets here." I pecked him on the cheek and made for the hallway.

"Wait. Wait! Now? But, where's it happening?"

I halted in the doorway. "I don't know. Honey, I've got to go!"

"But, when will you be back?"

"I don't know!" I ran down the hall and bounded down the stairs, hoping I hadn't awakened Hannah.

I'd just managed to rake a comb through my tangles and take a swipe at my teeth with my toothbrush when I heard the toot-toot of a horn in the street. Jangled afresh, I scooped my shoes and purse into my arms and bolted from the house in my bare feet.

Jean's grayish-blue eyes danced with a hint of amusement as I wiggled myself into her passenger seat and slammed the door on the birdsong of early morning, a sound I relished, but barely noticed in my excitement.

"Do you remember me telling you about Laura?" Jean glanced over her shoulder and pulled the car from the curb.

"I—think so." I ran through the list of names I'd penned into my calendar at our last coffee date. *Laura—Salome—Lila—Daisy…*

"Yes, but I thought she was due the last week of July." It was July third, and certainly too early for it to be safe for Laura to birth her baby at home.

"Yep," Jean said. "She'll be thirty-seven weeks in two days. I told her to go to the hospital when she called this morning, but she flat-out told me no. I said we'd come check things out. Who knows? She might not really be in labor."

I glanced at Jean as she drove. Her words took me by surprise and I repeated them in my mind, letting the realization that Laura's labor might be a false alarm sink in. A ripple of disappointment drained the nervous excitement from my system like soapsuds down a sink. I bent to put my shoes on and a dawning of common sense checked the disappointment. Hopefully Laura wasn't in labor. It would be better for her and for her child if she wasn't.

I straightened and leaned back in my seat to gaze out the window. In the right-side mirror, streaks of light had begun to pierce the layer of clouds hovering over the horizon. They lengthened as I watched, and reached ahead of the rising sun like the slender fingers of an outstretched hand splayed against the lilac sky. A trace of radiance appeared. The trace became a sliver, then the sliver became a crescent. Little by little, the molten orb swelled through the ever-brightening clouds until it emerged, pulsing in all its resplendence.

Just like a birth, except—and my mind drifted to my first exposure to birth.

I'd grown up mesmerized with expectant women. Most of my girlhood friends loved babies. I loved babies, too, but it was those great bellies, heavy with burgeoning life that captivated and struck me dumb with awe—I could hardly get enough of them until my first encounter with childbirth served to quell my enchantment with the process for a time.

One morning, my seventh-grade English teacher announced the assignment of multi-resourced research papers. Groans of displeasure began to rumble through the room, but Mrs. Minich hushed us with an upraised hand. "Hold on, folks, settle down."

Someone protested, and she aimed a finger toward the sound.

"Hey, now, I said settle down." She fetched a sheet of paper from her desktop. "I've got something a little different for you this time. There's a film to accompany each topic." She waved the paper in the air before turning to pin it to the corkboard next to the door. We quieted, intrigued. "You'll select your topic, and I'll order the film. You'll watch the films in the media room by turns after school."

We were given permission to look at the list. I felt a shiver of excitement as I squeezed myself through the gaggle of kids crowded around the board. The idea of watching a film for school was almost too much. My eyes scanned the subjects. Artificial limbs, ballet dancing, child labor, dentistry, the environment, firefighting, the military, police work, open heart surgery…

Open heart surgery. Cool.

Two weeks later, the movies arrived and our times in the media room were scheduled. My friend, Sherry, asked Mrs. Minich if we could have our turns on the same afternoon so we could watch together.

"What movie'd you pick?" I asked my friend as we met by her locker on our big day. She tossed a math book onto the floor of the tiny space, then slammed the door with a flourish.

I smiled. Sherry was so dramatic.

"Child labor. What'd you pick?"

I wrinkled my nose. "Child labor? What? Like vacuuming? Like folding laundry?"

"I dunno. Yeah, I guess. It was all that was left. I missed school the day Mrs. Minich put the list out and it was that or dentistry. Like I'd pick dentistry. I hate the dentist." She frowned and flashed her braces at me. "But I said, 'What'd you pick?'"

"Open heart surgery."

"Serious? Ew. I don't wanna see that."

"Well, I don't want to watch a bunch of kids do chores, either. I do enough of my own, thanks. But it was your idea to watch together. I will if you will." We started off down the hall, and I trotted along as quick as I could to keep up with my friend's long-legged, jaunty stride.

We started with my film, and it was fascinating. Though Sherry and I punctuated the viewing with all the grimaces and gasps you'd expect from a set of pre-teen girls, thanks to the surgical draperies shielding us from the human element of the procedure, we both handled it well.

As the closing credits spooled across the screen, I stood to turn on the lights.

Sherry hopped across the room to switch films. "That was so totally gross." She fumbled around with the VCR until the tape popped out.

"Ah, you're so totally gross."

She put her tongue out at me. I flicked off the lights and we settled back into our seats. The raspy sound of the film as it came to life shushed our banter and recalled our eyes to the screen.

Child labor. My mind drifted to the mounds of leaves my dad had made me rake into the garden the weekend before, then to the zillions of leaves still strewn around the yard. Boring. Why make a film about that?

Still, I'd promised Sherry I'd watch hers. Besides, if I stayed to watch it, I wouldn't be able to finish the yard that night. My sisters might even get it done without me. I smiled to myself over my good luck.

The fuzzy screen on the wall opened upon a scene, tugging my mind back into the room, but—*what the heck*? There, before my only scarcely sex-educated eyes, lay some unknown, unfortunate woman, flat upon a narrow table. Her face was hidden behind the rise of her huge abdomen and her quivering thighs were propped apart, exposing her privates without preamble or apology.

A man concealed in paper from cap to mask to shoes sat perched on a stool before her, his gloved hands clasped in his lap. Was he a doctor? Who could tell? Even his eyes were disguised behind a pair of thick-rimmed glasses.

Shivers tingled down my legs, my stomach knotted, and a shock of heat dampened my neck and colored my face. I wanted to escape, but found myself riveted to the scene. I clutched the arms of my seat as the woman moaned and squirmed a bit.

Except for the doctor, she was alone, and he made no move to soothe her.

My heart twisted with pity, replacing my sense of embarrassment. Then the pity gave way to horror as, with a groan, her unsheltered womanhood began to bulge and spread and stretch before a shimmering...

My word, is that the head?

The fringes of my vision began to blur. Beads of moisture sprang upon my brow. My guts plummeted toward the floor.

I stood, went instantly blind, and a sudden ringing in my ears deafened me. I could hear Sherry's voice, but could make nothing of her words.

I groped for the door and wrestled it open. My fingertips found the brick wall lining the corridor and I ran my palms over its rough surface until I reached the girls' bathroom where I staggered inside and collapsed onto the nearest stool. There, I ducked my head between my knees and soaked in a bone-chilling sweat while I waited for my vision to return and my roiling belly to settle.

*Oh. Oh! Oh, no...*I knew then I'd never have a baby of my own.

————

The rocking of the car as Jean pulled into a parking space before Laura's shabby tenement roused me. I jolted into the present, noticing my reverie had restrung the tension of my nerves. I followed Jean to the rear of her car, trying to force myself to relax as I slung my share of heavy and ungainly bags onto my shoulders and turned to face the building.

We bumped and stumbled our way up the narrow stairway. With every step, I assured myself Laura would most likely not be in labor, but once we'd squeezed ourselves into the apartment's front room, I knew she was.

I was assaulted by the pungent scent of birthing in the thick air. I recognized it on some primal level, possibly—despite the vow of my youth—from having birthed a baby of my own by then. Hard on the heels of that smell was the stench of dirty diapers, days-old dinner dishes, and unwashed bodies.

Laura's home was filthy. It was hot, too, though the sun was just risen.

I stood motionless in the doorway while my insides balled into a fist.

Laura sat cross-legged and startlingly naked on the floor on a stained and sheetless mattress, fished, I supposed, from one of the bedrooms and jammed against an equally stained sofa. Her stringy hair lay askew over her bare shoulders, and droplets of sweat stood on her nose. She was in the grip of a contraction and appeared unaware of our presence.

But Gary, her husband, looked up from his seat next to her. With a huge grin splitting his face, he jumped to his feet, nearly knocking Laura over. "Jean!" He boomed, crossing the room in a bound, "Glad you're finally here! This is kinda weirding me out!"

Laura grimaced and swore at him under her breath as she steadied herself and struggled through the remainder of the contraction.

Gary returned the curse with a scowl. "What a witch, eh?" He extended his hand to me. "Gary."

"Kim," I whispered as I took his hand.

"Nice to meet ya, Kim! Welcome to the freak show!"

Laura's contraction passed, and she let out a long, shuddery breath. Gary bounded back to her, giving her a jolt as he plopped himself down.

"Gary, you blasted idiot!" She swore again. "Quit thumping me!" Then she shot a glare at Jean. "And I'm not going anywhere, either!"

"Touchy, touchy." He poked her arm and glanced our way with another grin. "See what I mean? She's a regular witch usually, but today she's witchier than ever!"

Laura slapped his hand away as another contraction rose to engulf her and Gary parried her slap with a second poke.

I stood rooted to the floorboards, stunned by the crudity of the man, transfixed by the obvious intensity of the woman's labor, overpowered by the reek and filth of the stifling room.

Oh, God, what am I doing here?

A motion from Jean caught my eye. She'd already cleared a space for the bags in a far corner and was rapidly unpacking her gear. She beckoned me.

I blinked. I gulped. I staggered to her. Jean decided we'd stay.

Laura's contractions were coming hard and fast. I understood we might have a little time before the baby made her appearance, but we just as likely might not.

"Here." Jean handed me a roll of paper towels. "Fold ten sheets into a neat stack for me. Okay? Then, see?" She pointed past the flaps of a ratty cardboard box. "Open the package of under pads, and make a second neat stack. Fill the squeeze bottle with olive oil and tuck it into my tote here." She patted a little plastic basket filled with cord clamps, a box of gloves, a bulb syringe, packets of sterilized instruments, and her stethoscope. "Hook two trash bags over a doorknob, then find the baby blankets and washcloths."

I obeyed, willing myself to remain conscious and present, while Jean squatted before Laura and listened to her baby's heartbeat. The chores and the steady beat of the tiny heart would have done much to soothe my frazzled sensibilities, except Laura and Gary continued to pick and bicker at one another. Jean even had to ask Gary to be still a moment so she could hear well enough to take Laura's blood pressure.

I completed my tasks. I should have seated myself on the floor next to Jean, but I was battling hard to keep my wits about me and knew I'd do better if I could work at something. I scurried about the place and tidied it up. I found and pitched the poopy diaper polluting the air from the corner of a changing table, I washed the crusty dishes in the kitchen sink and scrubbed off the countertops, I wiped down the bathroom and scoured the tub.

Every now and then Jean's Doppler would send the sound of the baby's heartbeat echoing through the apartment, and I could hear Laura laboring, each of her contractions coming closer than the one before; each obviously stronger. And, still, unbelievably, in between the powerful workings of her body, Gary and Laura squabbled and cursed at one another.

I worked until there wasn't another thing for me to do but follow Jean's example and take my seat on the floor next to the travailing mom.

Jean did what she could to minister comfort to Laura, but the unceasing, even increasing tension between man and wife all but canceled her efforts.

At last, I decided to say something. I was afraid speaking up might offend Gary or end my apprenticeship with Jean, but I could bear it no longer.

"Uh, hey, Gary?"

"Yeah?" Gary looked up and flashed his boyish grin.

"Guess what?"

"What?" He bounced a bit and Laura swatted him.

I winced, but went on. "Labor's one of those times when your woman's always right."

Gary's grin gave way to gravity. He cocked his head in thought a second or two, then nodded and winked, "Sure—" He glanced at his weary wife. "Yeah, okay. Yeah, I get it."

That was it. Not another contrary word was spoken.

After that, only the drone of the fan whirring from a crooked window frame and Laura's breathings and heavings, sighings and moanings, whimpers and grunts and groans could be heard. One after the other, mighty contractions swept her frame. We whispered encouragement in her ears as we bathed her brow with cool cloths and pressed the small of her back until, in spite of the dirt and odors, the matchless magic of birth began to steal over my soul.

There was a pause in Laura's labor, as though her womb was catching its breath, and then she uttered a long, deep, throaty bellow.

Slowly, slowly—ever so slowly, a wrinkly, wet scalp began to appear and, in that instant, it looked just like that sliver of morning sun I'd watched as it pressed itself into view on the drive over.

Jean whispered, "Okay, Kim, catch the baby."

Surprised, but willing, I touched the baby's head with tentative fingertips, swallowing, blinking back a sudden wash of tears. Jean continued to whisper in my ear until the little thing slipped into my trembling hands.

But she was born limp and starkly white.

Jean took her from me, laid her on Laura's sweaty breast, and set straight to work with a skillful touch and sure breaths. My heart halted in my chest, and my own breath caught in my throat as a lifetime flashed past in some sixty or seventy seconds.

And then a steadily strengthening cry displaced the ominous silence, and a splendid wave of pink swept the pallor from the baby's skin.

Again and again, just like that glorious sunrise.

Chapter

FOUR

BEFORE I WAS A MIDWIFE, I WAS AN APPRENTICE. Before I was an apprentice, I was a woman. Before I was a woman, I was a girl. Before I was a girl, I, too, was a tiny baby.

I was born to Durrell and Mary Banfield through the witching hours of warm summertime, 1970, in the days when fathers were kept in waiting rooms and mothers were strapped to delivery tables. I was my mom's first baby, and the first grandchild on both sides of the family. I remember my grandfather telling me I came during the oat harvest of a particularly hot and humid spell the last season he planted the sticky things. I came ten days late after teasing everyone with a week's worth of contractions.

Once I began to come in earnest, I took a solid forty-eight hours' worth of labor to arrive, with my poor mother alone and tethered to her bed, worrying and squirming and sucking in lungfuls of nitrous oxide. She said it was deathly quiet in the delivery room when the sweating doctor finally managed to tug me from her body with a set of forceps. Mom was afraid I was dead and thought she could sense fear of the same in the silence of her struggling attendants. She told me the moment I was born, she was "put out," and, after some indeterminate period of time, was "brought to," and there I was, examining my surroundings with wide eyes. Fourteen months later, my sister, Kris, came along. Three years after that, Missy joined us.

I passed a delightful girlhood, my days spent devouring books, coloring pictures, collecting toads and woolly-bear caterpillars, chasing rainbows, rejoicing through thundershowers, conjuring mystical worlds with my sisters, admiring my mother, and trotting after my dad wherever he'd allow me—utterly cherished by folks who cherished one another unreservedly. Together and with joy, we worked and played, wondered and explored, imagined and invented, learned and stretched and grew.

When I was six, the day after my birthday, I gave my heart to God. We were just home from church and I asked my dad if he thought there would be peanut butter and jelly sandwiches in heaven. I adored peanut butter and jelly.

Dad said, "Well, you know you won't go there unless you give your heart to Jesus."

My eyes popped open. "What? Doesn't He already have my heart?"

"Have you ever told Him He can have it?"

"Hmm—" I thought a minute. "Not that I can think of—"

"Well, Jesus isn't going to just take it. It's yours. He'll only take it if you give it to Him."

"But why do I have to give it to Him?"

My dad took a breath and considered. He said, "Well, it's like this, Kimmy. God made the world—this big, beautiful world—then He filled it with people. Every day He visited the people—He loved them and they loved Him—and they would take walks through the world together, talking and laughing and enjoying each other.

"He did make a rule about the world, though. One little rule. He said, 'Please keep this rule—it will keep you safe and happy, and will keep us together.'

"But one day, the people broke His rule. And the breaking of the rule broke the friendship between the people and God, and it also brought meanness and disease and death into the world. And every person who's come after the first people have broken the rule, and have done other bad things as well.

"God was very sad about all that. God hated to be separated from us, and He hated that we were trapped into all that meanness and disease and death. But the breaking of the rule, and all the bad things the people did afterward—what God calls sin— had to be paid for, and the price had to be the death of the sinner.

"But Jesus, part of God, like the Father and the Holy Spirit, said, 'What if I became a person and pay for all those sins with my own death?'

"And God said, 'Hey, You know what? That would work. Let's do that.'

"So, Jesus came to earth and He lived his whole life here without ever sinning. He was killed by the sinners, but, because He never sinned, His death was able to pay for everybody else's sins and—even more! Because He never ever sinned, death couldn't hold Him and He rose up from the dead!

"Now, to be connected with God again, and to be able to go to Him in heaven after we die, we have to admit we're sinners and apologize, then accept that Jesus paid for our sins and give our hearts to Him."

"Oh, gosh, Dad! Wow! But when were you going to tell me? I'm already six years old! I gotta do that!"

Dad laughed. "Okay, Honey, but settle down! Settle down." He drew me into his arms. "How about we do it right after lunch?"

"After lunch? No, Dad! Now!! I gotta do it right now!!!"

And, so, we did.

"Jesus," I said after my dad. "I admit I'm a sinner—that I put myself ahead of others and ahead of you, hurting all of us. I understand my sins have separated me from You, that every sin I've done has to be paid for, and, since You love me and don't want us to be separated, You paid for my sins Yourself. Jesus, I'm sorry for my sins! Thank You for paying for them! Thank You for bringing us together! I do give You my heart! I do give you my whole life!"

I was only six, and I had only prayed a very simple prayer, but when I prayed that prayer, just following along after my dad, I felt Jesus pouring into me and was electrified. I went forward into my life constantly aware of Him within me.

I learned to read somewhere in there—before I started school, according to my mom—and I did love to read. Among my favorite books were the *Little House on the Prairie* series, the complete works of Sherlock Holmes, and the *Black Stallion* volumes, but the stories I loved best were those written by the old-time Scottish veterinarian, James Herriot. I wolfed down every last word Dr. Herriot scratched onto paper about his work, dreaming myself into the life and death dramas, one moment gasping in horror and the next, laughing until my sides gathered and stitched.

As much as I loved to read, what I lived to do was poke my nose into the manifold fascinating crannies and crevices of my grandparents' farm. I was charmed by the vegetable garden and in love with the apple orchard. I was curious about the aging threshers and tractors and tillers, intrigued with the burn pit, and enthralled by the defunct outhouse. I was impossibly enchanted with the deserted hayloft and derelict stalls, the haunted half-light a-swirl with a fine sprinkling of golden dust, each ghostly corner trimmed with the lacy filaments of ancient spiders' webs.

But it was the tiny stand of forest and slight, lively creek at the far end of the fields I reveled in most. I walked to the wood every chance I could get and with each step of every trip, I shed the trappings of my outside life. One stride at a time, their layers shifted to the ground behind me and were replaced with a sense of timelessness. I'd feel my inner self unfurl and expand into eternity. From somewhere in the depths of my girlish heart, I recognized the gravel crunching under my feet, the dust that eddied about my ankles, the streamlet skipping and singing its way through the endless shades of green ahead of me, and the great cobalt canopy of sky arching over my head were ageless and enduring. They existed—crunching and swirling, skipping and singing and arching—for all the generations before me and I understood they'd be there still through all the generations to follow. In my bones, I knew it was the artistry of Almighty God, and I knew I was His handiwork, too, and the thought poured the foundations and erected the framework of my life. It anchored and infused me, even then, with an awareness of belonging and purpose.

I was a scattered child, though. My parents often chastised me for my dawdling, daydreaming ways, while my teachers urged me to press better into my studies, each repeating, one after the other, "You have so much potential, Kim! You'd do so well if you'd try!" I promised to try, and meant to try, but was ever diverted from my promises by any number of interesting objects and ideas.

I had a good bit of difficulty with my schoolmates, too.

I never did quite fit in, preferring my books and crayons and the corners of the school yard to the silly and sometimes unkind games the girls in my class wanted to play. One day, I was told I could be part of the group if I'd quit trying to include the reclusive waifs who drifted along the edges of the playground. Another afternoon, I was offered a nickel from each girl if I'd agree to stop wearing the bright green polyester pants I was enamored with.

Middle school proved even worse.

The years between my twelfth and fourteenth birthdays were rough. Looking back, I see them as the cathartic necessities they were, forcing me down a path that would ultimately prove beneficial to me and, therefore, I'm grateful for them. While they were happening, however, I was purely miserable.

Six weeks into my eighth-grade year, our principal, Mr. Hicks, committed suicide after learning he had Parkinson's disease, and then my relationship with my best childhood friend imploded. I learned I was friendless—and friendless is no exaggeration—when I brought my tray to our table in the lunch room one afternoon, only to be driven from it with slurs and ridicule.

The aftershocks of that collapse resounded through the remainder of the year. All I managed to gather amidst the wreckage was I was too focused on my studies and too invested in my French horn, I was of the wrong appearance on every perceivable level, profoundly unfashionable, irreparably straight-laced, and of unfavorable values and faith. Through the remainder of the year, I spent most of my school hours ducking violent volleys of insults. Every day, in attempts to avoid the continual salvo, I ran to school, arrived at my classes as late as possible, hid away in the art room through lunch, and ran back home. I was devastated as friend after friend, without explanation, deserted me to join in the derision.

My parents had only vague notions regarding my troubles, as I rarely shared details. I was angry, I was embarrassed, I was disinclined to relive the experiences by describing them, and, really, I think I thought they knew what was happening.

The sunny nature I'd burst into life with rapidly morphed into a maelstrom of ire and resentment. The permutation annihilated my academic performance and corroded my behavior, generating incredible tension at home. By the end of the school year, I was drowning in turmoil and continually lashing out. My conduct was so rebellious and ugly my father told me, though he and my mom loved me very much, for the sake of my little sisters, they'd begun to look for another place for me to live.

About that time, the idea of home education was raised within our church, a little non-denominational community we'd begun attending when I was eleven. It was a place filled with and led by a group of edgy, energetic people who were passionate about living what they believed. They were artists and visionaries who hunted, fished, gardened, breastfed their numerous and naturally-born babies, and treated their kids like people. Their decision to educate their children themselves seemed to spring up easily from the fertile soil of their creative, earthy lives. My folks were older than most of the adults in the church, as my sisters and I were also older than most of the other children, so initially we felt rather misplaced among them. But my parents' decision to move us there was providential.

I'm sure I was the only child given a choice whether to submit to homeschooling, being as old and unruly as I was. When the concept was first proposed to me, I rejected it with vigor and, wisely, my parents didn't press. Then, school let out for the year. While I was still a handful, the altered environment of summertime calmed things down enough for me to realize how loath I was to return to the abuse I'd suffered in the classroom.

But the first year of school in the home was a nightmare. The work was harder, my study habits abysmal, and my once-tender heart steadily hardened under the deleterious influence of a ceaselessly simmering rage. The strain was relentless and palpable. My parents—offended, grieving, afraid for my future, unsure how to handle or help their sweetheart-turned-seething cauldron—hung with me like champions, though I pushed them to the limits of their patience and resources. Blowups were the order of the day. Mom would call Dad, Dad would come home, Mom and the girls would scatter, and the fight would commence.

The situation reached its climax the springtime before I turned fifteen.

Dad, for all our contentions, was still one of my favorite people and though I hid my anticipation as best I could, I looked forward to his evening homecomings—except on the occasions I was banished to exile.

One spring afternoon, having wreaked havoc with my mother yet again, I sat stewing in my room, watching for my dad from my bedroom window.

His aging Buick LeSabre rolled into the drive toward suppertime and my heart skipped a beat. I watched as he climbed from the car, bent to retrieve his briefcase, and headed up the walk.

A muffled but cheerful greeting rang out when he opened the door, and my heart took another stumble. I could hear my sisters' giggling voices as they welcomed Dad inside. I knew hugs and tickles and kisses were going the rounds and, though it had been a long time since I'd actively taken part in such pageantry, a ripple of sadness swept over me. I never would have admitted it, not to Dad, not to Mom, not to anybody, but I missed the time in my life when my heart was soft, my manner affable, and my life simple.

"All right girls, skedaddle." Dad must have noticed Mom was upset. I could just see her, standing to one side in her green and yellow patchwork smock, arms folded across her chest, face grim.

The rumblings of serious parent talk rose through the floor of my room. My breathing quickened and my heart increased its fluttering. They spoke too quietly for me to hear their words, but I didn't need to hear to guess the gist of what was said. "Well, Durrell, it's Kim. Truculent. Defiant. Antagonistic. Insolent. A bad example for Kris and Missy. More than I can handle."

Dad's footsteps sounded on the stairs, heavy and threatening, and each creak fanned a fresh gust of oxygen over my ever-smoldering emotions. I balled my fists and set my face.

The door opened.

For the life of me, I can't recall the details of the tangle I had with my mom that day, nor am I able to remember what my dad said when he entered my room. Only slivers of the evening remain clear in my recollections, but those slivers are clear indeed—shards of clarity stabbing through the ominous thunderheads darkening my soul.

Dad's jaw was clenched, but his voice, though tight, was calm to start with. He said something, I reacted badly to it, dashed past him, and made for the stairs. Dad followed me and, with more exasperation, with more desperation than I'd ever heard in his voice before, thundered, "KIMBERLY!"

I hesitated.

"Kim!"

In spite of myself, I turned toward him. Why I stopped and turned, I can't say. It was almost as though his voice was a tangible entity that halted my flight, held me in place, and forced me to face him. With one foot on the top stair, I glared at him.

Before I could open my mouth, Dad said, "Daughter, you're *ruining* your life! You're *destroying* it with your own two hands! You're here on this earth for a reason! God has an awesome plan for your life, but you're going to *miss* it if you go on this way!"

The rage erupted. With a roar of fury, I slammed myself back into my room.

Trapped in there with my wretched self, I churned and twisted like a cyclone, screaming and cursing. I tore the covers from my bed, swept the books from my shelves, yanked the clothes from my closet and drawers until, spent, I flung myself into the morass and lay facing the west windows, trembling in the wake of an inarticulate wrath.

The sinking sun set the frilly white curtains aglow and, by degrees, the beauty began to pacify me. I lay there, my eyes filled with light while the words my dad shouted burned themselves into my psyche.

"God has a plan for your life—God has a plan for your life—God has a plan for your life…"

My throat thickened as hot tears threatened to surface. I made an attempt to repress them.

As I grew from girl to young woman, I began to sense I was born for many magnificent reasons, especially with Jesus living inside my heart. The years that passed between then and the moment I was facing there in my bedroom, however, did their best to rub most of the shine from those sparkling sensations.

But in my room that evening, lying on my side on that rumple of clothes, bathed in a vision of shimmering cotton, the idea God made me on purpose—God had a plan for my life and wanted to do it with me—began to revive itself and set my every cell to vibrating.

With tears burning my eyes, I prayed. "God—Lord—You love me! You want to be with me! And you really did make me with a plan in mind, didn't you? Okay." And the tears became sobs. "I want that. I'm in."

Peace flowed in upon the utterance of that prayer, the first measure of peace I'd experienced in a long, long time, and I fell asleep right there on my bedroom floor.

Chapter

FIVE

A CHILLY WIND WHIPPED SNOWFLAKES INTO OUR eyes and teeth as my sisters and I laughed and ran around the parking lot with our friends, as eager to start our day as young fillies are to prance out into the sunshine come bright mornings.

A group of parents stood huddled around a man with a clipboard, clutching their jackets to their chins until the man, Mr. Siedlecki, one of our pastors and leaders of our homeschool endeavors, let out a piercing whistle.

Swarmed now by the children as well as the parents, he called names and pointed fingers until each of us was accounted for and stuffed into a vehicle. The next thing we knew, we were on the road, a long string of station wagons and minivans making their way north for a day of skiing.

My sister, Kris, and I were assigned to Karen Scherf's car. Jessica Witte was tucked in with us too and, almost the moment Karen pulled out of the parking lot, we were elbowing one another in an effort to strip off our scarves and coats.

Mrs. Hayes, another homeschooling mom, was riding with us and soon she and Karen were absorbed in conversation. I'd brought a book to read, but scarcely had I flipped open its cover when I heard Karen tell Mrs. Hayes something about a birth she'd been witness to a week or so before.

It had been three years since I saw the dreadful film that squelched my reproductive fervor, but the memory of it was so fresh in my mind I piped right up, interrupting the conversation. "Mrs. Scherf, you watched a birth? On purpose?"

"I did!" She flicked her blinker on and prepared to make a left turn onto Mission Road. "I'm training to be a midwife." She smiled and glanced back at me in her rearview mirror.

"What? And you enjoyed it?"

She glanced back again. "I loved it! I love birth! It's—"

I cut her off. "It's gross! It's horrible! I'm never going to have a baby!"

Mrs. Hayes turned in her seat to look at me. "Oh, Kim! What makes you say such a thing? I loved giving birth to my children!"

"Well, I saw this video when I was in middle school—" My belly began to churn at the thought of it. "And it was awful. Some poor lady was laid flat out on this table with her legs spread apart—just spread right apart! And some guy, I guess a doctor, was sitting there, staring right at her privates! And then, well, I guess the baby started to come—and, oh, my gosh..."

Jessie and Kris were watching me, wide-eyed. I swallowed. My mouth was filling with saliva and I felt a prickle of sweat at my hairline. "And she—I mean, her privates—I mean, you know, her bottom, her vagina..."

Kris gasped and clapped a hand over her mouth.

I swallowed again. "Well, so, this huge ball—I guess it was her baby's head—oh, gosh! It just pushed her bottom—or, you know, her vagina open wide—so wide—and—and—well, and I had to get out of there! I don't actually know how it ended. She probably got it out okay, but…"

I felt faint like I had when I watched that terrible film. My vision was a little fuzzy and I noticed a slight ringing in my ears. Kris sat transfixed, her hand still over her mouth. Jessie was staring at me. The two turned their eyes toward the women in the front.

Mrs. Hayes cleared her throat and shifted in her seat, opened her mouth, then shut it again and looked at Karen.

Karen broke the silence. "Kim, sweetie, I'm so sorry you had to see a birth like that. Now, I'll admit that lots and lots of babies are born just that way, but, you know what?" She slowed as the train of cars approached the entrance to the ski hill. "Some women have their babies at home with midwives and birth like that is really different from the birth you saw in that movie."

The next time we wedged ourselves and our snow pants into Karen's minivan, Karen brought a book along for me to borrow. It was *A Midwife's Story* by Penny Armstrong.

The tale was the true-life account of a homebirth midwife serving a secluded Old Order Amish community in Pennsylvania. I read it in nearly one sitting, with story after story weaving such an exquisite illustration of homebirth and midwifery, I closed it knowing without a doubt I'd stumbled upon the purpose God created me to fulfill.

I stroked the worn yellow book as it rested on my lap, a little dazed from having read for so many hours. Somehow, the tale reminded me of my favorite novel, *Christy*, by Catherine Marshall. A couple years before, I read Mrs. Marshall's story of a young woman who was plunged into the depths of the Appalachian Mountains to serve its primitive cluster of eccentric families as a school teacher, and was profoundly moved by the difference she made in their lives, even while they made their own indelible mark upon hers.

Yes. From the sense of significance that sparked to life as I roamed my grandpa's farm and fields and forest, to my exposure to the remarkable story of Christy Rudd Huddleston, to the moment I surrendered my life to God upon a tangle of clothing and setting sunlight, I knew I, too, was made to make a difference in life.

I looked at the book in my lap again and the spark burst into flame. I knew without a doubt in my mind God created me to be a midwife among the Amish, just like Penny Armstrong.

I rustled my mother up from a spelling test she was correcting.

"Mom!" I dropped the book on the test with a thump. "Mom, look at this! Look at this book Karen Scherf lent me! It's about a midwife who delivers babies for Amish people in their own homes!" I waited for her to express her amazement, then, impatient, went on without it. "Guess what?"

Mom's warm brown eyes smiled at me, despite the rudeness of my interruption. "What?"

"This is what I'm supposed to do!"

My mom was silent. The day I watched that childbirth film with Sherry, I came home and told her I would never have a baby. I told her I decided to never even get married.

"Mom?"

"Oh—" Mom picked up the book and ruffled through its pages.

What's that funny note in her voice?

"My goodness." She laughed weakly, then frowned. "How wonderful—except…" She leaned forward and tapped the book with one of her long, slender fingers. "Well—Honey, midwives generally aren't the ones who faint over labor."

Yes. Yes, I was worried about that too, but I snatched the book from her hand and parroted Karen. "Homebirth is different than hospital birth, Mom. Plus, if God's called me to be a midwife, I'm sure I'll be fine."

I set straight to work.

I'd overcome aversions to spiders and sharks and bats as an eight-year-old by poring over a set of picture books about them, forcing myself to touch and admire each image until an appreciation for the exceptional creatures dispelled my fears. I decided to do the same for birth, so I borrowed book after book from Karen in my quest. The first two I read after Mrs. Armstrong's book were *Heart and Hands* by Elizabeth Davis and *Special Delivery* by Rahima Baldwin, treasure troves of birthing imagery.

I spent hours alone in my room with those books, absorbing the pictures and, yes, sweating, and, yes, sometimes setting them aside awhile till my belly stilled and I could see again. But, as with the spiders and sharks and bats, over time, the intense visceral reaction those powerful images conjured was replaced with wonder and amazement. I read and re-read those books, and many others besides, and I allowed their missives of normalcy, of beauty, of sanctity to infuse my soul and transmute my responses to them.

Chapter

SIX

THREE YEARS LATER I WAS RELEASED FROM HIGH school.

I say released because, though I made significant improvements in attitude and approach to my education, my academic performance remained persistently less than stellar. My folks offered to provide me another year or two of homeschooling, but I heartily refused their offer.

I also managed to wiggle out from under the pressure levied on me to attend Nazareth Nursing College. Instead, I signed on with Carla Hartley's home study course, Apprentice Academics and, through Karen, slipped into the mysterious world of home-birth midwifery. I attended my first Michigan Midwives Association conference the autumn after my graduation and while there met a midwife I hoped to secure an apprenticeship with.

But, alas, as is so often the case, I was more interested in working with that midwife than she was interested in working with me. Naturally, I can't blame her. I don't know how crazy I'd be over the idea of taking a squeamish eighteen-year-old virgin on as my next apprentice, either.

I met a cute boy around that time, anyhow, and most likely wouldn't have been quite as attentive as my apprenticeship would have warranted. He was, after all, really cute.

His name was Brent Woodard.

I wasn't so sure of Brent at first. One of the decisions I made as I surrendered the reins of my life to God was, rather than wasting my time and energy searching out a man I'd be willing to marry, I'd trust God to bring exactly the right man to me at exactly the right time. Then, in order to strengthen my resolve to wait and to help me recognize the man when he finally appeared, I crafted a fantastic description of him. I wanted a man who loved the Lord more than anything—who'd dedicated his life to God and to his God-ordained destiny, just as I had. I wanted a man who'd appreciate and celebrate my strength and my potential— who'd realize I, too, was created with purposes to fulfill, purposes sure to extend beyond that of wife and mother—and who would consider it his sovereign duty to see all my purposes realized.

There were other things I wanted, besides. I wanted him to be frugal and practical and adventurous, to be handy and hard-working, to be an outdoorsman, to be brave and tenderhearted, strong and gentle, wise and fun. I wanted my family to approve of him, and I wanted him to share my vision for homebirthing and homeschooling our children. I also hoped he'd be tall and handsome and young.

I studied my depiction and recognized I'd likely have to be flexible about the tall and handsome and young part. Otherwise, I considered it spot on. Then I shared what I wrote with the women of my community and was informed no such man existed—especially not a tall, handsome, young one.

At first, I was surprised by their collective assessment, and then I was disheartened. And then I was resolved. I'd really wanted to be both a wife and a mother, but the more I thought about it, the more I felt I'd rather live my life unmarried than settle for less than what I'd penciled onto paper.

I spent the rest of my school years strengthening my resolve to remain single and sending all would-be admirers to my dad for re-direction until I woke one fresh Sunday morning in early June, about six weeks before my eighteenth birthday, with a strange sense of anticipation stirring inside me. That sense swelled as a voice whispered into my spirit, *"Today's going to change your life forever."*

I can still feel the excitement that sentence sent snapping over the surface of my psyche. I moved into the day buzzing with expectation, but, as the day progressed as predictably as the Sundays of my youth generally did, the buzz gradually tapered to a tingle.

Then, just as quick as anything, one unusual thing after another happened. I was invited to a neighboring city for the graduation ceremony of a bunch of semi-strangers. Though my dad initially said I couldn't go, he stepped entirely out of character and relented. On the drive to the ceremony, I discovered we were, in fact, about to attend the open house of one of those strangers. I was uneasy about being an uninvited guest, but what was I to do? My uneasiness increased when we arrived at the scene and I was abandoned by my ride. Fortunately, though, being a friendly sort, I was soon in conversation with the graduate's Aunt Rose.

Rose was interesting, and I was just beginning to relax into the surroundings, when a tall, athletic, brown-eyed, redheaded young man with the most dazzling smile and intoxicating presence stepped into the corner of my vision.

Whoosh.

The tingly buzz of electricity tantalizing me since morning surged into a crackling bolt of lightning, sending the day's second strange sentence zinging through my mind. *"And that's the man you're going to marry."*

A current of heat washed over me, stinging my skin crimson, spreading from my throat to my cheeks. I staggered backward slightly. A mild look of confusion crossed Rose's face, but she kept right on talking and my sense of civility forced me to return my attention to her, though I failed to hear anything else she said.

Good God Almighty, what is this? I don't know a solitary thing about the glorious boy before me—Hey! Geesh! Quit! Don't call him glorious! No, don't look! Don't look at him! Don't look at him again! I don't even know his name.

What I did know was I'd been assured by a good many reliable sources that the sort of man I desired was nonexistent. This guy's age and appearance only served to confirm there was no way in a million years he could be my future husband.

That's it! This is the plan of Satan himself! His evil attempt to distract and derail me from my destiny!

I spent the remainder of the afternoon doing everything I could to avoid him—to avoid Brent, for I'd learned he was Brent, and in fact, the very graduate we were celebrating—though the insane words I heard earlier ricocheted mercilessly through my head forever and ever afterward. I was to learn many weeks later he spent the rest of my visit trying to catch and meet me.

We had one close call at the doorway. I was coming and he was going. The nearness of him was heady, and I couldn't help but notice how nice he smelled, but I'd steeled myself well enough by then to return his friendly greeting with an uninviting, "Hi."

I hung in there, skirting and dodging until, at long last, my friends were ready to depart. I collapsed into their car, flaccid with relief until I learned, instead of going home, we were heading across town to visit with a family who stayed back from Brent's party because they were sick.

I was too worn out to be especially surprised, and soon I was chatting pleasantly with the coughing, sneezing family as if I'd known them for ages. Toward the end of our visit, which occurred in the driveway, now that I think of it, a member of the family asked if I'd like to take a job with them at a summer camp.

What? Seriously?

"Oh, I have a job lined up already, thanks."

"Well," Elizabeth said, "If you change your mind, or want to keep in touch, here's how you can reach me." She scribbled her telephone number on a scrap of paper that somehow happened to be handy.

I was completely enervated by the time I climbed the stairs to my room that night. Even so, and even while I was sure that handsome boy was a dangerous dart from the devil, I poked my head through my sister's doorway and said, "Brent Woodard, Kris. Remember that name."

Two weeks further along the path of my life found me working at Michigan School for the Blind's Camp Tuhsmeheta with Brent Woodard in the flesh. I panicked to find Brent there at the start, but Camp T proved the perfect place to inspect the warp and woof of a soul, as it's impossible to spend nine weeks of the hottest, driest summer of a lifetime working day in and day out with multifariously challenged children, and not discover what the people you're working with are made of. Brent revealed himself crafted of gold from the inside out, young and handsome as he was.

We spent the summer getting to know one another and, with every morsel of time we were able to steal together, we each were increasingly smitten.

Though I did nearly lose him over his misunderstanding of the word *midwife*—

"So, hey, Tony?" Brent said to a buddy after one of our talks in Camp T's kitchen.

"Yeah?"

"Yeah, so, Kim's nice and everything. Really nice. But I'm thinking she's not for me after all."

Tony looked up from the book in his lap. He knew Brent was crazy about me. "Why not?"

"Well, get a load of what she wants to do for a living—" Brent lowered his voice and Tony leaned in. "She wants to have other people's babies for them."

Tony sat back and frowned, shaking his head a little. "No, she doesn't, dude."

"Yes! Yes, she does! She just told me herself."

"No. She doesn't." Brent opened his mouth, but Tony held up a hand. "She doesn't want to do that. Look. Hold on." He nodded his head. "What'd she call it?"

"She called it midwife. She wants to be a midwife. She wants to be the person who gets in there in the middle—you know, in there in between the husband and the wife—for folks who can't have babies—to, you know, have babies for them. Mid—middle—wife. Midwife. See?"

Tony threw his book at Brent's head. "You're such an idiot. Did you really just graduate high school, or not? A midwife's like a doctor. They deliver people's babies."

"Whoa! Wait! Are you sure?"

"Dude—" Tony retrieved his book and went back to reading.

So, point by point, he made my list and, two years later, just a sliver past our twentieth birthdays, he proposed marriage with the help of all our friends, his entire family, a late-night ride through the countryside, and a stuffed tabby cat.

I accepted and we married four months later.

Chapter

SEVEN

THREE MONTHS AFTER OUR AUTUMN WEDDING,
Brent quit his job as a security officer at Meijer's Thrifty Acres to
attend Lansing Community College's Police Academy. I supported
us, earning seven dollars an hour working night shifts at a behavior treatment home for violent, developmentally disabled men. We
thanked God every suppertime that we'd hit a deer with our truck
a couple days before our wedding, as that fat doe, while leaving
the vehicle intact, provided every scrap of meat that graced our
table through our first year of marriage. We used the last little bit
of it up Father's Day weekend, two days after we cashed Brent's
first paycheck from the police department that hired him in Battle Creek, Michigan. We moved to Battle Creek in June.

Our first baby, due toward the close of the year, took root
within me three months before we moved and, by that time,
between my inability to secure an apprenticeship and the anticipation of her arrival, my yearning to become a midwife slipped
as far from my thoughts as the earth is from the stars.

We spent our first and last summer alone launching Brent into his new career, unpacking boxes, finding a midwife, and making friends at our new church. We also went on a three-day paddle on the Pine River, explored the town on our tandem bike, watched the sky fill with hundreds of hissing air balloons on Independence Day, took an evening to rinse mace spray from Brent's eyes, and spent hours upon hours in our wood-sided diesel station wagon with a city map unfolded on my lap, since the hardest part of Brent's new job was learning his way around. Battle Creek is the second largest city in Michigan by square miles and a pure labyrinth of twisting, turning streets.

Summertime drifted into autumn, and it was then I discovered Brent wasn't on board with our homebirth plans. The revelation came one evening over supper when I mentioned something about the homebirth I thought we were planning.

Brent looked up, his forkful of chicken rice casserole halting before his lips. "Homebirth?" he said with genuine surprise and a shake of his head. "We're not having a homebirth."

"Uh, what?" I almost laughed as I said it, sure he was just kidding around. He was always kidding around with me.

"We're not having a homebirth."

It was my turn to pause mid-bite. "But, we're seeing a homebirth midwife..."

"Yeah, well, we're not having a homebirth."

I was stunned. Besides the fact I thought I'd already cleared that hurdle with Brent while we were dating, I could only wonder, after all my years studying and talking about homebirth and midwifery, what he'd imagined I'd want to do once I became pregnant myself. Of course, now I understand he really hadn't thought about it at all before my pregnancy. Most young men do all they can to avoid thinking about womanly things like childbirth before they're forced to, but I didn't understand that then.

"Brent, Honey, please, wait a minute. Can we talk about this? Can I tell you why I want to have our baby at home with Jean?" A surge of panic began to make my chest feel tight, but I quashed it as I pushed my plate aside, summoning all my wits to the floor. Prior to our marriage, in accordance with our values, we'd decided that when our opinions were at odds, after adequate discussion and consideration, Brent would make the final decisions.

Brent put his fork down and pushed his plate away, too. "Sure."

I spent two full hours describing, from the science to the warm fuzzies, every single reason I wanted a homebirth. I was calm and respectful, even while I was desperate. Brent listened to everything I had to say, and I was hopeful he'd changed his mind—I'd been so convincing, I'd re-convinced myself.

I'd hoped in vain. When I finished, Brent leaned back in his chair, folded his arms across his chest, and said only three words, "Just not comfortable."

No questions. No comments. No further discussion required. Brent was "just not comfortable," and that was it.

I reeled—shocked, angry, and feeling bitterly betrayed. The panic I'd suppressed twisted my insides, threatening to eject the few morsels of dinner I'd swallowed.

But all I did was sit in silence, aware I was looking at far more than birthing preferences. I was standing face-to-face with my promise to honor my husband and his decisions, and I realized how I reacted would have an impact that would resonate throughout the lifetime of our marriage. That realization engulfed me like the breakers of a tempestuous sea, leaving me chilled, choked, and sputtering, but, after a moment or two I was able to say, "Okay."

And okay it was for about two weeks. I began to prepare for a hospital birth, managing to keep my anguish and anxiety over

Brent's decision a secret between me and God until, one evening, Brent headed in for what he thought would be just another night on the job.

Brent and his partner spent their shift as usual, responding to a variety of calls until they were dispatched to investigate a box of bloody clothing someone had found on a vehicle.

The officers arrived upon the scene and were led to the box. They took only a cursory glance at it and its contents. It appeared as it had been reported, a box of bloodstained clothes. It was suspicious and aroused the officers' curiosity, but, without any sort of noticeable crime having been committed, there really wasn't anything else to do besides take it to the crime lab. When the men were ready to do that, Brent lifted the box from the vehicle.

"Squeak."

The two men froze, then took off for Battle Creek Health System.

Brent said later it occurred to him on the drive how mortified he would have been had the contents of the box turned out to be, say, kittens, but the box contained, in fact, a baby. It was eventually discovered that a sixteen-year-old, with the help of her own mother, gave birth to the tiny girl and decided against keeping her. She was thought to be about a month premature.

The baby was taken to labor and delivery. Brent and his partner, unable to tear themselves away, spent the rest of the night standing by.

Regarding the baby, the hospital staff emerged heroic. The baby was saved and set on the road to recovery. In regard to the impending birth of our own baby, the hospital fared otherwise. Hour after hour, Brent stood silently in the shadows of the birthing floor, watching as doctors and nurses entered and exited the rooms of laboring families. He never told me exactly what he saw. I don't think he actually saw anything specifically objectionable. What he described for me when he returned, shaken and aged at the end of his long shift, was attitudes, perspectives, philosophies—attitudes and perspectives and philosophies out of step with ours. "Call the midwife, Kim," he said wearily, rubbing the kinks from his neck. "We're having this baby at home."

For the record, some seven or eight years later, while retelling that tale, Brent, with a stricken look on his face, turned to me and, right in front of the couple we were telling the story to, apologized. "I can't believe I thought I could tell you where you had to have our baby. Who did I think I was?"

Oh, how his words healed me. Though he'd changed his mind and allowed me my homebirth after all, I realized in that moment it hurt to have been so dictated to by my life partner. Had we given birth to Hannah in the hospital, no matter how smoothly it may have gone, the fact is, I would have suffered a deep and grievous loss. And the experience would have been sure to have cooled our relationship too, though I know I'd have tried with all my strength to forgive Brent and honor him through it. I'm so glad we never had to find out how difficult that might have been. Instead, between his change of mind and that beautiful apology, my love and respect for him flourished and grew, as did my ability to trust him and his decisions.

So, on a blustery evening in December, seven days before Hannah's due date, after spending the day feeling crabby in general and toward our golden retriever in particular, I eased into early labor, excited (though still kind of cranky) in the knowledge I'd soon be bringing our priceless baby into the light.

Having only had a few cramps and a single smear of scarlet goo in my panties, I decided I'd better go to bed—who knew when I'd be able to sleep through another night? With capricious gusts of snow-laden gales rattling the windowpanes, I passed the hours of darkness curled against the warm body of my young husband, waking from time to time as my womb squeezed me and my unborn bundle in a snug embrace.

The sun rose shrouded in a haze of thick flakes, and I rose with it, though I knew I ought to sleep in. But I was bursting with energy and breathless with anticipation. I rearranged my closet, scrubbed the bathroom and the kitchen, and vacuumed the living room, taking breaks only at the insistence of my unusually active bowels. When I considered the hour sufficiently decent, I telephoned my midwife and my mother to let them know something was happening.

Mid-morning, a set of yet-childless friends dropped over, and we decided it would be just the thing to go fetch our Christmas trees together. And it was just the thing to spend the day out in the crisp, spruce-scented air, searching amid the drifts for a tree that suited us while the squeezes came on with ever increasing strength. By suppertime they were strong and close, and I was pleased to find I could bear them, though I retreated to the solace of a shower instead of breaking bread with the group.

My mom called to see how things were going about the time I exited the bathroom. She lived two hours north, and I wanted her to be with me through the birth.

"Oh, no." Brent laughed. "She's not in labor."

I was near enough to take the phone from him and get my mother heading my way.

Once Brent was convinced I really was in labor, he prepped the room for the birth, and, entering it soon afterward, I was startled to find virtually every square inch covered in layers of transparent plastic drop cloth. In the days following the birth, I asked him both why he hadn't thought I was in labor and why he'd spill-proofed the room so excessively. He told me he sincerely hadn't thought I was in labor, since I wasn't, "you know, rolling around on the bed, screaming, or anything."

As to the plastic, he confessed his expectations of childbirth were more influenced by the explosively bloody films he'd been subjected to in the police academy than he realized. Between that and the "rolling around and screaming" bit, it really was no wonder he'd been skeptical about homebirth.

Though I never did roll about or scream, my once-scarcely noticeable uterus revealed the full measure of its potency in wave after crushing wave. I shifted endlessly between soaks in the salty waters of my bathtub to lying still as possible on my side on the twin bed tucked into the corner of the nursery—the whole of my being, all my substance, caught up in the rushing rhythms of my travail.

I vaguely remember our two families arriving around bed-time, with Jean following soon after. By then, if I wasn't in the bathtub, I was on my hands and knees. The pain in my back was astonishing, and I was nauseated and exhausted.

Our parents and my sisters whiled away the hours squished onto one sleeper-sofa, one rickety wooden rocker, and one sag-ging recliner while Jean, for the most part, left Brent and me alone.

And we liked that. After all, we'd gotten Hannah into me all by ourselves, and the very energy that gets babies in is the same energy that gets them out, and it works best in private. Here and there, Jean would slip in, listen to our baby's rapidly pattering heart, whisper a word of assurance, make a suggestion or two, then slip back out.

The hours passed as hours do, ticking away minute by min-ute, but that magical nighttime was measured for me by waves of indescribable sensation. My anchor amidst the waves was Brent, with his strong hands on my back, his knees supporting my cheek, his words imparting the courage I needed to face and embrace my body's awe-inspiring display of raw power.

Toward the wee hours of morning, as the waves climaxed in a crescendo of pressure, the growls and grunts that replaced my breathings and blowings drew Jean and my mother from the next room.

Jean examined me, and found I wasn't quite ready to push, though the urge was wholly overwhelming. Then Jean listened again to our baby's heartbeat and we discovered she wasn't tolerating the intensity of the labor so well, at least not with me on my hands and knees. In a flash, Jean had me on the bed, reclining against a stack of pillows and inhaling the cool stream of oxygen that issued from an age-mottled, lime-green cylinder. Jean listened to our child again, and we were relieved when she smiled and said, "Better." But I noticed her smile was thin-lipped and a crease formed between her gray eyes.

Strangely though, in that moment I was flooded with the assurance our little girl was okay—and that she was, in fact, a girl.

I wanted to lay my hand on Jean's arm and tell her our baby was fine, and I wanted to shout to Brent, "Oh, Brent! Here comes your daughter!"

But, as Jean smoothed away the last rim of my cervix with her gentle fingertips, all I was able to do was surrender to my body's mind-blowing impulses and push.

All on my own, with a groan and a shriek and with every shred of my might, I pressed our squirming, squalling baby through my blazing tissues and into Brent's massive hands.

And she was Hannah! And her wails saturated the air! And our own cries joined hers!

I reached down and swept her into my arms.

I know it sounds cliché to say our lives changed forever then, but they did. As we gushed and wept and laughed over the tiny life sprawled across my deflated belly, with the gorgeous blush of rose suffusing her bluish-purple skin and the fantastic coil of turquoise cord snaking from her navel and with each of her minuscule fingers and toes splayed wide as though in surprise, Brent and I looked up and our eyes met. The pools of our souls coalesced and we fell more deeply in love with one another than we'd ever been before, even as we fell headlong in love with our perfect baby girl.

Chapter

EIGHT

AMAZINGLY ENOUGH, MY APPRENTICESHIP WITH
Jean was her idea.

On a brisk January morning, six weeks after Hannah's birth,
Jean came over for our last postpartum visit. She scudded
through our front door followed by a stiff breeze and flurry of
snowflakes, and looked chilled through. I offered to make her a
cup of tea and we made our way to my tiny kitchen.

Jean scooped Hannah into her arms while I set the water to
boil.

"Ha-nnah—Hi, Hannah!" Jean laughed as Hannah rewarded
her with a smile as bright as her big, dark eyes. "Oh, my, does she
ever look like her daddy." She ran her hand over the blanket of
fuzz covering my daughter's head. "Minus hair."

Jean coaxed smile after smile after smile from my happy baby
as she sipped her tea. Our talk flitted here and there, and finally
lighted upon a reminiscence of my birth.

She set her cup down and reached to pull the scale, measuring tape, and stethoscope from her bag. "I still can't get over the faith you had in your body's ability to give birth, Kim. You inspired me, from the moment I walked through your door and you said, 'So, do you do twins? Do you do breeches? Do you do footling breeches? Because I'm having this baby at home!'"

We laughed.

Jean moved from the table to the living room and spread out her sling on the sofa. She laid Hannah in it and began to undress her. I perched on the arm of the couch to watch. The gentleness of her hands as she worked touched my heart, as did the affectionate way she talked to my girl.

Jean listened to her heart and checked her length, then she attached the old bronze spring scale to the sling and swung Hannah aloft. "And—it looks like she's seven pounds, nine ounces. Good!" She smiled at me as she returned the squirming bundle to the sofa cushions. "Let's get her diaper back on before she makes a mess."

I asked all my questions as Jean looked me over and jotted her findings into my chart.

"You know, Kim." She closed the chart and bent to stow her gear. "I think you'd make a good midwife. How'd you like to apprentice with me?"

A thousand thoughts flashed through my mind. *How did Jean know I want to be a midwife?* I hadn't shared the dreams of my youth with her. Desire surged to the surface, but I stamped it out. I was a wife and a new mother, and I considered those occupations incompatible with any school or a career.

"Oh!" I said. "Thank you for asking! I'm honored! But, no, I can't. Maybe when Hannah's grown up..."

I told Brent about our conversation over dinner that night almost as an afterthought. He was shocked I'd told her no. I was shocked that he was shocked.

"Brent! I'm a mom now."

"Yeah?"

"Well, I sure can't be a mom *and* a midwife."

"What do you mean? Why can't you? You don't have to do it full-time. You could just do a little."

Just do a little. Wow. Thank God for that man.

I called Jean the next morning and told her I thought I'd like to be her apprentice after all, but wondered if I could just do it a little at a time. She said just a little bit of an apprenticeship would be fine with her.

I hung up, flushed with hope and trembling with trepidation.

I wrote in my journal that March, "I've started reading the book, *Becoming a Midwife* by Carolyn Steiger. I can see learning to be a midwife and, then, actually *being* a midwife takes a lot of time, effort, and commitment. I want to do it, but not at the expense of my family. My family has to come first."

I meant what I wrote and, with that thought, I jumped in.

Eighteen months passed before Jean called me to attend a birth, but, while I waited for that day to come, I unpacked the books and study materials I'd accumulated before our marriage and formulated a plan to tackle them. After I finished *Becoming a Midwife*, I picked up Carla Hartley's *Helping Hands*. My journal from that season brims with the wisdom and advice of midwives with similar faith, values, and priorities I was eager to absorb.

I was reminded that midwifery truly is a calling. So many of us would say we *were* midwives long before we *became* midwives.

Yet, I was admonished midwifery is not about us midwives. It's about the families we serve and their hopes and dreams. It's about inspiring confidence and autonomy, and about education and encouragement and empowerment; never about accolades, never about reward, never about shining, never about rescuing— never, ever about delivering.

I was advised midwifery is also about having a clear head and solid footing. It's about being ready to love and respect, to accept and serve folks as they come.

I was warned there would be highs and lows. While the highs are gloriously high, the lows of midwifery are about as low as low gets.

I was exhorted to mind the needs of my family amid the extreme demands of midwifery, and cautioned to take care of myself, too—for if I ran dry, I'd have very little to give.

I read through those words again in preparation for writing this book and was touched to tears as I did. The way they helped me lay a healthy foundation for my years of midwifery study and practice is plain to see.

The next winter we moved from the cute bungalow where I birthed Hannah to a shabby, drafty, dramatically less expensive spot across town. Once we were settled there, Brent and I crafted a schedule that would allow me to both study and attend appointments with Jean.

I felt as though I had things well in hand until I attended my first two births.

Laura and Gary's birth was a mind-blower in so many ways.

I don't know what I expected from my first homebirth, but it wasn't exactly what I experienced that sticky, humid morning in July. To that point, I'd filled my young head with idyllic tales of crisp Amish families and earthy hippies giving birth in environs of peace and beauty and dignity. My own birth at home served to reaffirm the images summoned by those tales. Looking back upon my inaugural event from the vantage point of twenty-some years and more than five hundred babies, I can say it was unlike any birth I've attended. Still, in the moment, I had no way of knowing it was atypical.

I returned home from Laura's birth just in time for Brent to leave for an afternoon shift at the police department; the night shift he worked right before I rushed off to Laura's was a bit of overtime. I picked up the house and made supper, then, after I bathed Hannah and put her to bed, I retreated to the back deck to think and write about the birth of Laura's tiny baby as the heat of the day dispersed with the sinking sun.

> *8:37 p.m., 3 July 1993. I attended my first homebirth today, and it was a thrill and it was too much and it was gorgeous and it was frightening and I still can hardly believe it happened! The parents were a trip and their house was trashed and the birth was magic—and then the baby was born pale and silent! Jean had to resuscitate her! I was scared—frozen— but something inside me just knew she'd be okay. Babies are made to breathe!*
>
> *On the drive back to Battle Creek, I marveled at how, even while I'd waited so many years to begin my apprenticeship, it seemed the most normal, natural thing to have spent the morning helping a woman birth her baby and wash up her dishes. I'm a little worried about the way the smells and what-not affected me, but, surely, with time, I'll grow accustomed to all of that....*

Tired as I was—wiped out, really—I was excited
to see Brent and Hannah, and more eager than ever
to care for them again after Jean dropped me off. They
were fine without me, too, which was a relief. I think
this will work. I hope this will work!

When I returned home from the second birth, I was more
than a little worried about my reactions to our clients' environs.
They sprang up unsolicited and unwelcome, yet with such force!
I felt like Miss Huddleston in *Christy* with her impossibly sensitive nose and aversion to dirt and disorder, and the matter became
the recurring theme of my prayer times as I moved into the substance of my apprenticeship.

I began accompanying Jean to prenatal and postpartum
visits a couple times each month soon after Salome and Nathan's
birth. Looking back in my notes, I see on the very first of those
excursions, I met a starkly spare Amish woman and mother of
three named Ruby.

Though I wasn't slated to attend the birth of the baby boy
growing within her womb, I met him sure enough when, seventeen years later, his hand was badly mangled in a mill accident.

By then, I'd served as midwife through the births of a handful of Ruby's grandbabies, as well as at the births of a whole
passel of her nieces and nephews and neighbors. Ruby called me
about her son because it's commonplace for folks who've come
to trust their midwives to call them about all sorts of medical
issues. I'd been called upon many times to squint into ears, peer
into mouths, scrutinize noses, examine eyes, inspect rashes,
explore bumps, look over bruises, assess ingrown toe nails, listen
to lungs and hearts, draw blood samples, analyze urine, investigate the private parts of worried grandmothers, soothe minor

bites and burns and stings, and bandage a multifarious collection of superficial wounds.

I always made sure the families understood the only care I could provide in such situations was a bit of old-school mothering—actual medical evaluation and treatment would most certainly be superior to my attentions. Often, however, folks still desired I stop by, and I soon learned how far a seemingly fruitless visit could go toward easing transitions from homes to hospitals.

So, though I was aware I'd not likely be able to do much for the boy, I agreed to come to Ruby and her son. I was waved into the driveway and ushered into the kitchen by, I suspected, most of the residents of the district. My knees nearly gave way when I unwrapped the gauze that swaddled the disfigured appendage. It was bad, but I managed to gather myself for a brief inspection before I re-wrapped it and sent him off to Bronson Hospital. They really ought to have taken him straight there, but the grateful relief I saw on the faces hovering over me as I made my examination was well worth the price of a short delay in his treatment. And that's one of the hallmarks of homebirth midwives. They recognize their calling is to tend as carefully to the souls they serve as it is to tend the bodies housing them.

When I think back to the day I met Ruby, I have to smile. Had I any inkling then of the special moments she and I would come to share by the time we reached the far side of seventeen years, well, I suspect the scope and significance of that inkling would have been beyond my ability to plumb. But I smile all the same with tears sparkling in the corners of my eyes to realize I'd passed right by little girls I'd one day attend in childbearing as they scampered about in the sunshine of their mamas' peony-trimmed yards.

We went from Ruby's to Salome's, and there I was horrified to discover Jean meant for me to "poke the baby" or, in other words, to perform the newborn screen. That entails sticking the fleshy portion of a baby's tender, pink heel with a steel lancet, then squeezing and squeezing six great bubbles of his or her blood onto a sheet of blotter paper provided by the Health Department. I'd only been party to one newborn screen up to that point, and that was Hannah's. She screamed in my arms as Jean secured the specimen and the only reason I remained upright was the fact I was holding her.

I nearly quit right then and there. Jean let me off the hook when she realized the state of my mind, but warned me I'd be up the next time a newborn screen was on the calendar. I swallowed, wiped the sweat from my brow, and nodded my understanding.

The rest of that day—the rest of that autumn—I went from house to house with my mentor, mostly for prenatal and post-partum visits, occasionally for births. The plan was for me to attend a visit day per month and a birth per month, while studying as much as possible between times on my own.

I was a confusion of conflicting thoughts and emotions through the season. Even while I was overjoyed to have finally embarked upon the pursuit of my calling, I was plagued with doubt as to whether I possessed the strength and stomach required of midwives, and I was disheartened to discover I was far more immature and self-centered than I realized.

It became clear if I wanted to tend well to both my family and my studies, I'd have to make some serious lifestyle adjustments.

It became clear it was time for me to grow up.

Chapter
NINE

AND SO, I BEGAN MY APPRENTICESHIP ABOUT AS apt and agile as a newly born foal and it's a wonder Jean kept me on at all. But she did and for that I'll forever be grateful.

The decision to attend one birth a month suffered almost immediately, as did my plan to study between times. Soon after my first round of appointments, Jean called me to attend three births in eight days with her—two for Amish families and one for a set of teenagers who gave birth to a nearly nine-pound child.

The day after the third of those births, I discovered I was pregnant again myself.

Two weeks later, with a full, silver moon bathing the wintry night in ghostly light, we took off for the birth of a new baby in Niles, at the southwest tip of Michigan.

I had begun to feel a little more at ease attending births by the time this family phoned us but, as life so often is wont to do, it threw a number of screwy pitches my way to knock me off my game. First of all, the couple was late-to-care and birthing a mite early, so Jean hadn't yet driven to their remote home, a solid ninety minutes away. Second, the sky let loose a furious flurry of snow as we drove—our first storm of the season—obscuring the preternatural moonlight, as well as our view of the roads. Third, I got us lost. Fourth, the dad called Jean's state-of-the-art car phone to say we'd better hurry because his wife was "already five fingers dilated!"

We arrived around four-thirty in the morning, feeling panicky and annoyed with one another, wondering how many centimeters equaled the five finger tips of a grown man, and worried we'd missed the birth.

We turned onto the two-track driveway late, but still well ahead of dawn, and followed its twists and turns through a grotto of trees blanketed with snow until it widened before a small barn and even smaller house.

Our hearts pounding, we scrambled from the car, grabbed the bags of gear, and slogged through the drifts toward the door. But just as Jean raised her hand to knock, we noticed a neatly printed note taped to the frosty square of window, instructing us to make ourselves at home until the couple returned from milking the goats.

The incongruity of the note produced sighs and giggles as we squeezed inside, cleansing us of our concerns and our irritations. I was struck afresh with appreciation for the no-fuss, industrious sort of folk we served and, in light of the changes I wanted to make in my own outlook and way of life, I was inspired too.

I don't remember when they came back in, but I do remember drinking them in when they did. Colette and Collin.

Colette was thirty-six and birthing her sixth baby. She had two long brown braids in her curly hair, with smiling eyes to match. Collin was a massively-built outdoorsman, complete with unruly beard and overalls. When the two stamped through the door, we learned that all the kids were there in the house, asleep in the one bedroom they shared, so Colette planned to birth on the hide-a-bed sofa in the living room.

Collin kicked off his boots and shook our hands before crossing the room to stoke up the fire in the woodstove. Colette said hello as she shook her jacket out, hung it on a peg next to the door, then excused herself to use the bathroom, ducking past the fraying flannel blanket pinned up between the living room and the rest of the house.

It only took us a few minutes to have things ready to greet the new baby, so we were soon settled into the corners of the unadorned but cozy little room. And then the next twisting pitch was cast to perplex me. Jean whispered I needed to watch myself as Colette was a woman who preferred not to be touched a whole lot.

I was startled, and I began to fret. *Do I tend to touch our moms too much? Had I touched Colette?*

I hung back as she labored, worrying about the answers to those questions. I was almost obsessively careful not to touch her, and I cringed inside each time Jean was forced to, glancing quickly at Colette's face to read how she handled it.

Colette seemed to tolerate Jean's ministrations well and labored beautifully. Before long, she began to push a bit, hovering upright on her knees and clinging to the forearms of her stolid husband. Jean asked me to wring out a hot wash cloth for her to press against Colette's bulging perineum when, with the next grunty push, the baby slipped right out onto the mattress.

Colette and Collin gathered the child to their hearts, while I sat there with my jaw slack and the washcloth cooling in my hand. When Colette said she still really wanted something warm on her stinging bottom, Jean looked at me and the cloth and nodded, and I had a moment of scattered bewilderment, trying to figure out how to apply the cloth without touching her.

Finally, unable to think of an adequate solution to the dilemma, I reached out and put it against her bottom, intending to quickly slip my hand away but, before I could, Colette sighed with relief and sat down! Oh my! I was in an agony of concern. What would Colette think when she noticed my hand clamped against, of all places, her privates? Would Jean ever bring me to another birth? Minutes passed, my hand fell asleep, and the cloth cooled, but I kept my mouth shut, fretting in silence.

All at once, Colette looked down at me and said, "Oh, you poor thing! You must be so uncomfortable!" She shifted to release my hand, and Jean applied a freshly steaming cloth. The fact that I'd touched her appeared to have gone unnoticed. I wilted a little as I squatted back on my heels.

After a minute or two, Jean asked Colette if she was having any cramps or contractions, reminding her she still needed to birth her placenta. Colette looked up from cooing to her baby, and said she didn't think so. Several minutes passed, and Jean asked again. This time Colette said she thought she was, but, when Jean asked if she'd be willing to try to push it out, Colette found she was unable to do so. Twenty-five minutes passed with Colette assuming every conceivable position, trying without success to expel her placenta.

Jean straightened, stripped off her gloves, and rubbed her fists into the muscles lining her spine. "I don't know what's keeping your placenta inside, Colette, but it really needs to come out. I'd hate to have to take you to the hospital—"

Then the gravity of the situation seemed to register on the woman's face. She stood up and said, "Just a minute, I'll be right back." She motioned to Collin. They ducked behind the blanket hanging in the doorway and shut themselves into the bathroom. Jean and I exchanged surprised glances.

Fifteen minutes later, the two returned to the living room. "Here you go," Colette said cheerily, handing Jean a tiny trash-can filled with her placenta.

Two weeks later, I attended my last birth of the calendar year and my last birth for several months. I entered my sixth week of pregnancy, and a ferocious case of morning sickness was on the prowl for me.

Jean called early on a Thursday morning to say the Bontrag-ers, an Amish couple living in the Centreville area, were in labor with their seventh child.

We arrived at Naomi and Joseph's primitive farm to find Naomi seven centimeters dilated, but no longer actually in labor. She was far enough along we dared not leave, yet we didn't have a clue when things might start up again. Ah! Grand multiparas! Ah! The life of midwives!

All day we stayed, all night we stayed, and we stayed all the next day, too. I'd been feeling pretty yucky on and off that week, but, so far, I hadn't felt as sick as I had with Hannah, and I was hopeful I'd do okay through the birth of the baby—whenever the birth would at last occur.

We whiled away the time sweeping floors, folding laundry, scrubbing dishes, and washing eggs. The snowfall from earlier in the month had disappeared in an unseasonably warm spell, so, we went on a number of walks up and down the tranquil, leaf-carpeted gravel road before Naomi's house, of course, with Naomi in tow, kicking about in the curled and crumbling remnants of summer's glory and turning our faces toward the last rays of sun-shine we'd enjoy before winter's gray days set in for good.

Then the second afternoon rolled around and a vomiting jag began, right about the time the dose of castor oil Jean pressed upon Naomi kicked in.

As I mentioned, the family's home was an especially rustic one. They had cold pump water and a cast-iron, wood-fired cook stove in the kitchen, and they had a microscopic bathroom with a rusting flush toilet stuffed into what must once have been a pantry—but only one—which, thanks to the castor oil, was continually occupied.

The outhouse was available, nestled against the woodshed across the driveway, but I couldn't bring myself to hover in the dim light over the rough wooden seat and layers of decay as my stomach rebelled against the little passenger in my womb.

I'd dashed out to the antiquated privy when my disgruntled belly first began to issue its complaints, but hardly had to open the door to know it would never work for me. In desperation, I scanned the yard and settled myself beneath the great, craggy arms of a primordial oak.

The upheaval, much to my mortification, attracted the attention of Joseph's dogs, but Joseph, with only the slightest surprise crossing his face to find me huddled over the webbing of gnarled roots threading through his lawn, put the animals away in the barn and I spent the rest of the afternoon and most of the evening languishing in the comfort of that hoary old hardwood.

Little Frieda was born at bedtime amidst a flood of amniotic fluid, meconium (baby stool), and blood. By one o'clock in the morning, nearly forty hours after she'd picked me up, Jean dropped me off at home.

I was happy to find Brent was still on board with my pursuit of midwifery when I rose the next day, but my apprenticeship took a bit of a back seat then, and stayed there a couple months as that snarling predator, morning sickness, pounced upon and nearly felled me.

Chapter

TEN

I MANAGED TO SLEEP OFF FRIEDA'S BIRTH AND stay, albeit unsteadily, on my feet another couple weeks, but by the first weekend of December, a strange sort of morning sickness began.

I'd suffered morning sickness with Hannah, going stretches of two and three days without keeping anything down. But, though I lost ten pounds by the time I reached twelve weeks, those stretches were separated by spells of relative calm.

This time, I tossed my cookies no fewer than nine times per day for thirteen days straight, losing twenty-five pounds over the first four of those days alone. I did everything I knew to do, plus everything Jean knew to do. Finally, Jean told me to call the doctor.

I called our doctor's office on an overcast Monday morning, and explained what I was experiencing to the nurse who answered the telephone. The nurse said, "Ah, yes. Yes. A lot of mommies feel yucky when they're newly pregnant. Try to eat a little and try to drink a little, and we'll see you at twelve weeks."

Assuming she'd somehow missed what I'd said, I repeated myself. She repeated herself too. "Yes, a lot of mommies feel yucky when they're newly pregnant. Just try to eat and drink a little, and we'll see you at twelve weeks. Did you want to schedule that visit now?"

Taken aback at her remarkable thickness, lacking energy, and feeling increasingly nauseated, I ignored her question and made a final feeble attempt to secure her help. "Yes, yes, I know, Honey," she said. "And I'm sorry you're not feeling well, but, trust me, lots and lots of mommies feel yucky when they're pregnant. Just try to eat a little bit, and try to drink a little bit. You'll feel better soon, okay? We'll see you at your twelve-week visit."

And then she hung up.

I put the phone down, threw up into the mop bucket I kept at my bedside, glanced to see that Hannah was still busy with the set of brightly-colored Duplo blocks she'd received as an early birthday gift, rolled onto my side, and waited for Brent to wake from sleeping off the midnight shift toward dinnertime. Brent was indignant when I related my story to him, as was the doctor he managed to connect with shortly thereafter. The doctor offered to meet us in the emergency room, but I preferred to wait for office hours the following day.

At the doctor's examination, my pulse was a galloping 135, and my blood pressure was hardly registering at 60/44. I wanted to stay out of the hospital, so the doctor arranged for me to receive IV infusions at home a few days, hoping the hydration would settle my system down. He also consented to administer the vitamin B6 injections I'd read about and wanted to try.

For the rest of the week, I was on intravenous fluids and daily B6 injections, but by Friday, my state of affairs had deteriorated further. Besides remaining steadfastly nauseous and vomiting with regularity, I was indescribably weak, my skin had become so dry I left a film of fine flakes everywhere I rested, I'd begun having cramps that swept in formidable swells from my throat to my stomach, and my blood veins became so fragile I'd already had to get my IV restarted a couple times.

I drove to the doctor's office that morning for my final injection, concerned I hadn't even begun to improve, more than a little worried about what would happen over the weekend, and intending to make sure the doctor himself knew how I was, as I hadn't seen him since the visit earlier in the week. Alas, however, the nurse who administered my last shot happened to be the obtuse woman I'd talked with on the telephone the first time I called.

"Mrs. Woodard," she said, smiling sympathetically as she pushed the empty syringe through the flap of the sharps container, "I know you feel icky, but lots of moms feel that way when they're pregnant—"

Struck dumb by the near-ridiculousness of her robotic little speech, I burst into tears.

She stopped short, looked me fully in the face—possibly for the first time—then fairly ran from the room to fetch the doctor. I was sent home with a prescription for Phenergan, feeling better cared for and a bit more hopeful.

Sadly, the Phenergan failed to work. I muddled through the weekend, just as sick as ever, if not sicker than ever. Brent's parents came for Hannah Sunday evening, and I checked into the hospital Monday morning.

I spent a week there, puking incessantly and blowing through one IV site after another, frightening the nurses and baffling the doctors. Jean, meanwhile, managed to reach Tom Brewer, the obstetrician famous for his pioneering work treating preeclampsia and co-author of *What Every Pregnant Woman Should Know: The Truth about Diet and Drugs in Pregnancy.* He suggested I request total parenteral nutrition (TPN) infusions. I did, and my request was almost laughingly dismissed, though TPN therapy would become the standard of care for hyperemesis gravidarum within a decade.

But it wasn't then, so, with my whole mind fixed upon the innocent little soul struggling to take root inside of me, I clung to life, subsisting on the silvery fluid that flowed a drop at a time into my increasingly brittle veins while I spent my waking hours drowning in queasiness and hurling with startling violence. I hurled until I wet myself, hurled until the blood vessels in my eyes and cheeks ruptured, hurled until my bilious vomit was flecked with blood, hurled until my pulse hammered mercilessly upon my temples, and hurled until my esophagus was convulsed with rhythmic paroxysms that made me think of the uncompromising coils of a hungry python.

All day, every day I'd lie just as quietly as I could on my hospital bed, though I never was able to sleep in the daytime. But if I did anything at all, I'd hurl. If I tried to read, I hurled. If I tried to watch television, I hurled. Phone calls and visitors made me hurl. The faintest whiff of food made me hurl. Even the thought of food could make me hurl. My throbbing head and the spastic crushing of my insides made me hurl. I usually could fall asleep at night if I stayed perfectly still, breathing and breathing through the relentless waves of spasms, but one night, just as I was about to drift off, another of my IV lines failed.

It was always an ordeal, trying to start new IV lines in my flimsy vessels and though my nurse explored and tested several places, by that time, I'd blown through a dozen or more lines, and my arms were cloaked in bruises and collapsed veins from my elbows to my knuckles.

An anesthesiologist was called in to try, a thin, pale creature who never once looked at my face. He never spoke a syllable to me, either. He just took hold of my nearest arm with a hand so icy I could feel the chill of it through his gloves, and went to work, searching for a viable vein along the back of my hand. I told him all the veins of both hands had already been tried, though I thought the purple-yellow color of them should have made that obvious. He ignored me, and went on to make a thorough and torturous exploration. At last he gave up, grabbed my elbow, strapped it to a board, infused it with a bolus of Lidocaine, slid the catheter easily into the fat vein at the crook of my arm, connected the fresh loop of tubing to the bag of Lactated Ringers dangling from the pole beside my bed, stood up, and departed.

I let the breath out of my lungs and nestled better into my pillows, hoping I'd be able to swallow down the nausea that had begun to lap and foam in my depths and ease away to sleep, but as the Lidocaine began to wear off, little zingers of pain began to nip and sizzle from the site of my brand-new IV.

I sat up and flicked on the light, and examined the area. It looked okay as far as I could tell, but every moment the discomfort increased. I called the nurse.

"I'm sorry," I said as she bustled through the door, "this IV has got to come out. I don't know what's wrong with it, but it hurts."

"Uh oh." She crossed the room and bent to inspect it briefly, then straightened. "Well, fortunately, it appears to be a good line. We'd better leave it in, Mrs. Woodard. If we take it out, I don't know that we'll be able to get another started."

I looked at my arm again just as another stronger, sparkling surge of electricity crackled its length. I gasped and shifted it a bit to see if I could get some relief, but the sensations continued to intensify. "Oh, no—please—I don't think I'm going to be able to handle this for very long."

"Why don't I get you some Tylenol?"

"Tylenol?" I asked in disbelief, and tears clouded my vision even as the bile began to rise in the corridor of my raw throat. "How would you suggest I take Tylenol? I mean, I haven't swallowed a thing in two weeks—"

The nurse blinked. She was a kind-hearted woman, but she stiffened her spine. "Mrs. Woodard, this line must absolutely remain in place."

I brushed the tears from my eyes and gulped, determined to hold on to the meager contents of my stomach a little longer. "Listen to me. Please listen! I'm sorry, I know how I need this IV, but the pain is getting worse every minute, and I just can't stand it. I'll take it out myself, if you won't."

In the end, she fetched the nursing supervisor, and the nursing supervisor was able to find an unmolested vein on the underside of my opposing forearm. The offending line was removed, but the pain remained, and I spent a good many hours afterward heaving and retching and sending streams of bitter, neon-yellow, blood-streaked fluid into the recesses of my dusty pink emesis basin.

The next day, a PICC line replaced the IVs, and my doctor came in on his day off because "the nurses called me at home and asked me to come. They're afraid you're going to die." A battery of tests was ordered, and an abortion was hinted at. On the twelfth day of the ordeal, I was sent for a sonogram of my innards. I was told that evening something about how my liver looked suspicious, and I was scheduled for a repeat ultrasound the following day.

I never mentioned that to anyone. I don't even think I told Brent. By then, I didn't talk. By then, I hardly even thought. My memories of those last few days are remote and indistinct. But that evening, my parents went to a prayer meeting at their church where they requested prayers on my behalf—prayers specifically for my liver, as my dad felt in his spirit my liver especially needed prayers.

The next day, I woke and spent the morning throwing up, as usual, until it was time for the second ultrasound. When I was brought back to my room afterward, I fell asleep, though all the time I'd been ill, I hadn't once been able to sleep during the day. I slept from about noon till five o'clock. I awoke in the dark, and lay there awhile trying to assess the strange way I was feeling.

Then I realized I was no longer nauseated—I was hungry! And I wasn't just hungry, I was ravenous! A tsunami of joy and relief and gratitude crashed over me and I began to sing! I lay there in the dark, and I sang and sang and sang!

And the theme of my song was Psalm 36:5–6.

> Your mercy, O Lord, is in the heavens;
> Your faithfulness reaches to the clouds.
> Your righteousness is like the great mountains;
> Your judgments are a great deep.

Eventually a nurse came in, and I told her I was better and wanted to go home. She gave me a little plate of Jell-O, which I devoured in a bite, and said she'd call my doctor. When the doctor arrived, I told him I was better and wanted to go home. He raised his eyebrows, then recommended I spend one more night in the hospital, assuring me if I could keep a bit of breakfast down in the morning, he'd consider letting me go.

The next morning, I woke with my heart still filled with song, gobbled a bowl of oatmeal, kept it down, and insisted I be released.

I was home by bedtime.

Chapter

ELEVEN

IT WAS GOOD TO BE HOME AGAIN, THOUGH IT TOOK
a while to recover my strength.

By late winter I felt ready to get back to work with Jean and, not too many midnights after I told her that, I found myself kneeling beside a young woman as she and her husband brought their first rosy-cheeked child spiraling into the light.

It was a significantly challenging passage that left me tired and faint and vaguely nauseated, plus I felt sticky and soiled with the various odors and exudates of birth—but she did it! And I did it, too.

I peeled my gloves off, sat back on my heels to watch the sweetness unfold, and sighed as a delicious shiver tingled the length of my spine.

What a job! What a life.

I waxed reflective as I reveled in the joy of the new family—mom, dad, grandma, aunt, baby—noticing Jean and I were both part of and separate from the occasion. Midwives, I mused, are invited to take part in one of the holiest moments a family will ever experience; they're invited to tend and guard and ease the process, invited to help usher in the miracle. But midwives stay out of what's happening as much as they're able. The birth of the baby is never about the midwife. Long after she's fulfilled her duties, the family will remain, and the strength of their union will find its source in those first few moments of rapturous, undisturbed time.

I was snapped from my reverie when the new mother's contractions rekindled. Her placenta birthed nicely enough, but a glob of clotted blood somehow slipped away and plopped onto Jean's nylon-clad foot. Jean, always exceedingly prim, glanced down and said, "Oh, my!" Then she wrapped up the placenta, set it aside, rubbed the mama's belly to tighten up her uterus, took a step backward, wiggled a bit, jiggled a bit, said, "There." And she handed me her sullied stockings.

I smiled as I rinsed the nylons clean in the bathroom sink. From tenderness to entertainment, this was yet another facet of our fathomless job.

As I went about the various tasks of post-birth cleanup, it dawned on me the irksome squeamishness I'd come to my apprenticeship with was beginning to dissipate. I smiled again. *Oh, Lord! Thank You!*

Weary as we were, we went right from the birth to the nine appointments Jean had scheduled on her calendar. Somewhere toward the middle of that snowy and bitterly cold day, we discovered we had a flat tire. We'd just wrapped up a visit with Nora and Ivan Mast, our next couple due, and we noticed the flat as we pulled from their driveway. We climbed out of Jean's car as the snow began to fall in earnest and, with a generous helping of uncertainty, pulled the jack and crowbar from the trunk and commenced a fantastical wrestling match with the rusty lug nuts, each of us going at the things by turns and wearing ourselves out.

Nora must have caught sight of us from her sitting room window, for the next thing we knew, Ivan was plodding toward us, kicking eddies of snow in his wake. Ivan was a giant of a man and he looked for all the world like a steamer smashing through icy waves, his broadcloth coat stretched across the expanse of his shoulders and enormous, boot-clad feet only accentuating his size. He worked at his brother's sawmill a mile or two away, but happened to be home that morning with a sore throat. We were sorry to drag him outside when he wasn't feeling well, but he dismissed our apologies with a grunt and a wave of one massive hand. He had the flat off and the spare on with a mere flick of his wrist, nodded once, and plowed his way back through the drifts toward the house.

We went from Nora and Ivan's to see Delilah and Neal Mast and Reuben and LeEtta Byler—or, as the Amish would put it, to see Neal Delilah and Reuben LeEtta. Neal was Ivan's brother and the owner of the sawmill. LeEtta was Ivan and Neal's sister. Nora and Delilah were sisters. Reuben was from "away," but still somehow distantly related to everyone.

We visited six other families, all connected by blood and a pure maze of roads, before Jean dropped me home at the end of that everlasting day. I said goodbye and trudged up the steps of my home in a fog of sheer exhaustion, but deeply happy, too.

A couple weeks later, Ivan called to say he thought "it might be about time for us to come out." So, beneath a quiet, thickly-blanketed sky, we made another trip along the furrowed back roads of St. Joseph County.

Once Ivan helped ease us and our armloads of bags through the creaky side door of his ancient farmhouse, he asked if there was anything we wanted him to do. I said he could start a pot of water warming on the stove. "Water?" he said, gesturing toward the motionless windmill that stood between the woodshed and the barn. "I'm afraid there'll be no water today."

I was dumbfounded. I told him we absolutely had to have a supply of warm water for Nora and the baby. He returned his gaze to the windmill, looked back at me, nodded, and reached for his jacket. Jean and I tiptoed to the room in the back of the house where Ivan indicated we'd find Nora. She was flat on her back in bed, with her eyes closed just south of the handkerchief tied tightly onto her head. She made no sound when we entered, and I wondered if she was asleep. Jean said, "Hi, Nora."

Nora opened one of her eyes to a slit and looked at Jean.

"How's it going?" Jean asked.

Nora drew one corner of her lips toward her ear and shrugged a little as she shook her head.

"Still having contractions?"

She closed her eye, grimaced just a bit, and barely nodded. Jean asked if we could listen to the baby. Without answering, Nora pulled the fabric of her nightgown to her breasts, and there was the biggest gravid belly I'd ever seen. Within a moment, Jean had the child's heartbeat ringing against the walls.

"Good baby," she said as she set the Doppler aside and reached for her blood pressure cuff. "After your next contraction, may I check you?"

Nora made a little sound Jean took for assent, and I decided I might as well begin setting up, though it hardly looked to me like much was happening. I drew aside the navy curtain covering Nora's closet and stood a moment looking at the neat line of pastel dresses to one side, and pastel shirts and dark trousers on the other. Every dress and every shirt was identical, but for the color. A heavy black bonnet, an aging white *kapp*, and a black felt hat lined the shelf above the clothing. A hook held a pair of suspenders and a small, black purse. Beneath the hems of the dresses stood two pairs of sturdy black shoes and, next to them, a cardboard box.

When I saw the box, I remembered why I had the nerve to examine Nora's closet and I flushed, hoping I hadn't been noticed staring. I pulled the box free and carried it to the kitchen, just as Ivan came stomping back inside with a sloshing, five-gallon pail he'd schlepped from the neighbors, whose well was powered by generator. He began clattering about in the cupboards while I pawed through the box.

Ivan and I turned toward the bedroom at the same time, my arms filled with a stack of under pads, blankets, washcloths, neatly-folded paper towels, a squeeze bottle of olive oil, and a pair of trash bags. He dipped his head and extended a hand, so I trotted down the hall ahead of him and began to search for places to set things among the oil lamp and matches, the steel-rimmed spectacles, and the dish of straight pins covering the dresser top.

We soon were all three settled in with Nora, who scarcely made a noise, though she was, by Jean's estimate, eight centimeters dilated. I found a perch on the edge of the bed against the wall just as a contraction began to sweep over her. Without opening her eyes, Nora fumbled for and found my hand, and took it up in a powerful grasp as the pain twisted her face. Ivan sat at her other side with one of his thick, calloused hands in her grip as well. She lay perfectly flat and perfectly silent as her body had its way with her. Out of the corner of my eye I could see her unborn baby kicking about mercilessly between contractions, and my own unborn child rolled from one side of my belly to the other. I stole a glance at the man and woman on the bed beside me, laboring to bring forth their tenth baby. They each had strands of gray and silvery-white streaking their dark crowns, backlit and glowing in the light of a window, and I realized they were old enough to be my own parents. I sat there in fresh awareness of my youth and inexperience, humbled nearly to the point of embarrassment to find myself in their service.

Little by little, and still in complete silence, the veteran birther pressed her eleven-pound, two-ounce son into Jean's hands. He was received by his parents without fanfare, though the love they felt for him and for one another was every bit as perceptible as any amount of fuss would have been.

When it was time to go, Nora nodded her thanks. Ivan scrawled out a check for Jean, gave each of our hands a bone-rattling pump, and carried our bags to the car, naturally, without a single word.

Little Bea was born next on another overcast, drizzly morning, at yet another antique farm a few days later. We arrived just as the sky began to brighten.

Nora's sister Delilah (that would be Neal Delilah, thank you) was laboring furiously to birth her third child. I was blessed to receive that sweet peach of a baby girl as she slid earth-side and began to cry. The memory of it makes *me* cry these many years later. I can't imagine what I'd have thought had I known then I would receive Bea's first child some eighteen years later.

Ivan's sister, LeEtta, birthed her baby next, though the child came five to six weeks early and nearly stopped our hearts as she did.

LeEtta wasn't due with little Orpha until the first week or so of June, only three weeks before I was due to birth Paul. LeEtta called Jean in the early morning to say she thought we ought to come out and check her over, explaining she'd rototilled her garden patch the afternoon before and felt unwell since. She worried the baby might have turned to an unfavorable presentation.

We started off soon after her call and were stunned to find LeEtta in hard labor and nine centimeters dilated when we arrived. We worked feverishly to set up for the birth, knowing we could never get LeEtta to the hospital before the baby was born. Our foremost concern was the temperature of LeEtta and Reuben's bedroom, as the handful of balmy days we Michiganders had begun to enjoy had turned as coldhearted as a slap. Because the family heated their home with wood and the fire had been out awhile, we couldn't hope to whisk the chill from the air in time with the stove.

I dashed from the house to borrow a kerosene heater from a neighbor. We managed to warm the room and get the oxygen and other supplies in order before the tiny child made her appearance. No sooner were we ready, when out she flew! And she was fine. She was even better than fine, she was vigorous. Reuben burst into great, gulping sobs as LeEtta drew the squalling babe to her breast, and we sat back with tears prickling our eyes and rivulets of sweat trickling along our sides.

Gradually things settled down into the usual happy buzz that follows a good birthing and I began to putter about, tending to this task and that. When I stepped into the kitchen for something, I found the baby's two-year-old sister still strapped into her high chair from breakfast. The darling sat there through the whole thing without making a peep.

LeEtta was a marvel through the weeks that followed. Jean was obligated to refer the family to the hospital, but LeEtta just strapped that bite-sized gal to her chest and kept her there, feeding her every hour around the clock until, according to Jean's admonition, the baby had "a butt."

The birth was an especially intense one for me, with LeEtta's baby being so close in age to my own unborn child. Until then, Paul's birth seemed a long way away, but I took one look at that wee baby, went home, purchased our supplies, and set up for the birth. Then, of course, Paul waited another eleven weeks to come.

The last baby's birth I attended before I had Paul was Nora's and Ivan's first grandchild, born to their oldest daughter, Abigail.

Abigail's Keturah came three weeks before Paul's due date, on one of the hottest of hot summer days. Jean called at three in the morning and asked if I would please drive down and help her, though I'd already decided I was through attending births until after Paul was born. I drove an hour north to Lansing the night before for my sister-in-law's wedding shower, but agreed to come. I made it to Jean and Abigail by first light.

The nearly nine-pound baby arrived five hours later. It was, as ever, a most miraculous event and as always, I was honored to be there, but by the time I found my cumbersome body half-crammed beneath the bed in the sweltering heat in order to help catch Keturah, I decided it was ludicrous for me to still be attending births. That afternoon I told Jean I was finished with birthings until my own new baby was born and at least two years old. She took one look at my sweaty, disheveled state and agreed.

I drove home, sticky and fighting to stay awake, but marveling, too, as I thought back over the year I'd just passed.

I'd witnessed the births of thirteen priceless souls.

That thought alone was almost more than I could grasp as with it came the potent recognition I was actually on the path to becoming a midwife.

I don't know what I would have thought had I known then I'd go on to catch many of the grandbabies of the families I attended with Jean through that first year—or what I'd have thought had I known my own daughter, then a wispy, whimsical two-year-old, would also become a midwife and serve those very same families.

From the distance of a quarter century, I see it was as if I were sowing seeds that first year, seeds that would yield generations of harvest.

Paul was born on another supremely hot summer's day, thirteen days past his due date. Once I was through the nightmarish morning sickness, my pregnancy with Paul was as pleasant as my pregnancy with Hannah. It was better, really, since the insidious fear I'd be unable to handle the pain of childbearing I suffered throughout my time carrying Hannah was beautifully dispelled when she made her appearance upon the earth. I felt so good and was so regularly with Jean that, more often than not, we forgot to do my prenatal visits altogether.

A couple weeks after the birth of Keturah, a week or so before my due date, I scheduled one. Jean came by and what do you know, Paul was presenting breech. We hadn't yet heard about chiropractic techniques for encouraging breech babies to turn, so she used the information we had at the time and suggested I perform a series of tilt exercises. I tried them once, but they felt wrong somehow and I couldn't bring myself to try again. I told her Brent and I weren't concerned about having a breech baby. She asked if she could bring a helper along to the birth if he stayed breech, but I told her we'd rather it just be the three of us.

Paul stayed breech until his due date. On his due date he flipped head down, stayed that way a day, then flipped back. Another week went by, and he flipped head down again and this time he stayed put.

I was peaceful with him being overdue until the day before he was born. I woke up that day and just felt done. I called Jean to come over and met her at the door with a glove, informing her my cervix needed a good stretching. Brent had attempted to check me the night before, but had only aroused my wrath by insisting I was completely dilated. I'd tried to explain he thought that because he was feeling Paul through the upper wall of my vagina. "Go back further," I said, wriggling a little at the discomfort. "Go around his head—way around his head. My cervix will be way back behind his head."

He felt around some more. "Babe," he said with enthusiasm, "I really think you're all the way open! Why don't you give a little push and see what happens?"

Disgusted, I told him he could get his fingers right on out of me.

When Jean checked me, she said, "Hmm—I wonder if we're wrong about your dates. You're pretty thick and closed still. Not really open at all."

I told her we weren't wrong about my dates and insisted she give me my stretch. She said she didn't know if she could. I told her I knew she could and that she must. She said it would probably hurt.

"And the birth is going to hurt, too! Please, Jean, try."

She sighed and set to work, and the next day I had him. I imagine I would have had him the next day regardless, but it made me feel better to have done something to encourage him along, and sometimes a lady filled with baby just needs a little something like that.

I rose the next morning with a backache and a big blob of bloody goo in my underpants. By the afternoon my body was fully committed to its appointed task, and by bedtime it was finished.

Brent called Jean's pager at five o'clock, even though I told him not to. My contractions were only ten minutes apart and I knew she was at the movies with her son and nephew, but he called her anyway. Instead of calling back, she came right over. As she walked through the door, my contractions shifted to five minutes apart.

Brent and I left Hannah downstairs with Jean until our families arrived. Then Jean left Hannah with Brent's mom and came upstairs with my mom. We'd invited Brent's mother to come up with Hannah and, though I wanted Hannah in with us for the birth, the idea made her uncomfortable, so she and Hannah stayed downstairs.

I began to push around eight o'clock. Jean, noticing my Kodak Star 110 pocket camera on the countertop and remembering how I'd been sad we didn't get any pictures of Hannah's birth, picked it up and began snapping away.

Brent caught Paul, just as he caught Hannah. I mentioned some weeks before that I wanted to catch our baby myself this time, but he said, "Hey, now, you get to have him—don't you think I should at least be able to catch him?"

My heart was moved and I couldn't refuse. I pushed our second wiggly, wet mass of life into my lover's embrace while Jean talked us through it with her soothing voice, even as she snapped picture after picture.

I pushed and shifted and pressed our son through the flames of my unfolding tissues and the cramps that clamped down like a vice on my hips until his head slipped into view. With another shift and push, he began to emerge, his head cupped in one of Brent's palms, his back cradled in the other. I reached down to take him up, just as I had Hannah, and Jean managed to capture an image of that exact moment.

Oh, how I love that photograph! And, though we'd not have ever thought it possible, our love for one another grew even longer, even wider, even deeper.

Hannah was brought in soon after Paul was born and, with her willful, blonde curls hemming her shining smile, she leaned over him and said, "Hey, Baby." And he opened his eyes and looked straight into her soul. She was the first person he saw on this earth, and they've been fast friends ever after.

Paul's birth was a beautiful moment, but one we enjoyed amidst the strain of substantial change and ever-increasing demands upon our time.

A few months before Paul's birth, though Brent often worked in excess of sixty hours per week patrolling the streets of Battle Creek and I embarked upon a career that wrested me from our home without warning and kept me away for indeterminate lengths of time, we decided to officially start and lead a youth group for our church.

Brent had been meeting informally with the church's teenage boys for about a year and the gatherings were such a hit, the teenage girls in the church began to clamor for their own place in the group. As we talked about expanding to include the girls, we realized we needed to explore whether this was just a neat idea or whether this was something God was calling us to. The kids demanded a serious commitment, the kids were worth a serious commitment, and a serious commitment it would be—far more so than we were able to divine at the time, though we were plenty intimidated. We were only barely grown ourselves and hardly qualified to teach or lead others.

But we did one thing right, and that one thing we established as the Woodard family *modus operandi*. We set apart some weeks to pray.

As we prayed, we felt assured God truly was calling us to serve the youth of our church. So, having nary a clue what we were doing, we flung ourselves into what would ultimately be twelve years' worth of weekly meetings, juicy bites out of Brent's vacation times, a sizable chunk of our budget, loads of work, hours and hours of prayer, and a life steeped in other people's kids that would wind up being about as marvelous as marvelous gets.

A couple months after Paul was born, we decided to move. Brent wanted to move because the neighborhood we were living in wasn't a good one by any stretch. My argument for staying was, considering we spent our whole marriage up to that point struggling to make ends meet, the cheap though unsavory place we had seemed a total blessing.

But Brent was bent on getting out, and he could be as stubborn as the last week of winter. He saw things happening in the homes around us, things he refused to describe to me, and he wanted to distance us from them. I yielded, but when he came home one afternoon to tell me he found the perfect spot for us out in the country for more than double our current rent, I attempted to reset my heels in my former argument. He told me while he felt positive he made enough money to pay that rent, he'd come to suspect budgeting and bookkeeping weren't his strong suits. He asked if I'd just "look things over" and see what I thought, then he smiled that irresistible smile of his, and passed me a partially crushed cardboard box filled with crumpled papers.

I spent the next several weeks toiling over that box every spare moment I could find—moments spare to be sure with a busy toddler in one hand and a constantly nursing baby in the other. I did my best work through the night times as Hannah slept. I'd put Hannah to bed, then I'd lie down with Paul in the center of our king-sized Goodwill mattress, doze a smidge while he nursed to sleep, ease away, surround him with pillows, switch on the monitor, sneak downstairs, and make the most of the next two hours. I did the same at his first waking. I'd hit the sack around the time of his second, and then I'd sleep through all his others. By the end of those weeks we were thrilled to discover we had plenty of money and I had a knack for handling it. I shifted gears then and spent the dark hours packing.

Though I had a lot to do during that time, I also had a lot of time to think, and I thought a lot about who I was and how I felt I was doing with my life.

Thirteen births, thirty-seven prenatals, and twelve postpartums comprised the first year of my apprenticeship, and it was an experience without parallel. But it was an eye-opener as well, dragging much of my idealism into view to be inspected and jettisoned. It's one thing to read stories and watch films about birth, but stories and films are edited, even the most realistic. Plus, we humans tend to focus on and romanticize the things that interest us.

It was a privilege to have been part of those thirteen births and a relief to discover Brent and Hannah were okay with my absences. I discovered I loved midwifery and homebirthing even more than I'd thought I would, but I learned, too, it's inconvenient and demanding in ways I didn't anticipate. I was surprised at the way my heart would start and sink every time the phone rang, surprised to find I rarely felt ready or even especially willing to go when summoned. Fortunately, once I cleared the departure hurdles and plunked myself into Jean's passenger seat, I was pretty okay about heading out and, even more reassuring, once I was in a family's home, I was very glad to be there.

But I was disappointed to find I appeared to lack everything required to be a midwife. It was a gift to work with Jean and demoralizing at the same time. Day in and day out, Jean tended to countless families, spanning numberless unreasonable hours and punishing miles, while faithfully tending to her own family. And she did it with supreme professional excellence—seeming

never to need sleep, drink, food, or the bathroom, never befoul-
ing her clothing (except for those stockings) or mussing her hair.

I, on the other hand, attended barely a handful of visits and
births, and was still only scarcely able to keep my family in a state
just north of chaos. I fell asleep everywhere I sat down, I was
forced to rummage around our clients' cupboards for sustenance,
I *always* needed to use the bathroom when either a mom was
spending a few hours in it or when a baby's birth was imminent,
I consistently found myself kneeling in puddles of broken waters
and blood, I was regularly smudged with poop, very commonly
splattered with urine and vomit, and I'm certain my hair never
even began to approach respectable, let alone attractive.

Jean possessed vast stores of knowledge and wisdom and
experience and intuition I barely recognized or understood, even
in hindsight. Time after time, I thought things were going fine
when she suddenly, though gracefully, leapt to handle some
mysterious and scary snag or complexity. The leap I'd make
would be from thinking things were fine to wondering what the
heck just happened.

And I discovered I wasn't *entirely* beyond feeling woozy when
circumstances warranted a measure of wooziness, though I was
improving. I was growing accustomed to the odors of farmyards,
unkempt houses, and birth, but I still felt woozy over lancets,
needles, scissors, and the pain those instruments inflicted. If any
sort of metal tool we used produced discomfort in a mom or her
baby, the battle for consciousness was on. Later, for I wasn't part
of any transports that first year, I learned I also had a problem
with hospital procedures I felt oughtn't be done. From screwing
monitor probes into tender baby heads, to unnecessarily rough
vaginal exams, to premature cord clamping, to babies being
whisked away from mothers—all those sorts of things would send
me groping blindly for the floor.

By the time I wrapped that first year with Jean, I could see the call to midwifery required qualities and abilities I lacked. With a steadily sinking heart, I realized the calling of wife and mother required qualities and abilities that, at their heart, were much the same. As I realized that, I realized, with a heavier heart still, how I did as wife and mother was immeasurably more important to me than my performance as an aspiring midwife.

As a girl, just as I crafted a portrait of the man I wanted to spend my life with, I painted a picture of the woman I wanted to be: godly, honorable, reverent, loving, gentle, joyful, kind, forbearing, generous, humble, graceful, compassionate, self-disciplined, beautiful, intelligent, selfless, focused, strong, industrious, creative, wise, encouraging, and inspiring. I also planned to be a masterful cook, a fabulous housekeeper, and a rock star in bed. Yes, admirable in every conceivable way—a blessing to my husband, to my children, to all the world around me—poised to leave a legacy of blessing in my wake. I entered my adulthood confident I was called by Almighty God to be a glorious woman who would pursue and master the vital vocations of wife, mother, and midwife.

Wifehood, motherhood, and midwifery, however, were soon to prove the sternest and most faithful of my life teachers. In showing me who I was under my own fickle and fallible powers—selfish, know-it-all, inflexible, perfectionistic, and controlling, impatient, quick-tempered, legalistic, judgmental—and would drive me into the arms of my Savior, my Transformer.

But it would be a while before that happened.

All I could see as I passed the hours of night filling cardboard banana boxes with our possessions was, for all my desires and all my intentions, I was anything but the ethereal creature of my dreams, and I was heartbroken over it.

Heartbroken. Angry and depressed, too.

So depressed.

Chapter

TWELVE

SLEEP DEPRIVED AND DISPIRITED, I CRASHED UPON our arrival at the tiny slate-blue house on Stillson Road, and all my attempts to resurface floundered.

Every day I sank deeper into my deleterious, damning conclusions. The things I'd come to recognize about myself were true, but how I chose to handle those truths was destructive. Supposing the success of my life was up to me, I supposed those things were condemnations, even sentences. I was disappointed with myself. I was ashamed of myself. I was angry and frustrated and afraid. And I was tormented with guilt for failing to be happy with my lovely life—with my handsome husband and my beautiful children and with the potential to realize my dreams.

Depression.

Depression is stealthy and subtle. It took a while before I recognized I'd become wedged beneath the onerous thumb of depression, and by the time I did, I was a suicidal mess. I actually think it took becoming suicidal for me to realize I was suffering depression.

Somewhere after Christmastime I confessed to Brent I was depressed and needed help.

Brent hugged me tight and told me he would help me. I hugged him back, thanked him, and said I thought I needed something more, like the pastor or the doctor. Possibly both.

But we were young, and under many misconceptions in those days. Somehow, we'd come to believe depression wasn't a thing that could be treated. We believed it was a thing to pray through and snap out of. I'd begun to doubt that myself by then, but Brent was still convinced. Years later, as with our near-hospital birthing scare, when Brent came to a full realization of what could have happened, he apologized to me for refusing to allow me to go for help. But in that moment, refuse he did. I was displeased with his decision, but I accepted it. I felt it would be a violation of our marriage to seek help in the face of his refusal.

Left to my own devices, I redoubled my efforts to wrestle myself free. I memorized my favorite Psalms, began a regular exercise routine, read self-help books, and wrote in my journal. Every month or so my sister, Kris, would send me an eight or nine-page letter from her home in Arizona. I clung to her letters. I haunted the mailbox for them and when one appeared, I'd tidy the house, fix supper, nurse Paul, wake Brent, leave him with the kids, and go find a quiet place to read it through a few times. A friend of mine whom I think suspected I was depressed, Deb, began calling me every afternoon. Jean would call from time to time, too, cheering me with birth stories and plans to resume my apprenticeship.

In spite of the moderate success of my efforts and the priceless bright spots Kris, Deb, and Jean provided me, I deteriorated. By springtime I concluded my miserable presence was harming Brent and the children, and I thought about suicide every day. If I hadn't been such a dreadful coward, so afraid of pain and of going to hell, I'm sure I would have done it. And my hesitation to do it made me feel even worse, because I just *knew* if I was out of the way, Brent and the kids would have the chance they deserved to find a better wife and mother.

My journal entries from those opaque days are filled with prayers, though, in truth, all my journals are filled with prayers. The Scriptures that meant the most to me then were those describing all things as possible with our Almighty God. A passage that especially resonated with me was Colossians 1:27: "…Christ in you, the Hope of Glory." Another was Proverb 23:7, "As he thinks in his heart, so is he." I understood from the start I was called to do amazing things. What took a climacteric event, even an epiphany to realize was I'd only be able to do those things if I allowed Christ to really *be in me*. To be and do all I felt I was created to be and do would flow out of that—out of connection with, out of relationship with, out of friendship with Jesus Christ Himself.

I began to cry out to the Lord. Literally. Usually in angry, accusing tones. A regular cry was, "HEY! You PROMISED in Your Word we get to be MORE THAN OVERCOMERS! Well, this isn't it!" And then I'd huddle, half-fearing, half-hoping a bolt of lightning would strike me from the earth.

Around this time my parents attended a weekend workshop they really enjoyed called From Curse to Blessing, and they invited Brent and me to attend another with them in May. I was disinclined.

No, truthfully, I was bitter and jaded and skeptical, and the idea of attending that conference filled me with fury. I knew for sure I needed to go. It was a workshop designed to bring to the surface issues troubling us, plus sessions spent in small groups for sharing about those troubles and receiving prayer.

Having already spent so much time in sincere, yet seemingly fruitless prayer, all aspects of the event were grossly unappealing to me. But I was desperate, and I felt obligated to my family to give the thing a try.

On the way there, I prayed. "Okay, Lord, here's the deal. I'll go to this conference and sit through every minute. I'll humble myself and do whatever's asked of me. That's my part. Your part is You'll come fix me. If we get to the end of the weekend and I've done my part, but You haven't done Your part, I'm going to go home and kill myself." Again, I wondered if He'd strike me dead with lightning for talking to Him that way—oh, how my views of Him have changed—but reasoned it would at least get the job done.

By the end of thirty-six hours I was fine.

It wasn't the talking, it wasn't the sharing, it wasn't the praying, although I'm sure the atmosphere created by those things facilitated what happened. It was as simple as the Lord showing me a single, simple thing that changed everything. It was as if He reached over and tapped me on the shoulder, pointed, and said, "Hey, Kim, look at that."

I looked. I looked, and I saw a thing that was there all the time. I looked at it and my eyes were opened to it, and seeing it released my heart and soul from it, and a torrent of releasing was unleashed, and that torrent rippled on and on, and I think it's rippling on to this day.

An interesting element of my dissatisfaction with myself as a wife and mom, I discovered, was linked to some issues I had with my dad and the way he parented me.

It took a while for those issues to surface, I think especially because he was really such a very good dad. I think *because* he was such a really good dad, and because I didn't want to complain about my really good dad, I pushed the issues I had with him away, back, down, out of my sight, and out of my mind where they were able get a hearty fester going.

Through my season of depression, those issues began to rise to the surface and I realized I was boiling with hurt, anger, and bitterness. The way I'd chosen to handle my feelings was to vow and declare I'd do things differently when I became a parent, failing to realize that to make such an oath was to take matters into my own hands, rather than to go to my Heavenly Father for comfort and healing and release—to make myself my own god, and to shackle myself to the fetid condition of my heart.

There at the conference, the Lord showed me plainly how corrosive the decisions I'd made had been. Then, in the very next moment, He delivered me from them.

How? In a flash, He showed me my dad's heart. He showed me how completely my dad loved me, and how he invested himself heart and soul in the betterment of my life. He showed me how every painful error my dad made was made while trying to benefit and improve my life, while trying to bless me.

He pointed me past my dad's actions to my dad's heart and in that moment, my heart broke for him and I was set free—just as simple as that.

When the conference came to a close, I drew my dad aside to apologize for having held him in judgment and dishonor, and to thank him for being such an excellent dad.

When Brent and I were alone that evening I reached for his hand and said, "Guess what, Honey? I'm okay now. I'm all better."

I could plainly see he was worried I had a mountaintop experience of some sort and that once I hurtled back to earth, I would likely be disappointed and worse off than ever. He tentatively voiced something along those lines, and I decided against arguing with him.

I knew I was better, and knew time would prove it.

Chapter

THIRTEEN

I REALLY WAS BETTER AND BY THE END OF THE
week, Brent knew I was, too.

From that simple weekend, one step at a time, I walked away
from the blackness and into the light, and I've never gone back.
A line or two from my journal reads, "Coming in for a land-
ing—the high's wearing off. But I know God met me and worked
a change in me. If I want to walk in that, I've just got to stay
connected with Him. Jesus inside of me will surely change me—
change how I think and how I behave. Thanks, Lord. I'm ready
to get to know You better. You've promised to be my Source—if
I'll only let you. Lead me wherever you want—I'll walk with You.
I'm going to grab onto Your Hand and never let go."

The first thing I did in the wake of that deliverance was
renounce and shun that devilish entity, perfectionism. I understood, while I should always put forth my best effort, it would be
"Christ in (me)," and "Christ in (me)" alone that would accomplish the "impossible" things I felt called to do.

That realization swept over me like brisk winds gusting over the shores of Lake Superior.

Encouraged and rejuvenated, I took a bit of time that summer to think about and establish my priorities and goals, then instituted routines and disciplines to safeguard and fulfill them. The routines and disciplines have morphed over my years, but the priorities and goals, founded on my undying sense of purpose, while broadened and clarified from time to time, have remained essentially unchanged.

I began to actively cultivate my friendship with God, opening each day with "Good morning, Friend! Here I am! Have Your amazing way with me!" I began to read and write, I poured myself into my family with renewed vision, and I began to tend better to myself as well.

I applied myself to those things, yes, imperfectly, but with all my heart, trusting God would handle what my imperfections left wanting, and what initially required robust measures of self-denial and hard work gradually transformed into the delights of my life.

I did another thing, too. Remembering, "as he thinks in his heart, so is he," I re-crafted my description of who I felt God was calling me to be, asking God to help me bring that description to life and then with "ask, believe, and receive" in mind, I transformed that description into a prayer of thanksgiving that goes something like, "God! I thank you that I am…" fill in the blank and fill in the blank and fill in the blank.

While this also has metamorphosed through the years, the heart of it remains the same and I still pray through that list nearly every single day. The results have been miraculous.

Jean invited me to start back with my apprenticeship around the time Paul turned one. Though the purist in me wanted to wait until Paul was two to start attending births again, I remembered I'd decided to lay the purist away and got going.

Besides, the first two babies due were being carried by the first two couples I served as an apprentice and the third baby was hidden within my own sister, Kris.

Laura and Gary, parents of the first baby I received, were first again.

They moved between additions to their family, though their new place was really no improvement over the last as far as I could see. We made our way into another seedy neighborhood, thumped and bumped our way up another narrow staircase, and tumbled through the doorway of another grimy home to meet a full-term, full-sized, vigorous baby girl toward two o'clock in the morning.

Salome and Nathan birthed a week or so later and, happily for her, their daughter came more swiftly than their son had. We were summoned south toward the end of a warm June night and welcomed the fresh baby to life a hair's breadth before dawn.

The family by this time had moved to a place of their own, an older farm a few miles west of their first home, beautiful in every way an old homestead can be beautiful, with so much of it reminding me of my grandfather's place.

The rumble of loose gravel beneath our tires drew us through the center of a green wood lined with broad, gnarled sugar maples and presented to us the simple white house with side porch, front porch, and archaic lightning rods. A neat but crumbling cement walk connecting the house with the barn wound amidst a conclave of mature lilac shrubs. The barn was whitewashed while my grandpa's was red, but both appeared to have sprung from the earth itself, with heaps of rocks for feet and the silent promise that a great many wonderful treasures lay beyond their giant, creaking doors. Stone-footed silos flanked its sides and, standing opposite, the blades of a windmill brushed the darkening sky.

The evening breeze, redolent of moist, rich soil, teased our wayward wisps of hair as we headed up the walk and a chorus of tree frogs rose and fell like swells upon the surface of a lake. A scruffy mutt barked a greeting and led us to a door that creaked open just as we reached it.

We passed the night in a web of enchantment, its strands comprised of a lamp flickering on a countertop, shadows dancing in the corners, the slightest flutters of curtain hems, the sonorous tones of a masculine voice, the musical notes of one feminine, a slow inhale, a shuddery exhale, a moan, a groan, a hush, and then a resounding wail.

We were ready to go home, as the Amish would say, by fore-noon. Nathan handed us each a grocery sack and pointed us to the garden in back of the house. We stepped past a woodshed bedecked with weathercock and cast-iron dinner bell into a plot of earth riotous with life.

We buried our toes in the loam and basked in the golden light, filling our sacks and our stomachs with strawberries, juicy and sweet, and with crisp green beans, then headed home, our souls a-brim with goodness.

Then my sister, my lifelong friend, my very own Kristen Marie, had her first baby.

Kris married Ron Ratkos on New Year's Day, 1994. Soon after their wedding, Ron took a teaching job at a high school in Cochise, Arizona. Kris called that September to tell me they decided to get pregnant the next month so they could come back to Michigan in July for a homebirth with Jean and me. I told her not to get too wrapped up in that plan, as babies generally get conceived on their terms versus ours, but, wouldn't you know it, she called back toward the end of November to say she was pregnant and due exactly on Paul's first birthday.

According to plan, she and Ron returned to Michigan after Ron's classes let out, and they settled into our folks' home to wait for the baby to come. One evening, Kris went out to enjoy the waning of the day on the porch swing. The swing broke, Kris fell to the gray lacquered floor with a thud, and Daniel dropped into her pelvis.

Ten days later she was in labor.

Kris called at bedtime to let me know her waters broke and her contractions commenced. I called Jean, eager and anxious to get on the road, but she told me to go on to bed and call her again once Kris's contractions were three to five minutes apart, and lasting a minute.

Of course, she was right, but go to bed? Oh, gosh! How could I?

Kris called every so often and it seemed to me she was in good, serious labor though she said her contractions never would last past forty seconds. I badgered Jean to no end—obviously, I never went to bed—but she, fully acquainted with how long a first-timer can take, held fast. A final time on the phone with Kris around one in the morning revealed she and Ron thought the way to time the length of a contraction was to mark it from its beginning to its peak. So she was having contractions three minutes apart that lasted ninety seconds, and had been for some time. My mind detonated!

By the time we arrived, Kris was seven centimeters and feeling pushy. They felt the intensity pick up while waiting for us and, unsure how much longer it would be before either the two of us or the baby arrived, they roused two local midwives from their beds. The midwives, Amy and Cathy, went back home once we were settled in. Kris was completely dilated a mere half hour later.

And then things slowed down. Kris carried Daniel in a posterior (facing front) position through most of her pregnancy. Though he seemed to have shifted to the anterior (facing rear) at her prenatal with Jean a couple weeks before, it appeared he'd swung back around. That's a tough way for a woman, especially for a first-time mom, to birth, because a baby's head will fit through a pelvis much better when it faces its mama's rear.

After Kris pushed fully an hour with negligible progress and a scattering of non-reassuring fetal heart tones, Jean straightened in her seat and said, "Ron, this would be a good time for you to say a little prayer."

Ron said a prayer, Daniel's heartbeat steadied, Kris's pushes became increasingly effective, and little Daniel surfaced with the rising of the sun. Ron received him with reverence and passed him to Kris, and my life hasn't been the same since.

Every birth moves me. Every birth changes me and expands my heart with love until it aches and throbs, but having helped my sister bring forth her firstborn child is comparable only to the experience of having helped my daughter bring forth her first child. And that experience is truly beyond description. To this day, I'm amazed I survived it. I nearly drowned in the love.

Chapter

FOURTEEN

I RETURNED FROM KRIS'S BIRTH AND TURNED MY
attention to a trip Brent and I planned to take with the youth
group to Toronto the last week of July.

It was to be the first of many trips we'd take with the teenagers over the course of our tenure, trips that, one by one, served
as catalysts for our ever-strengthening commitment to them. The
trips were almost like labors, almost like births. Intense. Hard
work. Costly. Painful. Enjoyable. Metamorphic. Metamorphic
for each of us, even for our own children.

That first trip coincided with the first time one of our group's
members faced a significant trial, and the events of that summertime provided a crash course in how to negotiate and lead people
through turbulent waters. It launched us into a lifetime of prayers
for wisdom and grace and strength; a lifetime of investing, of
persevering, of stretching, of maturing. We served from our hearts
and with all our hearts, and I'm blessed to this day with the friend-
ships conceived, carried, borne, and nurtured through those years

of service. Though naturally not everyone was dramatically transformed for having been part of our group, I'm still amazed at the way God was able to use two terrifically young and unqualified people simply because we were willing to be used.

We were confronted with the trial only days before we were to take off for Toronto. It was brought to our attention one of the young men in our company, Nate, had engaged in behavior that promised to usher in some serious consequences.

Brent and I spent an evening praying and talking. We were caught between the hard place of concern for the group as a whole and the solid rock of our concern for the young man in question. By the end of the evening, we decided to offer Nate the opportunity to stay with the group provided he confessed and renounced his wrong-doing beforehand. We shared our decision with the church's pastor and he made it clear he felt our decision would prove a mistake.

But Brent was Brent, and with his trademark, obstinate, cross-armed, spread-legged stance offset by his most disarming smile, insisted it would be a mistake to do otherwise.

Ours was a group of self-professed Christ followers. We believed, as followers of Jesus Christ, even as we enjoyed the gift of His salvation, we owed it to Him to yield to and embrace His commands, to treasure and keep those commandments, understanding they were issued with our highest good in mind. We didn't expect perfection. Our imperfection is, after all, the whole point of needing a Savior. But we believe when one of us stumbles, yes, when one of us sins, an admission and disavowal of that sin is vital both to destroying the sin's power in the individual's life and effecting a restoration of the individual's heart.

We didn't consider that every single sin committed should be dealt with publicly, but this particular sin's result would soon become very public and with a whole group of wide-eyed souls looking on, we felt it should be made clear, while we loved Nate without qualification and always would, membership within our group was conditional. And voluntary.

We called everyone together the night before we were slated to leave for Canada.

The pastor opened the meeting himself with a reading of Proverbs 10:12: "Hatred stirs up strife, but love covers all sins." He closed his Bible, folded his hands over it, and nodded to Brent. I was a little thrown by the intro, but Brent was unaffected. He smiled and nodded at Nate.

Nate, noted at that point in his life for being rather arrogant and rarely contrite, pursed his lips, raised an eyebrow, and stared back at Brent.

Brent smiled and nodded again.

Nate closed his eyes, harrumphed, sat back in his chair, crossed his arms, frowned at Brent, sighed dramatically, then, at last, began. "Well, I guess I have to 'confess my sins' here or I'm 'out,' so—" And he went on to say he'd messed up, "about like most of you, I bet if you'll be honest—but I'm real sorry and I just hope you'll let me stay."

The second hand of the clock on the wall made the only sound in the room, ticking each second away for what seemed an age. I sat there in the heaviness, my mind teeming with nebulous thoughts.

Wow. I guess the pastor was right. We've just made a terrible mistake.

"Well—okay..." The pastor said, clearing his throat and shifting a bit in his chair. "Have you anything to add, Brent?"

Brent took it all in with his chin on his fist and his forefinger hooked over his nose. He pushed his chair back, set his feet, unfolded to his full height, stepped across the room, knelt down on the floor, laid one of his big hands on one of the young man's knees, looked into his face, smiled his wonderful smile, and said, "Let's pray."

I slipped from my seat and knelt next to Brent, laying my hand on Nate's other knee and, for a great many ticks of that clock, we were silent.

Oh, Father, have Your way here—
Tick..tick...tick...

At last, Brent breathed, "Oh, Father, I thank You for Nate—"
Tick...tick...tick...tick...tick...tick...tick....

And all at once, Nate crumpled in upon himself and began to sob. As he sobbed, he poured out his whole soul in one of the most profound expressions of humility and sorrow and desire to be rightly joined with the Lord I'd ever heard.

His prayer ran like a modern-day version of the fifty-first Psalm.

> *Have mercy upon me, O God, according to Your lov-*
> *ing kindness: according to the multitude of Your ten-*
> *der mercies, blot out my transgressions. Wash me*
> *thoroughly from my iniquity, and cleanse me from my*
> *sin. For I acknowledge my transgressions: and my*
> *sin is ever before me. Against You, and You only, have*
> *I sinned, and done this evil in Your sight: that You*
> *might be justified when You speak, and be clear when*
> *You judge...Purge me with hyssop, and I shall be*
> *clean: wash me, and I shall be whiter than snow.*
> *Make me to hear joy and gladness; that the*
> *bones which You have broken may rejoice...Create*
> *in me a clean heart, O God; and renew a right spirit*

within me. Cast me not away from Your presence; and take not Your Holy Spirit from me. Restore unto me the joy of Your salvation; and uphold me with Your Spirit. Then will I teach transgressors Your ways; and sinners shall be converted to You. Deliver me from blood guiltiness, O God, God of my salvation: and my tongue shall sing aloud of Your righteousness. O Lord, open my lips; and my mouth shall show forth Your praise—

We were quiet a while after he finished, each one amazed by what we saw and heard. Then Brent prayed a beautiful blessing over him and wrapped him in his strong arms.

The next thing we knew, another of the young men began to weep and asked if we would please pray for him, too. Before the night was out, we prayed for every youth in the room as they wept and admitted their own sins and renewed their commitments to Jesus.

We were on the road to Canada first thing the next morning, still feeling like we'd been caught up in a dream.

And the group. The group was never the same again.

December 1995 found us purchasing our first home. It was an ugly red ranch with mustard-yellow carpet. I didn't like it, but the price was right, and it sported four wooded acres, a field just right for football and campfires, and a swimming pool. I felt at peace about it the minute I stepped from the car when we went to look it over. Brent did too, so, I packed us up, made a pot of sloppy joe sauce and a giant batch of cookies and, between our friends and the teenagers, got ourselves moved in a single day. Though I never did come to like the paint or the flooring, and we never changed it, because we just couldn't afford to, it proved the perfect place to see us through the next six years of rearing children and wrangling teenagers.

It was around that time we began to plan the teen group's first mission trip in earnest. Brent spent a Christmas break in Guatemala during his senior year in high school and was so moved by the experience he came away fully committed to his faith as a Christian. He was determined to provide the youth in our group a similar opportunity.

Brent's outlandish plan—one providing a most apt illustration of him if there ever was one—was to collect the group, pop us on an airplane, fly us to Guatemala, and trust God would use us in some stupendous way, with no know-how, no contacts, no Spanish, no nothing. I was terrified.

Thankfully, just after the turn of the year, a group from Youth With A Mission (YWAM) in Elm Springs, Arkansas, visited our church and presented us the option of joining with them on a short-term trip to Mexico they planned for June. Brent took them up on their offer and I nearly fainted with relief. They said all we'd have to do was get our group together, fill out some paperwork, raise the six hundred dollars per person, and get everyone to Arkansas.

Eleven teenagers were interested in going, plus the two of us and the spectacular Geneva Goheen, a woman from our church who helped us with the group from its inception until she went into full-time mission work herself. With the exception of Nate, the young man who kicked off our moment of catharsis the summer before, the kids who signed up to go were a younger set, fresh out of middle school.

We were certainly novices, which made me nervous, but we were excited and positive the brave kids willing to come along with us would have experiences similar to Brent's.

We were kind of freaked out, too, only secretly. The fundraising and logistics of the trip were daunting. Six hundred times fourteen is eighty-four hundred. We had to raise eight thousand, four hundred real-live dollars, plus find someone willing to let us borrow or rent a dependable vehicle big enough for our bodies and our stuff. We had to collect the mounds of paperwork necessary to take a passel of minors out of the country without their parents, a task equivalent to teachers attempting to get homework assignments turned back in to them. And we had only three months to get it all accomplished.

Ours was a church of thirty or so families and while we were given permission to embark upon the proposed adventure, not a single adult besides Geneva believed we could, or even should, attempt it. We were apprised of that dim opinion regularly. For twelve weeks, our phone rang off the hook, and we were cornered and lectured at every church event we attended.

We weren't sure we could pull off the endeavor either, but we did feel called by God to try, so we faked confidence, then prayed and worked like crazy—and we stopped answering the telephone.

And, truly by the grace of God, we pulled it off. We prayed through every single element of the trip with those kids, then we managed to earn every penny we needed with those last pennies appearing mere days before our scheduled departure. We managed to talk the local Catholic church into renting us one of their fifteen passenger vans, even though their official policy was to never rent out their vehicles and even though we were taking it for two weeks and sixteen hundred miles. We managed to get every form filled out and collected, including notarized permission slips and birth certificates. Finally, somehow, we got all fourteen bodies plus two weeks' worth of gear wedged into that van at three o'clock one sultry June morning.

We showed up at YWAM's front gate just before midnight at the end of a hideously long day, rumpled and grouchy, but with our envelope of birth certificates and permission slips under one arm, a box of cash and coin rolls under the other, and the kids with all their stuff intact and in hand, too.

Our little group was mixed in with several other groups to form a behemoth assembly of 244 people. I almost wrote we blended in with the other groups, but I'll be honest. Most of the 244 were straight-laced kids from the Dakotas and Nebraska. Our group (apart from the girls), though plucked straight out of our church, was a group of hoodlums. They talked junk, picked fights, broke the rules, and otherwise did all they could to anger and embarrass us. Brent spent most of our first four days there collaring, lecturing, and apologizing.

But on the fourth day into the trip, we witnessed a miracle. The miracle, as miracles often are, was disguised as a catastrophe. One of the five or six vehicles we were rolling toward Mexico in broke down right at the border and we had to spend three days camped out in a nearby church while it was repaired.

While we waited, our leaders, most likely at a loss for how to occupy so many teenagers in such an uninteresting location, decided we would practice the skits we planned to use during our street ministry times.

So, there we were, stuffed into the church's sanctuary, watching those skits—and, my gosh, I was taken aback with their power. Designed to bypass the barriers of language, they were simple productions, but in their simplicity, a deeply stirring portrait of Jesus was painted: a picture of His tender heart and His willingness to stoop into our darkness, His willingness to shoulder our darkness and His intent to heal and restore us to life, whatever horrors it cost Him.

In a rush, my journey with Him was on display in my mind, from my surrender to Him at six, to my recommitment to Him at fifteen, to the moment He delivered me from the stranglehold of depression.

Tears threatened to well into my eyes and the pressure made my throat ache. Self-conscious, I glanced around to see if I was the only one so affected by the performances and I noticed Brent was gone. Instantly, the tears dried up as I wondered who he caught doing what and, sure enough, there he was in a far corner with one of our guys.

But he was with Ryan.

Ryan, though a bit on the sullen side, wasn't one too often caught up in the foolery of the group. He almost didn't come with us to Mexico at all.

We made it our policy to invite everyone, but to badger no one. We only wanted those who really wanted to come to sign on, and Ryan didn't sign on until we were four weeks out. On that day he pulled into our driveway, plopped onto our sofa, heaved a sigh, and said, "Fine. I'll go."

Brent said, "Why?"

Ryan said, without a spark of enthusiasm, "God told me to."

Now there they were, over in the corner. Brent had an arm resting across Ryan's shoulder, and their conversation appeared impassioned. My first inclination was to respect Ryan's privacy and leave them alone, but an urge to join them began to rise inside me and was soon irresistible.

As I slipped in beside the two, I was startled to find Ryan crying. I was even more startled to find Brent crying as well. As it turned out, Ryan, for the first time in his life, profoundly moved by the skits we watched, surrendered his life to the Lord.

I began to cry, too.

Over the next few minutes, one by one, every single kid in our group joined us and also began to cry.

It was just like the summertime before.

Standing in a huddle, wrapped arm in arm, with the tears and snot flowing freely, those kids spent the next ninety minutes telling us their sins and committing their lives to the Lordship of Jesus Christ.

We went on to spend our time in Mexico visiting orphanages and hospitals, lending our backs to construction projects, passing out food and clothing to families in need, and sharing the hope of our reinvigorated faith. We returned to Michigan with a brand-new group of young folk and three phenomenally weary but jubilant adults.

Chapter

FIFTEEN

WE FELT THIS WAY AFTER THE CRISIS WITH NATE the summertime before, but we were even more aware in the wake of our trip to Mexico that God was doing something extraordinary with the young men and women He entrusted to us. That awareness dawned almost with a chill. It was exciting, but it was sobering, too. So much potential. So much responsibility. So much fun. So much work. So many opportunities to mess up!

Even while the kids remained kids prone to all varieties of buffoonery, the real-life changes flowing out of those encounters with the Lord were significant and authentic, and we wanted to press forward with them, wanted to ride the momentum. We began to plan a second trip to Mexico.

Simultaneously, I began to wonder if I could both help Brent with the group and manage my apprenticeship. Not only that, but I was about to begin homeschooling our children. The magnitude of each endeavor weighed heavily upon me. I had serious doubts I'd do well with even one of those things; could I hope to do well enough with each to justify the attempt? I wavered along the blade of that disquieting question for weeks before I had the nerve to raise it with Brent. Yay or nay, I dreaded the answer.

I finally admitted my fears to Brent from the dark warmth of our bed one night. He switched on the lamp, rolled over to look into my eyes, and smiled. Oh, that smile. "Kim, you're called to do all three of these things. I know it. I don't know exactly how you'll get them all done, but I'm sure, since God called you to them—called you to these amazing things—He's also got a way planned out for you to do them." He pulled me into his arms and I snuggled up to him, laying my ear against his chest so I could listen to the reassuring thud of his heart. "And I'm with you, Honey. We'll just keep it before Him in prayer, and do it!"

Redemption rapidly became one of my favorite words as I began settling more deeply into my new lifestyle. I began to rise early enough to spend the first portion of my days in prayer and study of the Bible, finally managing to read through the entire thing for the first time in a lifetime of calling myself a Christian. I went on to read it again and again and again, and from cover to cover. Every day I read it, and I found it to be indeed a living, ageless, timeless, relevant Message. Nothing has done more to affect my transformation than my immersion in the Word of God. Through it, and through my times in prayer, a continually flowing stream of fellowship with my most precious of friends, my God, sprang forth—an ever-increasing fountainhead of all my heart and vision, all my courage and strength, of all my life and ultimately, what would sustain me through all of my days.

I dove into my commitment to lifelong learning with a reading of Gordon MacDonald's gem of a time management book,

Ordering Your Private World, and was captivated with his idea that the hours of our lives were given to us as a vehicle for the fulfillment of our callings, while our callings flow out from our lives centered on Christ. I went on to read *Experiencing God* by Henry Blackaby, and was enthralled with his suggestion that the Lord is always at work around us, and His invitation to join Him in His work is far more for the sake of our relationship with Him and with others than it is for the sake of accomplishing tasks. That put me in mind of a thing Brent often said to me: "Remember, Kim, the tasks exist for the people, not the people for the tasks."

I also scrounged up and studied all I could about natural living, altering my diet and exercise regimes until I finally managed to shed the sixty extra pounds I found slathered onto my hips and middle at the conclusion of my pregnancies, as well as dramatically improving my health and quality of life.

And joy of joys, my marriage to Brent and our relationship with Hannah and Paul exploded into a thing of beauty eclipsing my wildest imaginings and would blossom more gloriously with every passing year.

Still, despite Brent's encouragement and the strides forward I was making in the private portions of my life, I held back from midwifery. If Jean called, I responded, but I didn't volunteer for anything beyond her calls.

The handful of births I attended that year were good ones, though the one most dear to my heart, my second sister's birth of my second nephew, concluded with a trip to the hospital.

Jean volunteered to help Missy with her birth free of charge if she'd come to Battle Creek, as my folks' home two hours north was a little far to commit to in a Michigan wintertime, but Missy preferred to stay put, and she hired the midwives we met in Kris's labor to attend her.

Missy labored beautifully, but just as she approached the point of birth, her baby's heart rate began to falter.

Fortunately, the trip to the hospital was quick and the baby was stable upon our arrival. A friendly, bustling doctor came in, asked what happened, pointed for the nurse to listen to the baby's heartbeat again, nodded his approval at its rate and pattern, took a peek at Missy's nether-parts, and said, "Well, why don't you push this baby right out?"

So, she gathered herself, gave one mighty heave, and Jonathan slithered into the doctor's hands, though he arrived stunned and in a flood of lightly stained waters—a splashing of meconium. The doctor cut his cord and passed him to the nurses. The nurses laid him flat upon his back and began to suction him.

I watched with my heart in my throat as Jonathan struggled to breathe past the flurry of fingers and tubing until, driven by my experience and instincts, I could take it no longer. My little nephew lay there damp and exposed, his chest retracting and his nostrils flaring with each valiant attempt to suck in a breath. I slipped my naked hand among the gloves and tubes, rolled him toward me onto his side, rubbed him firmly between his tiny shoulder blades, and said, "Hey there, Baby."

He opened his brilliant eyes, looked straight into mine, and began to wail.

I returned home from Jonathan's birth to learn, once again, Laura and Gary were expecting a baby. Laura and Gary, the couple whose tempestuous first homebirth launched me into my apprenticeship—and the couple whose simpler second homebirth re-launched my apprenticeship after Paul entered our lives— would now be the couple to launch me past my self-imposed hurdles, back into my apprenticeship afresh and for good.

We made our way west one evening to find their home just as grungy as ever, but this time it felt like a homecoming. We arrived in time to hear how the girls were doing in school, pausing from set-up to admire the photographs and sheets of artwork plastered on the refrigerator and the pop bottle terrariums standing in a row beneath the mudroom window. Gary, mellowed a bit with the years, made me a cup of strong coffee and told me about his new job while I sipped it. We congratulated him for kicking cigarettes—he was so proud of himself—and, later, after a third lively girl was born, we kidded him over his household teeming with females.

Oh, the bonds that form betwixt birthing families and the midwives who serve them. Strands of love. Brightly colored threads. A part of our contribution to the masterful tapestry that is this wild, oxymoronic life. I read a blog post recently titled, "A Letter to a Midwife's Mamas," by a woman named Carrie Blake. In it, Carrie expressed her desire for the families she served to remember how amazing *they* were through their birthings, rather than remember her name or the part she plays serving them. She feels if she does her job well, she'll hardly be thought of in the retellings of the stories.

It's a beautiful piece and her point resonates with me. And still, there's often something special that develops between the families I serve and me, especially those I return to serve time and time again. I don't ask them to do it, but when they spread wide their generous arms and welcome me into their hearts and homes as one of their own, inappropriate and unprofessional though it may be, I jump right in.

And Laura and Gary and their three glorious girls, for all their idiosyncrasies and improbabilities and indecorousness, will always possess a place in my heart of their very own.

Chapter

SIXTEEN

THAT FALL WE STARTED HANNAH'S HOMESCHOOL
education, an enterprise that ultimately spanned eighteen years
and culminated with her emergence upon the world as a full-
fledged midwife.

I, on the other hand, began to attend prenatal and postpartum days with Jean again, as well as an increasing number of
births. I helped Jean tend several families I'd get to serve many
times over, and it was then I was introduced to the Amish community north of us. By then, Jean had taken a second apprentice,
Nan Vandecar, to help her with the southern community of
Amish families. I was sad my stint in the south ended, but I
accepted it as I knew there was no way I could attend every family Jean had penned into her calendar.

The community to the north was a close-knit, nourishing one,
and the first family I served there was the Neuenschwanders. Kathleen and Ezra were parents already to one daughter, proprietors of

a small Holstein dairy farm, and they came to care tickled and grateful to be carrying a second child.

I did my best to pay attention to the route we took to their farm, as Jean told me she wanted me to be ready to drive myself to the births. She lived a good deal farther north than I, and although she planned for us to travel together whenever possible, she expected there would be many times she'd have to go on ahead of me.

I printed the names of the roads carefully into a notebook as we crunched their lengths—Ionia, Nashville, Valley, Kinsel, Shaytown, Ainger, Bradley, Chester—and took note of land-marks: a bridge spanning a crook of the river winding through the county; an algae-covered pond filled with painted turtles; the tiny village of Vermontville; the corral of shiny black workhorses with snowy-white legs and manes and tails; Caleb's Apple Orchard; and the freshly mown hayfield with the great pile of fieldstones at its corner.

Jean flicked on her blinker and we turned from Ionia onto Kinsel. We rumbled past a cornfield bordered by a copse of oak and cherry, then passed a tall, white barn with twenty or thirty black and white cows mooing and milling around its rear door.

"Here we are." Jean flicked her blinker on again. We rolled slowly up a drive encompassing the sprawling white house and pulled to a stop next to a sidewalk bordered by a hitching post and beds overflowing with sunshine-colored mums.

We followed the walk to a rear door of the house and reached it just as it swung wide.

"Hello and come on in!" said a tall, slender woman capped in white and covered in a dark purple smock. Her eyes were a-sparkle and her lips spread in a bright smile. "Ezra'll be in soon—Oh! Why, here he comes now!"

We turned to watch the stout, apple-cheeked Amishman cross from the barn toward the house with just as brilliant a smile on his face as his wife's. "Howdy, howdy!" he called as he came, removing his straw hat as he reached us, revealing a throng of messy auburn curls.

"Hello," Jean said. "Ezra, Kathleen, this is Kim, my apprentice."

"Kim!" The two nearly said at once. "Pleased to meet you!"

We entered the tidy home, and I could see at once Kathleen's favorite color was violet as everything that could be reasonably painted, dyed, or tinted that hue was. It had the effect of making the air itself feel like a lovely shade of lavender.

As we began the prenatal, I was touched at how involved Ezra was in everything we did and said. While many fathers attend the prenatal visits, it isn't too often the Amish dads are able to. Most work "away," either in factories or employed to other Amishmen with larger farms or businesses, as small-scale farming is inadequate to support constantly growing families and the men find it impractical at best to attempt to take a day off just to attend a prenatal. But Ezra managed to support his family by his dairy, and so was able to come in for every single prenatal. Between his eagerness to be involved and his many thoughtful questions and musings, his presence was a pure delight to us and to his wife, who clearly adored him.

At one of our visits, the subject of underwire bras came up. Kathleen must have had a question about them, though I don't remember what it was. In response, Jean said this, I said that, Kathleen added a thought, and on we talked. When Ezra threw in an observation, we three nodded our heads in agreement until it dawned on us how irregular it was for an Amishman to make any sort of comment about any sort of bra at all.

All eyes turned to him and he blushed the deepest red blush I've ever seen. "Ahhh—" He stammered, "But—I suppose—well then, yes. Yes, and—how would I know, eh?"

Kathleen, Jean, and I burst into laughter and, with a look of relief on his scarlet face, Ezra joined in.

And so began a sweet association that would carry through six or so years and four babies.

The first of those babies came shortly after that first meeting. Kathleen's unborn baby spent the better part of his last few weeks in the womb flipping from head down to breech and from breech to head down. It was stressful, but it certainly provided an excellent learning opportunity for me. Every time their squirrely son flipped breech, Kathleen knew it by the nausea his hard, round head pressing against her stomach caused, and we paid the couple many an extra visit to assess the situation and to game-plan.

Happily, Kathleen went into labor when the child's head was down and the feisty little thing came quickly and easily, though Kathleen startled us with a profuse bleed. Jean and I worked in concert to stem the flow of blood and to work the placenta out. It birthed, the bleeding stopped, and Kathleen recovered well, though I was shaken. I went home to study the physiology and management of the third stage of labor—the birth of the placenta—at length.

When Kathleen became pregnant again, she entertained us with a story that reminded me the Amish don't tell their children anything about pregnancy or childbirth. "So," she laughed, "I was reading the children a story the other day before naptime. They were leaning all over my belly, and the baby was just kicking at them like mad. Finally, Ruby, our oldest, said, '*Mamm*! What on earth is going on in there?'

"I thought our secret was out!"

Kathleen birthed a fat, ten-pound child on Father's Day. Two years later, she birthed a second fat child on the very same date.

A few weeks after Kathleen and Ezra's first birth with us, I attended a birth on my dad's birthday.

The family lived in a roomy, brand-new place on a private lake, but the house wasn't quite finished when the baby decided it was time to head on out. Mama wanted her child to be born in the house, however, and her husband managed to complete the master bedroom and bath just days before she went into labor.

As big as the dwelling was, it sported only the one finished bathroom—the bathroom the laboring woman elected to hole up in through her entire labor. As is ever the way of things, I began to sense the call of nature around midnight and by one o'clock I could resist no longer. I zipped out to squat as discretely as I could at the edge of the yard, and wound up surrounded and serenaded by the family's small pack of yodeling hounds. Thanks be to Jesus, the baby's daddy was unable to come investigate the ruckus since he was stuck in the tub with his wife.

He ended up catching the baby in that tub, though he hadn't intended to. His wife was reclining against him in it and Jean and I were kneeling quietly in front of them. The tub was kind of tucked into a corner, with one of the narrow ends pointed into the room. All of a sudden the woman said, "Oh! Here it comes!" And she stood up and leaned forward with her hinder parts aimed away from us so we couldn't reach to catch the baby! Thankfully, she had her parts and her emerging baby aimed right at her husband. Cool as anything, he caught the squirming child and passed it to his wife between her legs as she sat back down.

Three years later, again, on the very same day, we attended the birth of another baby in that family.

Less than a week later, Jean called to ask if I was up for an adventure. She was on-call for a fellow midwife, and one of the midwife's clients called, in labor with twins. Jean told me a second midwife was on her way, so I'd only be the third hand there, but I was overjoyed to be invited and willing to do anything I was asked.

Off we flew up the coast of Lake Michigan. I can't remember when exactly we got there, but I know we made it well ahead of the other midwife. We set up, and very soon after, the first baby, a tiny five-pound, four-ounce girl, issued forth from her mother's enormous belly. She came at fourteen minutes till midnight and as we settled in to wait for baby number two, we realized if he didn't come pretty quickly, the twins would have different birthdays.

And what do you think? Yes, that second child came twenty-four minutes past midnight of the next day. A fat, seven-pound, ten-ounce boy. Mama had a bit of a heavy bleed with the birth of the placentas, but it was manageable and the third midwife made it about the time we got it resolved. I felt sorry she missed the unusual birth and sorry Jean had to do without her, but I was aglow for having had the chance to help receive both splendid babes.

When Jean called at dawn a few days after the twins were born to invite me to help her with the Eicher family, atypically for me, I was eager to go. We soared northwest along M-66 for a spell, then, as was our wont, began to wind our way along an intricate network of back roads.

We were reveling in a glorious, long-lived autumn where every tree and every vine and every shrub was a conflagration of coppers and crimsons, every pond gleamed and every field was set afire, every stream sparkled and glittered with reflections of gold. All the earth and sky, even the atmosphere itself, shimmered and seemed almost to hum.

I was lost in the flaming sunrise until Jean slowed to take a narrow two-track that threaded its way through a thick forest of white pines. My mind vanished again among the dancing light and shadow of the wood by the time the two-track widened and arched into a clearing hosting a handcrafted saltbox house and a barn trimmed with a split-rail fence.

A passel of boys gushed from the house as we began wrestling gear from the depths of Jean's car.

"Mamm! Mrs. Balm iss un koma! Mrs. Balm iss un koma, Mamm!"

I smiled to see they were eight in number and looked for all the world like a set of Russian nesting dolls with identical crowns of black curls, snapping black eyes, and homemade, well-patched trousers.

"We're here to help you, Mrs. Balm," the tallest of them said as he swung Jean's cumbersome suitcase from the trunk.

"Ya! Ya! Here to help!" A chorus of voices chimed in. Every bag was claimed and carried to the house amid considerable scuffling and scraping and vying for position. The two littlest boys, having failed to find anything suitable for their tiny hands to hoist, appeared bereft and on the point of tears until I passed my purse to one and my water bottle to the other.

We burst through the side door of the house and into a kitchen where two capped and aproned women, the proud mother of the boys and their one and only sister, were standing over mounds of bacon and numberless eggs as they splattered and sizzled in three colossal cast-iron skillets. It made for a welcoming sight and a wonderful smell, to be sure, but the midwives in us were quick to guess there wasn't nearly so much labor going on as there was when the woman phoned Jean.

"Boys!" A man's voice boomed as the family's father strode into the room. "I see you've made yourself useful! Good work! Now, wash up your hands for breakfast and be back in a jiffy!"

He stepped between his wife and daughter to give each a kiss on the cheek before turning to greet us. The man was tall, with trousers and eyes and curls to match his sons, only his curls were streaked with iron.

"Ladies, welcome!" He smiled, then glanced at his wife and spread his hands, "We're honored to have you here, though we're none too sure it's time for you to be here after all."

The woman sighed and nodded as she reached to flip the eggs in the pan farthest from her. Her cheeks were pink from the heat and beads of sweat stood out upon her forehead. "None too sure, is true. I thought I was going good. I had pains all through the night, and by rooster-crow I could time them. But things slowed down some once the boys got up and around."

"Should we check you?" Jean asked.

The woman cast doubtful eyes stove-ward, but her daughter said, "Oh, I can handle breakfast and the boys from here, *Mamm*."

"Can you, dear?" Her mother said as she sighed. "Then, yes, I'd like to be checked."

The woman, Alta, a veteran birther of forty-six years, slowly climbed the stairs, untying her apron strings as she went. She draped her apron across the topmost railing and pushed the door to her bedroom open.

I gasped.

I'd already noticed and enjoyed the fact the unusual home was a masterpiece of carpentry. Every wall and ceiling was paneled in wide slats of knotty pine, the floors were vast stretches of multi-hued hardwood, the support beams standing sentry throughout were the trunks of great trees, and the railing lining the stairway was made of logs.

But the bedroom was the jewel of the place. Every stick of furniture was crafted of meandering logs and twisting branches polished to a deep shine. A handstitched seven sisters quilt of greens, blues, and purples was spread across the gnarled four-poster bed and set to glowing by the shaft of sunlight streaming in through the wide-open, unadorned windows.

Alta smiled at my response to her room as she removed her *kapp* from her silvery head and kicked her sandals off her feet. "Do you like it, then? My Marvin is an artist."

I looked at Marvin with admiration, but he just smiled and hooked his thumbs into his suspenders.

Alta was seven centimeters dilated, but scarcely contracting any longer. Like Naomi Ann and Joseph of my first baby-catching year, she was too far along for us to go back home, but there was no way we could know when her body would kick her back into labor. Jean gave her a solid stretching and came away with some blood on her glove, which was encouraging, and we settled in to enjoy a day—hopefully only a single day—with that most intriguing family.

Marvin and Alta taught their sons themselves because the closest Amish school was at some distance, and the couple wasn't willing to send them to school among the English. Marvin allowed the boys to postpone their studies a while in order to guide Jean and me on a tour of their homestead.

We met the chickens first, the Black Ameraucanas and the White Cochins with the wildly-feathered legs.

"*Glehsh du unsawh chokies? Die sin di oyyawh fon di chokies,*" one very little boy said, holding a greenish-blue egg in each hand.

"What did he say?" I asked an older boy.

"He asked if you like our chickens, and wants you to know they're where our eggs come from. He especially likes the green eggs."

"Ah! I see! Yes, I love your chickens and, my, what wonderful eggs!"

Then we stroked the soft muzzle of the gentle jersey, the *koo*, who provided the family with milk and rich, yellow butter, and was regaled with stories about the many calves she'd borne. We said hello to the tall brown Standard Bred, the *gol*, who'd pulled the family buggy from before the children were born, as he tossed his glossy black locks and searched their grubby hands for carrots.

We watched the red wattle hogs, just called *piggies*, scratch their backs against the fence posts and were enlightened as to whom would be bred and whom would be butchered and whom would be given to grandma.

We inspected the dusty workshop with its contents in all stages of creation, breathing in the fresh, clean scent of new-milled lumber, and reviewed the row of misshapen pumpkins languishing on the vines in the garden before returning to the house to admire the double wedding ring quilt taking form on a sturdy frame in the corner of the living room.

When the older boys turned to their studies, we amused ourselves with the younger ones, reading stories, taking walks, piecing puzzles, tossing pebbles into the creek rippling along the borders of the wood, and so spending the hours until the children were fed and bathed and sent to bed.

No sooner had those many males been stashed away for the night than Alta's pains resumed and rapidly gained strength.

With a full moon smiling down on us through the unembellished windows, Alta paced the length of her room with her hands upon her hips, blowing and breathing through the contractions as they swept through her. Between each one she paused in her pacing and said, "Oh, thank You, Jesus! Thank You!"

The hands of the clock ticked past nine and approached ten and Alta climbed onto her bed and pressed her new baby into the moonlight.

"Oh!" Alta breathed, taking the rapidly pinking child from my hands and raising it aloft before drawing it to her breast. "Oh, Dad! Look! Finally! We finally have another girl!"

Chapter
SEVENTEEN

AS THAT BRILLIANT AUTUMN BEGAN TO FADE, SO did the life of one of our friends.

Beth Moody, wife to Ken and mother to Ryan, Chad, and Ethan, after standing strong and fighting hard for many months, lost her footing and succumbed to breast cancer at the age of only forty.

Ryan was the young man I found crying in a church corner with my husband on the way to Mexico a half year before. Chad, Ryan's younger brother, was there, too, and had also committed himself with tears to a relationship with God.

I often wonder what would have happened with those boys had they not encountered the Lord when they did. They'd been rocketing away from the values and faith of their parents prior to that trip when, through it, He exploded into their lives, showing them His heart of love and mercy, and snatching them into the safety of His arms before the full fury of illness and death was able to crash in upon them.

Even so, they suffered the loss of their mother very deeply and Brent spent countless hours with the boys and their father through the days and weeks, and even the years following her death, becoming almost a second dad to them.

Beth's death struck me in a way that took me by surprise, struck me in a way I was to learn over the next few years would be the way every such death—the deaths of young spouses, young parents—would strike me.

Amidst the sorrow of the present, I experience those losses, those deaths with a tremor of both memory and foreboding, with a tingle of déjà vu and a prickling of premonition.

That feeling crept over me when I read Catherine Marshall's account of losing her young husband, Peter, as well as when reading Elisabeth Elliot's story of the loss of her even younger husband, Jim.

I felt that way when Dan, the pastor who performed our wedding, lost his wife, Cher. I would feel the same way in the year to come when Brent's childhood friend, Silas, left a wife and tiny daughter bereft after a car accident and, then again, when another of our pastors lost his wife and the mother of his un-grown children the year after that.

Did I know, somehow, Brent would lose a battle with cancer only ten years after Beth lost hers, leaving Hannah and Paul without a father and me a widow? How could I? And yet, there I was and there I would be, shivering beneath the chill of that eerie, uncanny sensation.

We passed a rather subdued Christmas season in the aftermath of Beth's passing, but maybe something of a better one, as we found ourselves sifting the important from the less important, reminded not to take our loved ones for granted, inspired to cultivate a lifestyle of gratitude, and holding one another more tenderly.

We crossed into the new year and though I could sense its presence lingering in the recesses of my mind, by degrees, the specter of death ebbed, then vanished.

Soon I found myself on the way to enjoying a winter and spring full of birthings sprinkled with all manner of youth events and adventures with our children.

We spent a brisk afternoon at Jean's seeing clients in late January. Hannah had her school papers spread over the tabletop. Paul was busy with a pile of Leggos out in the living room. I was appreciating the opportunity to work with my kids nearby. Our last client of the day, Katie, mother of two exuberant boys, appeared to be in early labor with what would be her third son.

As we wrapped up our visit, I glanced at my two and said, "I guess I'll go on home and get my ducks in a row since it looks like Katie will be needing us before long."

Hannah looked up at me and said, "Mom, are we your ducks?"

We arrived at Katie and Luke's home around nine-thirty that evening, and the first thing we saw as we climbed from the car was their gigantic German shepherd, blocking the path to the front door.

He was a gorgeous animal, but he'd revealed himself before as less-than-friendly, and we had concerns about getting past him should we arrive with no one to greet us.

I can't tell you how many times we've had issues with folks' dogs. I actually love dogs, especially German shepherds, but every now and again, we encounter a dog who prefers to keep his family to himself and often those sorts of dogs are the very dogs allowed to run loose around the homes we're supposed to try to get into in the dark of night.

When we mention our apprehensions to the parents-to-be, the unfailing, universal response is, "Rover? Oh, no! Rover won't hurt you! Rover's never hurt anybody."

Since then, partly per my experience with Katie's dog, I've learned to reply, "I'd rather not be the *first* to get hurt by your beloved animal." I make it clear that if they expect me to exit my car from its spot in their driveway, their growling, slavering ball of loveable fluff will need to be put securely away.

We made it past the dog when we arrived because Luke was watching for us, then opened the door and called a greeting as we pulled in, but it was a bit different when, later in the night, we decided we needed the birth stool.

I scooted out to fetch it from the car—my, was it ever frosty by then—and when I turned to dash back into the house, there was that dog, hackles raised and growls rumbling from his massive chest. It took a bit of doing, but using the stool to keep him at bay, I made it back inside in one piece.

At a postpartum visit only weeks later, I arrived to find the dog missing. I asked after him when I came through the door (I was always on the lookout for him), and was told he'd been destroyed after relieving a man who'd come to work on their house of one of his testicles. Ah, yeah. Yikes.

But the baby! Katie and Luke's third son slipped out just a smidge after I made it back inside, slick as a pat of butter, even with his arm up beside his head.

The family went on to birth a fourth son two winters later, and that child proved more thoroughly lodged within his mom than his older brother. After several painful but fruitless hours of labor, we suggested Katie get down on her chest and knees, hoping the attitude would encourage the child to wiggle himself into a position more favorable for birthing.

Katie was disinclined to wave her rump about in the air, but we talked her into it, fairly promising it would make all the difference. She finally agreed, but decided to direct her derriere into a corner of her bedroom for modesty's sake.

She'd no sooner settled in there when her oldest son, aged about six and allowed up past his bedtime to witness the arrival of his newest brother, entered the room. He cocked his head at his mom's unlikely pose, looked askance at the rest of us, marched over to the corner, bent double, took a good look at his mother's lady bits, stood back up, popped his hands smartly onto his hips, and announced, "Nope! No baby yet!"

Katie rolled her eyes while the rest of us dissolved into fits of helpless laughter.

Winter melted into riotous springtime, and we spent the season serving a set of three sisters married to a set of two brothers and a cousin clustered along Ainger Road, again to the north.

The families, all Grabers, ran Graber Dairy together, and the success of the enterprise, small as it was, allowed the men to stay home from the factories. But every member of each family old enough to work worked on the dairy, and worked hard.

Two of the sisters, Treva and Leora, had children besides the babies they were expecting, five or six little people between them under the age of seven. Anna Mae, the youngest of the three and newly married, was filling with her first, and the fluster of excitement that surrounded her was contagious.

All three women were pregnant and due within weeks of one another, and Jean and I found ourselves on that little stretch of road nearly every week for a number of months, hopping from house to house to house.

As is the way of the Amish, the older children were kept in the dark regarding the impending arrivals. The most they'd been told was that, while Jesus brought new babies to families as He saw fit, it was possible a baby or two was on the way to theirs.

Exactly how Jesus brought babies was left to their imaginations, and was the topic of much lively speculation. The children never appeared to question what they'd been told, but it was plain to see they suspected Jean and I somehow were involved in the enigmatic proliferations of their families, seeing as how we were constantly there in one of their homes with our mysterious bags, asking questions—in English, no less—handing their mothers paper cups to take with them to the bathroom, examining the little white sticks their mothers brought back, wrapping their moms' arms in balloonish sleeves that trailed strange tubes, poking their mothers' fingers and squeezing drops of blood onto tiny machines that blipped and beeped, scribbling everything into folders, and scooping up tape measures and other odd lengths of tubing to before whisking their mothers away into bedrooms where all sorts of cryptic whisperings would seep out to them through the cracks and keyholes.

Jean and I were sure to pay a visit nearly as soon as one of those cuddly new babies appeared, bags yet in hand. We set to work, stripping the babies naked and swinging them aloft in fuzzy slings, then we pressed those lengths of tubing to the tiny chests, pressed beeping things beneath the little arms, and poked the wee feet until big bubbles of blood dribbled onto slips of paper. Then, again, Jean and I ran off to the bedrooms with their mothers for fresh sessions of inexplicable murmurings.

But most baffling of all were those late nights or early mornings when their fathers rustled them from their snug beds to rush them, half dressed and hair askew, down the road to their aunt's house where they were forced to spend whole days at a time. Ordinarily, they loved to spend the day with their cousins, but there was always something off about those sorts of excursions, and they found themselves drawn to the windows facing their own homes. And by golly, every time, there in the driveway would be Jean's little gray car!

Later, they were allowed back to their homes and, well, by that time they just about knew what to expect: brand-new babies tucked into the crooks of their mothers' arms!

Leora had her baby first. Vera had hers six days later. Meanwhile, the children shifted things into high gear, their faces, all eyes and ears and whirling minds, studies of concentration. They peeked inside our bags every chance they got, stood on tip-toes to peer into our vehicles, plastered themselves against the bedroom doors, and hopped about beneath the windows, struggling with all their might to puzzle out the riddle.

One day, they woke to see Jean's car down in Anna Mae's driveway. Some while later, Leora and Vera noticed all their children old enough to walk had disappeared. After something of a frantic search, the women found the missing kids crouched beside a defunct silo, directly across the road from Anna Mae's house.

"And just what do you think you're doing over here?" Vera asked breathlessly when she and Leora reached the spot.

"Well, look!" The oldest of the group said. "Jean and Kim are over there! We think they're helping Jesus bring Anna Mae and Seth a baby, and we're going to catch Him at it!"

Of course, the children were herded back to their respective homes in a hurry, but Jesus, as it turned out, was in no rush to bring little Matthew. Come to think of it, little Matthew wasn't all that little, either. He shoved his way into the world around four o'clock in the morning, tipping the scales at nine pounds, nine ounces.

Toward five, Seth trotted down to the barn to share the happy news, knowing all the adults would be there milking. Soon there was a light tap on the door and Leora and Vera's smiling faces materialized in the circle of mellow lamplight cradling mother and child. They were pungent from the hour they spent pressed into the soft sides of their black and white friends, but beside themselves with such joy and eagerness to welcome the newest little soul into their family, no one seemed to mind the smell.

Anyway, it would be the flavor of the child's lifetime, an aroma to bring him back home, no matter where he might find himself.

Chapter

EIGHTEEN

AFTER ANOTHER SPRING FILLED WITH FUNDRAISING events, we took off again for Mexico. We had more kids signed up for this trip, so Brent was forced to rustle up two vans, but Brent and I were the only adults going, so we each had to drive the whole nineteen hours down and the whole nineteen hours back, and we did it in two straight shots.

I had all the girls in my van and Brent had all the guys. Our first trip down, we left Hannah and Paul at home, but this time we brought them along. It made for an exceptionally interesting experience, let me tell you. Hannah was a doll, as usual, but we hadn't quite figured out how to handle Paul, though he was nearly three years old by then. We considered ourselves good parents until he was born. After that, we choked down our helping of humble pie and said a lot of prayers asking God to forgive us for the uncharitable thoughts we'd had toward some of the other parents we knew.

On the three-day drive from Arkansas to Monterrey, several of our group came down with something like strep throat. About a third of the seventy persons in the group fell sick before the trip was over, including Hannah and me. Upon our arrival, a tarantula and a bunch of tiny scorpions were spotted, and Paul got away from us two or three times while we were unloading the buses. Finally, Brent scrounged up a scrap of cord and used it to tie Paul to his belt loop. And, yep, he kept Paul tied to him until we made it safely back home.

Our first night there, with Brent dangling over the edges of one of the two bunk beds in our room, and both the kids and me squashed into the other, I worried over the bugs and the illness and my son's penchant for escape. I had a little trouble falling asleep.

It wound up a positive experience, even though, if memory serves me, I spent most of the trip hand-washing our laundry and unclogging toilets.

The morning we packed up to head home, I remember sitting on one of those little bunks with Brent, watching our kids play over and around the four duffle bags filled with our things. As I sat there I realized, despite a houseful of belongings waiting for us back in Michigan, all we really needed in the world was in that twelve-by-twelve-foot concrete room.

I reached over and squeezed Brent's hand as a wave of that premonitory sensation I felt in the wake of Beth Moody's death caused my heart to skip a beat.

We made it back home safely enough and Brent and I got straight back into policing and midwifery while Hannah lost her first two teeth, Paul mastered the basics of potty training and broke his foot, a drunk driver totaled our ancient Honda, I took our teen group's two girls on a three-day canoe trip along the

Ausable River, Brent was formally invited to join the church's leadership, our church's lead pastor stepped down from the ministry, and we lost two members of Brent's extended family.

By this time, Brent was in his fourth year with the group, and his sixth year as a police officer, and he dearly loved both. He was such a great man! A great husband, a great dad, a great friend, a great cop, and a great pastor. He was even-tempered, clear-headed, brave, funny, discerning, tough, tender-hearted, cagey, genuine, and amazingly instinctual.

And did he ever have stories to tell!

One evening, he was sent to the home of a man who beat an opossum to death with a stick, then stashed it in his fridge for his evening meal. One of the man's neighbors called to say the guy's porch was covered in blood. Brent was ushered through the man's house along a trail of blood spatters that led to a refrigerator containing only a six-pack of Coors and a giant silver bowl filled with the dead animal. The man was so kind as to invite Brent back for the barbeque.

Another time, he was called to the home of an elderly woman complaining of intruders. It took only moments after his arrival for him to realize the intruders were visible to her alone. He really could have left then, confident she wasn't in any danger, but his giant heart kept him there until he was finally able to ascertain that the "intruders" were the five or six magazines on her coffee table. He read them their rights and locked them in the cruiser.

He was in car accidents with two drunk drivers, one while on duty. He suffered a serious back injury during a foot chase the year after Paul was born. He was flagged down once to resuscitate a baby shaken unconscious by her grandpa. The baby didn't make it, and Brent spent a long while cuddling Hannah that evening after work. He was sued after a drug dealer he was attempting to pull over struck another vehicle and killed its passenger—ironically, also a miscreant. He was waved down one afternoon by a woman on the edge of birthing her eighth child on the sidewalk a few blocks from the hospital. She kept her legs together and he got her there just in time.

Never was there such a hard and selfless worker as Brent Woodard. He worked seasons of alternating shifts, generally six months of night shifts—the exhausting, but potentially thrilling shifts—followed by six months of evening shifts, the exhausting, busy, babysitting shifts. He'd either have Mondays and Tuesdays off, or Tuesdays and Wednesdays off. One of those nights per week, week in and week out, year after year after year, he spent leading youth group meetings. He had two to three weeks of paid vacation per year, and one week of every one of those vacations he spent taking the teenagers somewhere outlandish, usually on mission trips. Every spring for four or five years we hauled huge groups of kids to weekend Teen Mania events, and two spring weekends we took the kids all the way to Arkansas for YWAM events.

Most of our adventures involved some sort of do-it-yourself vehicle repair job, conducted by Brent, and it seemed we always had at least one teenager tagging along whom Brent had fished from a juvenile delinquency program. The group already was a colorful one, and, between the regulars and the guests, whether at home or away, we were continually entertained with an assortment of shenanigans. We had kids firing off firecrackers in the middle of the night; egging cars; mooning as many people as possible; disappearing, getting lost, committing crimes; losing their things, losing our things; drinking way too many Mountain Dews and getting horribly sick; toilet papering our trees and filling our yard with political signs; sneaking a construction drum complete with flashing light onto the diving board of our pool; and going bonkers after eating whole packages of No-Doz. They knocked the side window from a vehicle we'd rented as we flew along an Indiana expressway; informed us it was "inappropriate" we insisted on bringing our kids with us everywhere we went; scorched the hairs off their legs while leaping over toilets set in the centers of giant fires; and chucked rocks clear over our garage and into our forty-five degree pool. There were wrenchings of knees, sprainings of ankles, getting bitten by poisonous spiders, catching and spreading viruses and bacterium, smashing themselves up on their skateboards, threatening suicide, attempting suicide, getting pregnant, starting fights, damaging wildlife, insulting friends and family, insulting innocent bystanders, and keeling over dehydrated no matter how many times we instructed them to drink water instead of soda in the 110-degree Mexican heat.

But then, we also had them sidling up to us with their homesicknesses, heartbreaks, hopes, fears, secrets, dreams, and confessions. We did a lot of listening, a lot of hugging, a lot of arbitrating, a little advising, and a truck-load of interceding while doing our best to hide our surprise and shock, horror, and sadness. It was demanding, and I don't think we ever felt equal to the task, but it forced us to press into our relationships with the Lord and with each other. It proved rewarding work. Most of the time, it was really fun too.

My journals from that period are overflowing with the triumphs and agonies of those exhilarating, frustrating, exhausting, potent years. My young heart was coming to life. The sense of who I was and what I was meant to do was maturing. With my hand squeezing the life out of Jesus' hand, my struggle to alter my way of living, marked as it was with myriad messy missteps, began to have the effect I'd hoped for.

Reading through those old journal entries brings back all the hopes and fears and longings of that time. The woman I am now was a newborn babe then! The nuts and bolts of today's daily life, the things I do without a second thought, then took such effort to achieve. And the accomplishments of my life to that point were yet germinal—fragile, vulnerable seedlings. I hear the echoes of my youthful, passionate heart as it cried out, straining to overcome, to rise victorious, and it makes the tears sting my eyes and the gooseflesh tickle along my arms.

Twenty-year-old scribblings: page after page filled with my burning to be and do everything God created me to be and do, plus all my worries I'd fall short. Our trips to Mexico always intensified my yearnings and returning to the humdrum of our daily lives increased my apprehensions.

Seeing to the never-ending tasks of wifing and mothering engulfed most of my time, energy, and motivation. Once I managed to get everybody up in the morning, fed, dressed, discipled, gentled, educated, entertained, trimmed, bathed, nurtured, and tucked back into bed at night intact and happy, there was little left for tending aspirations. More nights than not, Brent returned from work to find me snoozing beside the kids with some half-read storybook spread across my chest, my intention to study pushed off yet another night.

I loved what I was doing—I did! But I loved what I wanted to do, too, and every day that went by without hitting those books served to increase the nagging uneasiness I felt over my chances of accomplishing anything of significance beyond parenting.

I spent an evening opening my heart with all its desires and concerns to Brent, and I found him a tremendous encouragement.

He was always such an encouragement. This is what I wrote the next morning.

I DON'T WANT TO WASTE MY LIFE! I was afraid it was getting wasted, both by my ineptitude and by the mundane, but Brent talked to me about how the Lord really is using me here and now in many ways, and that I shouldn't worry. He reminded me I have to be faithful in little things first, letting the little tasks God's given me to do now develop my character and prepare me for bigger jobs ahead. So, I don't want to get distracted by looking too far into the future. I have to live here and now. I must pay attention to what the Lord is telling me today, to do my best with what He's given me to do today. No task— not scrubbing a high chair or washing a dish or folding a shirt— should be considered meaningless. Certainly, not rearing Hannah and Paul, or being wife to Brent. Thanks for showing this to me, Lord. Show me how to live today with excellence.

My mom also was an encouragement, reminding me the most amazing accomplishments of any life are comprised of attendance to regular, daily tasks. I spent a while ruminating on that in my next quiet time.

Reading my Bible this morning—reading and thinking about Naomi and Ruth, reading and thinking about Hannah, reading and thinking about Esther, I realized these extraordinary women really were just as ordinary as I am.

They mostly lived simple lives, just like mine. They nursed babies and changed diapers, they cooked meals and washed dishes, they folded laundry and tidied messes, they trained their children and cared for their husbands. They struggled to rise mornings, failed to find anything flattering to wear, battled morning breath, and endured bad hair days. They worked hard and longed for a smidge of playtime—or at least a quick nap. They dropped, enervated into bed nights, then surely lay there awhile in the dark, waiting for sleep to come—or a frightened child, or an amorous spouse—wondering if they could possibly be making any kind of meaningful difference on the earth, hoping they were making a difference...

Then, amidst the tedium and ennui, God remembered the desires of their hearts and, right in the midst of their ordinariness, called them to life. He imparted vision, and He infused them with the strength and resources they needed to live lives of spectacular significance. And they went on to live lives recorded and remembered for years and years to come, probably amazing them even more than their lives and accomplishments amaze us, if they ever actually fully realized the amazing nature of their lives and accomplishments at all.

It's kind of thrilling, though also rather sobering, to realize our lives will have an effect, will be remembered, will possibly even be recorded.

A couple weeks later, on my twenty-sixth birthday, I woke to find a card Brent wrote and set out for me. In it he said,

> *I don't tell you enough how much you mean to me, Kim, but I hope you know all the good you've brought to my life. I'm so glad God picked you for me, because I didn't realize at the time what qualities to check for. I just knew you loved the Lord, and were hot. But I was blessed way beyond what I expected because you're so much more than those things. Your love for*

*God is so deep and true, I know your desire is to be
closer to Him and I know your prayers do much more
than we see, because they're humble and consistent.
I care so much about the way my kids are handled,
and I'm blessed to be able to say I've never observed
a mother treat her children with so much tenderness
and kindness as you. Your enthusiasm for life has
changed me. It's been a slow change, but more and
more I want to learn new things, to look at and
admire nature, to grow in my relationship with God.
I thank God for you. I'm so proud of you. A little
over eight years ago, when I first saw you at camp, I
was convinced you were the woman for me. Now
every day I see why God brought you into my life. If
I ever do anything GREAT, you'll deserve a lot of the
credit. I don't think I've ever said this before, but,
thank you for laying down all the many things you
could have done—mission work, art, midwifery, college—to marry me and raise a family with me. I know
God will bless you for doing that, and He'll one day
give you all the desires of your heart. Happy Birthday
to the most beautiful woman of all times. I love you.*

Oh, how I needed that!

Looking back, I see how invaluable those early years with
their numerous lessons were. They dug and set the footings for
the life I was meant to live. I see very clearly now the strength
and resilience I'd need to face the storms in store for me were
fashioned through that first decade of my adulthood.

Chapter

NINETEEN

RING! RING!

"Hannah, can you get that?"

Ring!

"Yes, Mama!"

Ring!

"Hello, this is Hannah. Oh, hi! Thank you! Yes, she's right here. She's just pooping."

Pooping? Really? Who's she got on the line? Oh my gosh.

But, of course, I was pooping.

"Here you go, Mom. It's Mrs. Balm. She said I sound so grown up on the phone!"

"That's great, Honey, but, hey, can you hang on to it a minute till—" I was relieved it was only Jean but still, I lowered my voice and nodded my head toward the door. "—I flush and wash my hands?"

"Oh, sure!"

"And?" I nodded again.

"Oh! Oh, yes! Sure, Mama!" Hannah twirled around and skipped from the bathroom. "Mrs. Balm? Mama will be right with you. She just wants to flush the toilet and wash her hands." She dropped her voice to a whisper. "And I think she still needs to wipe."

So, I guess telephone etiquette will be the next thing I add to the homeschool curriculum...

I could hear the smile in Jean's voice when I finally managed to retrieve the telephone from my very own Chatty Kathy, but the subject was serious. She and Nan had been all day with Naomi and Joseph Bontrager, the family from my first year of apprenticing, the family we'd spent most of two days with, the family with the kindly old oak that had sheltered me as my insides struggled to accept the new soul alighted within.

"Kim, we've been over here since yesterday, and Naomi's been dilated to a nine since daybreak. She's tired. Joseph's tired. Nan and I both are tired. I feel like I've tried everything. It's her ninth baby, I think it's big, I think it's cock-eyed, and you remember how she bled last time. Would you be willing to come down here?"

Would I be willing? I sure was willing, and I was just flattered beyond speech Jean felt she needed me. I still wasn't to the point of feeling especially need-worthy, though, and I hadn't a clue what she thought she'd get out of my appearance. But I hastily scribbled the directions to Naomi's house, found someone willing to stay with the kids, dashed out the door, and threaded my way south.

I arrived to find Naomi had retreated to the toilet to try to sit through five contractions there; one of Jean's favorite little tricks. Jean and Nan were sitting at the kitchen table looking fairly beat. I had a chance to think on my way down about what Jean said on the telephone—ninth baby, nine centimeters, big, cock-eyed, heavy bleed last time. I tried to think what I'd do if I had to do the birth by myself and decided I'd settle on a go with McRoberts—a sort of squat-on-your-back position that allowed a woman to really get her pelvis open while resting a bit at the same time—though I imagined Jean already tried that, and probably more than once.

"She's feeling pushy in there on the toilet," Jean said.

"That's hopeful!"

"But she's felt pushy on and off for hours," Nan added.

"Oh."

"She's tired, but her vitals are good and the baby is good." Jean's gaze shifted toward the window facing the backyard. "But I already told you I think it's big and off-kilter. What do you think?"

"Have you tried McRoberts?" I asked.

"She just won't go in it," Nan said. "She won't hardly do anything we suggest."

Jean sighed. "I was surprised when she said she'd go sit on the pot. It's the first thing she's agreed to try since we got here." She turned to look at me. "This is the first hard birth she's had, really. That other birth you helped me with wasn't hard except for the waiting. Once her labor started it came quick, just like all her others. Her last one came quick, too. I almost missed it. Nan did miss it. I think she's waiting for it to just fall out."

"Well," I said, "if it were up to me, I'd try McRoberts."

"Okay. Why don't you go in there with her and suggest it? Maybe she needs a fresh face and a fresh perspective."

I tapped lightly on the bathroom door, and Joseph called, "Come on in."

I pushed the door open enough to peek my head in. Naomi was sitting on the stool, breathing through the last of a contraction with an elbow propped against the window sill and her opposing hand squeezing tightly to one of Joseph's. Joseph twisted his neck to look at me and smile grimly as I slipped inside, but Naomi kept her forehead pressed against Joseph's middle. She was wearing a threadbare nightgown and a pair of thick woolen socks pulled up to her knees. Her eyeglasses were cast upon the countertop and her head was wrapped in a loose-woven kerchief fringed with silvery strands of hair that escaped the tight knot pinned to the nape of her neck.

Joseph rubbed the small of Naomi's back, almost as though he were trying to rub away her pains. Naomi took in a big draught of air and sat back a little as she blew it out, making those stray hairs dance about her face as her breath ricocheted off Joseph's belly. She looked at me with weariness in her pale blue eyes and discouragement etched into the lines of her plump face. "Kim." A tear sparkled in the corner of one of her eyes. "I don't know, but I don't think this one wants to come, Kim."

I knelt on the floor in front of her and laid my hand on her knee. "I'm sorry you're having such a rough time of it, Naomi."

Naomi nodded her head and the tear trickled into the crinkles lining her eye.

"But the baby wants to come. Of course it does. Your baby is just having a rough time, too." Naomi's eyes filled and swam in the tears as I talked. "I know this birth isn't going like you're used to births going, but you're so close! You're almost there."

"I don't feel a bit like I'm almost there, Kim."

"You are, Naomi! You're nine centimeters! But you're gonna have to let us help you. You've got to try to trust us."

The tears began to stream down her face. "I do trust you, but it's so hard."

"I know."

"But I do trust you."

"Okay then." I patted her knee. "So, come lie down on your bed, and let's see if we can't get this over with."

"Lie down on the bed?"

She began to shake her head, but Joseph said, "*Kom, Mamm.* The ladies know what you need to do. Come to the bed." She sighed and nodded, and let Joseph help her to her feet.

I don't think I've ever seen a person walk so slowly in all my life. It couldn't have been any more than thirty paces to her bedroom, but it took her at least five contractions and the full support of her husband to get her there. She'd take five or six excruciatingly short and shuffling steps, have a contraction while clinging with all her might to Joseph, then take five or six more steps and have the next contraction. Finally, she made it to her bed, though it took the span of two more contractions to get her up on it.

At first, she just flopped flat out, but with all sorts of coaxing, we persuaded her to curl her chin to her chest and convinced her to allow Joseph and Nan to pull her knees toward her shoulders. Just as she did, a mighty contraction swept her stocky little frame, and with it came a powerful urge to push.

Jean was across the room, getting her Doppler for a heart tones check, when Naomi surrendered to that urge. With a herculean thrust and a great surge of meconium and blood, the baby's head appeared. I was the only one positioned even close to between Naomi's legs, so I reached out my gloveless hands and received the baby's body as it swam into the day.

Amazingly, for all the gooey mess she was birthed through, the child set the air to ringing with a stream of indignant cries. I plopped her, goo and all, onto her mother's belly and reached for a baby blanket.

Naomi collapsed against her pillow, her wet eyes wide with surprise, but as the baby continued to wail, she seemed to suddenly realize she'd had the baby. "Joey, get me up, will you?"

Joseph and Nan helped prop her up. Naomi took one look at the child sprawled and hollering across her, and she scooped it to her breast and began to cry right along with it, "Oh! It's passed! Oh! It's passed! Oh! Oh! It's passed!"

And then, as we three ladies set to work on the mess, a priceless stream of new parent talk began to flow between the relieved and grateful couple.

"Oh, Mother, you did it after all!"

"I really didn't think I could, Joe. It was so hard! So hard. Oh, but, Joey, look at her. Isn't she just the prettiest little thing?"

"I don't think she's so little, though she is awful pretty."

"No, she isn't so little, is she? Why, look at her head. Is that a big head, do you think, Joe? Do you suppose she's alright with such a big head?"

"Of course she's alright, Mother. Of course she is! Why, just look at her! She's extra smart is all."

"You think so? Well, okay then. She does look smart though, doesn't she? Look at her lookin' at us! Joe, I think I don't want to have any other babies. I think this baby had better be it. What do you think?"

"I think that's fine, *Mamm*. I think that's just fine."

I drove home from the birth feeling I'd passed a milestone. Jean never needed me like that before. I was so caught up in the good feelings, I got turned around on my way home, so turned around I had to knock on a stranger's door for directions out to M-66. I still wasn't sure I was midwife material, but for the first time, I felt like a serious contributor.

Chapter
TWENTY

AGAIN, THE TELEPHONE RANG. "KIM?"

"Kris!"

"So—why do you think I'm calling?"

Squeals and laughter erupted, and tears began to flow.

The children, piqued by the noise, ran in from the living room to dance about my legs.

"What, Mama? What, Mama? What Mama?"

"Aunt Kris is going to have a baby!"

"A baby! A baby! Yay!"

And the news was doubly sweet since, the winter before, she'd suffered a miscarriage. She'd gotten pregnant again, according to plan—she wanted to have her babies in the summertime so she could give birth to them with me in Michigan—and she was due on my birthday. Then she'd called on New Year's Eve to say she'd begun to bleed a little. Her midwife came out the next day and confirmed the child had died. Over the next few days, labor began. She gave birth to a tiny, silent person, complete with face and hands and feet, and she and Ron buried the little thing among the roots of a mulberry tree sheltering their yard.

Never had I felt so far away from my sister, my bosom friend. I remember pressing my forehead against the windowpane in my bathroom, and the harsh feel of the cold glass mirrored the sense of desolation that began to settle over me like a fog rolling in from the lowlands. I grieved both the loss of the child, and my inability to be there with my sister through it.

By the time Kris and Ron conceived again, my sorrow had subsided to a muted ache, and the news there was a new child revived and assuaged that sorrow all at the same time.

The challenge with the subsequent pregnancy was the baby was due in March, and so would have to be born in Arizona. "Kim, do you think you can come? I can't imagine having my baby without you!"

I went to work straightaway on Brent. My first order of business was to convince him to let me go for the whole five weeks Kris could safely birth at home.

"FIVE weeks, Kim? You can't be serious."

But of course, I was dead serious.

Next, I had to convince him it would be perfectly fine for the kids and me to travel out by bus.

"By BUS? No way. I've seen the folks who get on and off those buses. Take a plane."

"But, Brent, do you know what three airline tickets would cost? We could never afford it in a million years! Hon, I'll be careful, you know I will. I'll keep my money in my shoe, and we won't talk to anyone. And I'll take the pepper spray!"

"It's gotta be a long trip, though. How long is it? I know you already know."

Yes! He's weakening!

"Forty-eight hours, but that's not as long as it takes us to get from Michigan to Mexico—I mean, geesh! That trip takes five whole days!"

"Um, five days—getting off to sleep nights."

"Well, yeah. Still, only two days! Plus, it's not like I'd be doing the driving."

The next day I was on the telephone with Greyhound.

On the third Thursday in February, I packed our bags and the next afternoon, Brent drove us to the bus station. It was a frigid day, with a fierce, blustery, side-sweeping wind stippled with fine shards of icy snow. The bus lumbered in and rolled to a stop, the kids and I gave Brent our hugs and kisses goodbye, and, with a credit card tucked into my right shoe, a little wad of cash stuffed into the left, a police-issue vial of pepper spray in the back pocket of my ratty jeans, a bag filled with books and raisins and a can of Lysol slung over my shoulder, and a tiny hand clasped tightly into each of my fists, I climbed aboard with the kids. We found three seats together, and the bus heaved away from the station with a sigh and groan as we waved goodbye to Brent. He smiled as he waved back, but I could see the uncertainty on his face as he stood buffeted and abused by the weather. I knew he was second-guessing his decision to let us go for so long and, especially, to go on a bus.

Overall, it was a good trip, though it had its interesting moments, make no mistake. Taking my two little people to use the filthy bathroom while the bus pitched us about was a challenge. Thank God for the Lysol.

Keeping the kids busy and entertained mile after mile after mile was interesting. One thing in the bag came out at a time and was used until their attention spans were spent. Virtually all the other children who boarded the various buses we rode over those two days would sooner or later make their way to our seat to take advantage of the stories and coloring books, games and snacks. A couple times we had a pretty sizable group crowding around our knees and elbows. Hannah, my ray of sunshine, loved all her new friends with all her heart. Paul, my little cumulonimbus, was rather more conservative.

On our stops we'd purchase a meal to eat once we climbed back onto the bus, then we'd walk around a bit, stretching our legs for as long as possible.

Night times were interesting. I was glad to find two sets of seats for the three of us right across the aisle each night. Hannah lay over her two seats while Paul lay over his seat and me.

Nighttime potty breaks on a Greyhound bus with a disoriented toddler were definitely interesting—and thankfully, also without incident.

The people we encountered on the bus were the most interesting of all. I'd intended to keep to myself on that trip, but it was on that trip I discovered just how spectacularly friendly our little Hannah really was. Everybody who sat near us became a cherished friend, privy to all the details of Woodard family life. Our full names and birthdates, our telephone number and our address were shared with all, and everyone learned our destination, too. Our reward for her gregariousness was unlimited attention and gifts. One man gave us a partly devoured Snickers bar, another gave us a half bag of chips, and another gave us two whole packages of tootsie roll suckers. One man, Don—yes, we learned his name, thank you, Hannah—traveled along with us nearly the entire trip, choosing the seat directly behind or kitty corner to ours every single time we switched buses. We met another man at the Dallas bus station where we waited from nine in the evening until one in the morning for a new vehicle. The station was crawling with people, and there wasn't an open seat anywhere. I'd stacked our bags against a wall and begun spreading my sleepy kids over them, when a fortyish man with a swastika tattooed on his left earlobe, dressed all in black leather from his broad-brimmed hat to his calf-length trench coat and cowboy boots, offered us his chair. I tried to decline, but he insisted while dislodging the kids and shouldering our bags and practically plunking us into the coveted seat with his own two hands.

So, with Hannah and Paul stretched across my lap, I listened to the man's life story amidst the tumult and cacophony of our bewildering surrounds. When we boarded the new bus, Don took the seat behind us, and the man with the swastika took the seat in front of us. By two o'clock, the whole busload of souls seemed to have fallen asleep, and a peaceful night ensued. I suspect the lot of us would have slept on a good while through the morning, but at seven sharp my son snapped awake. He stretched and yawned and announced at the top of his lungs, exactly like Robin Williams in *Good Morning, Vietnam*, "Iiiiiiiiit's wake up tiiiiiiiiiime!"

A stir rippled through the sleepy crowd. Paul smiled at me, looked around, and noticed the man in front of us had removed his leather hat from his head and had a perfectly circular bald spot right on the back of it. Before I could arise from my befuddled state and shush him, Paul leaned forward and shouted, "Mom! What happened to his hair? Mom! Don't ever cut my hair like that! Hey!" Then he leaned farther forward. "Hey, Mister, put your hat back on!"

It seemed to happen in slow motion, the way car accidents in movies do. Fortunately, the guy was good-humored and still spent the rest of the day, which, incidentally, was the rest of our trip, talking to me as though it never happened—albeit, with his hat on.

Don sat quietly behind us, listening. He seemed a little jealous. About an hour away from our hopping-off point one of the kids finally asked, "Are we almost there, Mom?"

Kris, Ron, and Daniel lived in a tiny house in a tiny village called Cochise, east of a sprawl of mountains. It had a minuscule school with crookedly dangling swings, a post office, and a very small scattering of residents. Was there an antique shop there, too? I can't remember for sure, perhaps there was; it was an old store of some kind. Every yard in the place was dust, though here and there you'd see a gnarly tree. Kris and Ron had a handful of gnarly trees.

It was dry, dry, dry. Two or three times while we were out there, random workmen would stop over to drink right from Kris and Ron's garden hose without a by-your-leave. I was told that was typical in the arid land. Long-eared, long-legged jackrabbits abounded, and hawks did, too. Kris warned me to be wary on my walks of the feral pigs. They were called *javelinas*, and could be dangerous. Railroad tracks lay near to the village, and we'd often hear trains rumble by.

Kris and Ron borrowed a camper for the three of us to sleep in during our stay. It was nestled between the sunrise and the sunset, south of the house, beneath a matchless canopy of stars; I'd never seen stars like that in all my days. One by one, they'd wink into the night until the dazzle made my head spin. I loved staying in that camper. It kept me right out there under the sky. It was hot during the day and cool at night, but not as hot as it would be by summer. It was a nice change from the Michigan chill we'd left behind.

Cochise was neighbor to another tiny town called La Playa. In English, *la playa* means the beach. It was near a dry lakebed where the sand hill cranes congregate in winter. We always had a lot of sand hill cranes in southwest Michigan in summertime. I'd see the tall birds walking about the farmers' fields, each pair with a downy brown baby or two. And what a racket they make mornings and evenings as they come and go from the waterways. Kris told me about the cranes when she first moved out there and I liked to think how it might be we were enjoying the very same birds. It made me feel connected with her.

Early on the tenth of March, a couple weeks after we'd arrived, somewhere around three, Ron rapped on my door to let me know Kris's waters had broken and her labor started. We all meant to remain in bed awhile, and Kris and Ron did. I tried to stay down, but couldn't. I crept indoors and curled up next to the furnace and drifted in reverie while I waited to be needed.

My thoughts wound backward to the time just before I married Brent when Kris, with tears trickling down her cheeks, told me she loved me so much she'd happily live out the days of her life as my servant, and would even spend them sleeping at the foot of my bed.

I smiled. Now it was me at the foot her bed, truly *her* servant.

But I didn't spend too much time reminiscing there in the dark. Kris's labor proved short and ferocious, and Emily surged to earth like a flash flood.

Ron called the midwife, Danna, and Kris's friend, Kathy, while I scurried about seeing to the things Kris wrote on a list for me to do when her labor started.

The women arrived and I completed my tasks just as the sun began to peek over the horizon, and we three settled into the corners of Kris's bedroom, intent on being what midwives are famous for being: unobtrusive, available if needed, invisible if not.

Almost in a single breath, Kris felt the urge to push, and there came Emily, springing from the depths of her mother with both her hands upon her flaxen head.

I scurried about in the afterglow of Emily's arrival, whisking away the mess and fixing breakfast and getting lost in the timeless image of mother and child, my heart brimming with wonder that I was, yet again, invited to take part in such a holy moment.

A neighbor fetched the children before Emily danced from womb to world, so once Kris and Emily were tidied and tucked away in bed, I was sent to bring Daniel back.

I walked him home piggyback with his chubby arms encircling my neck and his soft cheek pressed against my ear. As we bounced along he asked, "What did my baby sister say, Aunt Kimmy?"

"Well, she didn't say anything, Daniel. Babies don't talk till they get big like you."

We went inside, and Daniel ran on his stubby little legs, straight to his mom's bedside. Emily made a squeak as he leaned over her and said hello, and Daniel turned to me and said, "Look! She's talking! See, Aunt Kimmy? Babies do too talk!"

I eased off to sleep that night—out in that cozy camper under the wild spray of stars—thinking.

I replayed Emily's dramatic entrance, so swift and with that flourish of hands overhead. Though we couldn't know it then, Emily would grow to be a gifted ballerina, and I like to think she hinted at her calling in life right there at her birth—her long, graceful arms extended as she pirouetted forth.

I smiled as I recalled my retrieval of little Daniel and our trudge through the village's dusty streets. Some years later Daniel would send me a picture he drew of our walk, complete with a pair of pennies pasted on for our heads.

Then my throat thickened a bit as I thought again how, not-withstanding Kris's passionate, sob-choked declaration to me in our youth, it was me kneeling in service to her—and through one of the most wondrous of life experiences. Little did I know the advancing years would find me twice more at her feet—four times total, and during the fourth time with my own daughter serving at my side. The gift of their trust through those priceless seasons, the opportunity to serve them through the inexpressible intimacy of their births, the chance to be right there as my nephew and each of my nieces emerged upon the world—there are very few things I treasure more in life.

The next four weeks were lovely—long, golden days blending one into another. Mornings, I made breakfast for Kris and all the children. Afternoons, I strapped my yummy niece to my chest so Kris and Daniel could nap together. She'd snuggle in and doze off, and I'd go about cooking and cleaning and caring for the family. Brent came out on the Greyhound for our last week in Arizona and, oh, was it ever good to see him!

He stepped off the bus, dropped to his knees, and gathered us to his chest in one long, breathless moment. When he stood up, he looked at me and shook his head. "I cannot believe I let you and the kids travel across the country on that bus. What was I thinking? We're never, ever doing that again."

We'd agreed to purchase a vehicle that belonged to a friend of Kris and Ron's there in Arizona, but it wasn't ready to make the trip to Michigan. Ron and Kris volunteered to drive it to us when they came for the summer, so we took Ron and Kris's old station wagon home. We left on a Sunday evening and were home twenty-eight hours later. Three days after that, we were on our way to Lansing for another weekend teen event with thirty-eight kids and nine leaders in tow.

It was really amazing to watch the teenagers learn and grow, and the growth made the work worth it. I mused about the group in my journal that spring. "The youth group is like an apple tree laden with boughs of fresh blossoms, some still closed, most just opening, a few beginning to swell with the first signs of immature fruit. This precious tree, just awakening, stretching upward in the sunlight and spicy spring zephyrs, needs to be carefully tended—it needs to be protected from pests, pruned, watered, and fertilized. It needs to be stung by bees. It needs to embrace the elements. It needs to push its roots down deep and spread its branches wide if it's to bear good, ripe apples. God, help us to be wise, diligent, skillful gardeners!"

I could have said the same about our growing children, too. A friend, noticing our struggles with Paul, had the courage to give us a child-rearing book upon our return to Michigan, and it was just what we needed. We tweaked our parenting style a bit and were rewarded with happier children and a more peaceful household. Even more importantly, we found ourselves as parents equipped and positioned to rear our children more effectively and with a clearer vision. Another entry in my journal reads, "Hannah's doing very well with her school work, she's so bright! And Paul asked me the other day when I would start teaching him 'school things,' so I set him to work at the dining room table tracing the alphabet and numbers. Sometimes I feel exasperated. Poked, prodded, tested, and questioned nearly to the point of death. But this morning, I feel grateful to be the mama of these interesting people. Being Hannah and Paul's mother is making me into a better person."

Chapter
TWENTY-ONE

ONE MIDSUMMER MORNING, JEAN TELEPHONED ME.

"Hi, Kim, Irene's in labor."

"Okay, awesome, I'll get ready."

"Get ready and just go, I'm in Berrien Springs, finishing up with a mom here."

"Oh. Okay."

I broke into a sweat and a rush of adrenaline hit me like a headache, but it sure did get me out the door in a hurry, and my thoughts carved a circuitous path upon the surface of my mind through the whole drive there.

Oh, my goodness. Oh, dear God. Oh, Lord. Oh, Jesus. Please be with me. Shoot! Turn on H Drive South or G? G. I think G! Yes, G Drive. Then what? 14 or 14 ½ Mile? Oh, good grief! Will I ever learn these roads? Oh, gosh. What if the baby comes before Jean? I barely have any gear! Yes, okay 14 ½ Mile.

Oh, my goodness. Oh, dear God—

I'd thoroughly soaked my t-shirt by the time I pulled into Irene and Steven's driveway and shifted into park. I climbed from the car just as a small flock of children bounded from the house to meet me. "Do you need help with your bags, Ms. Kim?"

No. I needed no help with my bags. I had only one very small, very inadequate bag. "Thanks, kids, but I think I've got it."

"Okay, then come in! Come in! Come in! Mama says we're having a baby today!" And they danced me to the door.

I followed the children inside and was relieved to find that although Mama did indeed appear to be in labor, there ought to be plenty of time for Jean to join us.

"Hey there, Irene."

"Hello, Kim!" Irene crossed the room and wrapped me in her long, slender arms. Her perfectly round belly pressed into mine and the scent of homemade peppermint soap filled my nostrils. She released me and I stepped back to marvel at her. She was a homeschooling, homesteading mother of five. Not Amish, but as close to Amish lifestyle as it gets, with a day-to-day, dawn-to-dusk existence congested with never-ending work. Still, she looked scarcely out of her teens, and seemed continuously bubbling over with joy. She and her girls were typically clad in simple dresses, aprons, and head coverings while her boys were clapped into overalls. Everybody wore warm tans, bright eyes, and uninhibited smiles. Nobody wore shoes.

This day though, Irene donned a white cotton nightgown dotted with blue rosebuds, and her dark hair was wound into one thick ringlet that coiled over her shoulder.

"How's it going?"

"Good I think! I think very good. I've been having regular rushes since before sunup."

I smiled. I liked that she used Ina May Gaskin's word for contractions.

I set my bag on the table and began to rummage for my fetoscope and blood pressure cuff, opening my mouth to respond as I did, but before I could say anything, she added, "I guess I'd like to be checked."

My smile disappeared. A shiver of adrenaline skipped down my thighs. I swallowed. Up until then I'd performed a grand total of three cervical checks, and felt anything but qualified to practice on the magnificent woman standing in front of me. Before I could stammer an answer, however, Irene groaned and bent over her countertop, elbows propped between the bowl of fresh soil-flecked strawberries the girls brought in from the garden and the cup of black-eyed susans one of the boys collected for her from the edge of the forest surrounding their little farm.

She stood there, groaning and blowing and swaying her hips. The flower-sprigged nightie swished back and forth, back and forth.

I swallowed again and attempted to collect my wits.

Irene puffed out her cheeks, then blew the breath out with a great flapping of her lips as she stood up. She pressed the heel of her hand over the small of her back. "Whew!" She shook her head and beamed a smile at me. "That was really good! Strong!"

"Um, yeah. It sure looked strong."

"So, how about that check?"

"You want me to check your cervix?"

She cocked her head. "What else would you check?"

I laughed weakly. "Yes, well." I waved a hand through the air. "Irene, you should know I've only checked three cervixes so far."

"Then I'll be your fourth! How hard can it be?"

I was loath to hurt her—loath to hurt anyone, for that matter, unwittingly, accidentally, or otherwise—but neither was I especially confident in my ability to make an accurate assessment. As it turned out, the check didn't bother Irene at all and I found her dilation, as well as her effacement and station, easy to measure. I did re-check my guess with the tape measure, shamelessly and right in front of Irene; five to six centimeters, mostly thinned out, and about a negative one.

Knowing the baby wasn't going to slide out before Jean got to us eased my nerves, and I went about the tasks of listening to the baby's heartbeat, taking Irene's blood pressure, and setting up for the birth while reveling in our wonderful profession and humming a little tune.

Jean arrived about an hour later and, about an hour after that, Irene smiled, sucked in a lungful of oxygen, and eased a tiny, black-haired beauty into her husband's calloused hands amid the whoops and cheers of her older beauties.

The experience proved a turning point for me. Though I was attending births regularly and feeling more and more like I understood what was going on, I had worried myself into a state of inertia over the potential for my inexperience to mar our clients' experiences. I'd found myself holding back and hesitating to do the things I was learning to do—things I was supposed to be learning to do. It was hard to do things fumblingly Jean was able to do with grace, especially as I felt the families we served deserved better than my fumblings.

The revelation provided by this birthing woman was identical to the one I had when Hannah was a baby. One evening, as I sat considering her innocent face, I realized, for all my good intentions, it was certain I would cause her a measure of pain in life. The realization broke me down and I cried and cried until I thought to talk to God about it. We talked and He dropped the thought into my soul that things would be okay if I'd just keep asking Him for help, then do my best, stay humble, be honest, and be ready to take responsibility for my mistakes.

That proved a vital lesson for parenting, for marriage, and for midwifery, too. I came to recognize it as an essential lesson for all of life. Possibly even the chief of all life lessons out there, though the virtue of replacing expectations with gratitude seems right up near the top as well.

That birth and the gift of its lessons were exactly what I needed as I moved through the months to come. I began doing some postpartum work on my own as early as my second year with Jean, but it wasn't until the fall following Irene's birth that Jean began to send me out to do a prenatal visit or two by myself on occasion.

The first time she called on me to see to a little grouping of prenatals on my own, I blanched and almost refused. Then I remembered what I learned at Irene's birth, breathed a deep breath, and jotted down my instructions.

Ironically, the appointments turned out to be the least of my difficulties. The difficulties were in the minutia. First, I had to find the ladies. None too simple for a directionally dysfunctional driver (at the time). Second, more often than not, I had to introduce myself to the ladies when I appeared at their doors. This was awkward, as most were supremely shy Amishwomen and a couple of them hadn't even heard of me!

Knock, knock.

Footsteps—A swish of curtains....

Hmm. Am I at the right house?

I'd take a step back, re-read the house number, and compare it to the number I'd scrawled into my notebook. *Well, I think it's the right house...*

Knock, knock, knock.

The curtains swished again and the door cracked open. A fraction of a white *kapp* and one eye appeared in the crack. "Yes?"

"Hi there! Ruth?"

"Yes."

"I'm Kim—Kim Woodard."

"Yes?"

"Oh, um, Kim Woodard, Jean's apprentice."

The door opened a little farther. "Oh? Jean's apprentice?"

"Yes. Jean sent me to take care of your visit today."

"Oh. I didn't know Jean had an apprentice."

What?

"Oh! Well, yes, she sure does. I guess she didn't call to say I was coming?"

"Well, she might've, but the phone's in the barn, you know, and I don't check the messages too often."

"Oh! Well, I'm so sorry to surprise you!"

"Yes."

"Um—so—may I come in?"

"Oh. Well, I suppose."

Third, I'd have to explain why I was there instead of Jean and then I had to deal with their obvious disappointment they'd not see Jean until their next visit.

I think at those early solo visits I copied out nearly every word that was said. More times than once I called Jean right there on the spot with our questions and concerns. If Jean was hoping for quiet days off when she sent me off without her, it was a pretty long while before she got any.

Chapter

TWENTY-TWO

THE TELEPHONE RANG OFF THE HOOK AND SENT us weaving our way among the whitewashed barns and corn-fields of Barry and Eaton Counties all through the fall of that year, tending to ever so many strong moms and delicious babes while the chill in the air ripened the apples and set the treetops ablaze.

A slim first-timer who'd worried us to no end through her pregnancy for her inability to gain more than twelve or thirteen pounds produced an eight-pound, nine-ounce daughter. Where she hid that child, we'd never know. Our first clue she was birthing a chunky one was the four hours she spent pushing.

Another two first-time mothers birthed daughters fewer than ten hours apart—the first of them slipping into the world in a shaft of mellow afternoon sunshine, the second bursting forth in the midst of a windowpane-rattling thunder and lightning storm.

One afternoon had us scudding northeast to Esther and Henry Yutzy's for the birth of a second daughter. Esther opened the door and astonished us with a cloak of honey-gold tresses that shifted and shimmered from her crown to her bare heels. We listened to her baby and assessed her blood pressure, then Henry took up a boar bristle brush and went to work on his wife's glorious hair while we set up for the birth. There was something so intimate, so nearly holy about the way he ran the brush through her gleaming locks, it felt almost like love-making. I blushed and turned my eyes away.

Then we passed the early hours of another evening on a tiny back porch in a wash of sunshine and a cloud of brilliant ladybugs, waiting for a baby boy who bounded forth with his cord clenched into his wee fist.

We slipped under the spell of each singular event, and they all blurred into a season of gold-trimmed enchantment as we rubbed backs, rubbed necks, rubbed bellies, stroked arms, stroked legs, bathed sweaty brows, brushed away stray hairs, held buckets for puking, held buckets for peeing, wiped away mucus, wiped away poop, massaged feet, looked deeply into mildly frantic eyes, nodded our heads, whispered our encouragements, crooned and hummed and rocked, rocked to the singular rhythm of birth.

More and more frequently, I monitored vitals, checked cervixes, caught babies, received placentas, clamped cords, and performed every sort of examination. I helped manage fetal distresses, malpresentations, shoulder dystocias, resuscitations, retained placentas, postpartum hemorrhages, and hospital transports with increasing proficiency, though thankfully those sorts of things rarely occurred.

That winter, Jean set me to work revising chart forms, policy papers, and informational articles, while I attended more prenatals and postpartums than I ever had before. I was stretched even further when Jean went away for a vacation and had her calls transferred to my telephone. Every call had me spread out over my office floor, buried in my books.

I studied more on my own too, with most of my study sessions inspired by the things that happened at those births. I'd come home and page through my books and read, read, read— many times, I admit, perched on the toilet or soaking in the tub at some indecent hour of the night, determined to absorb all I could while what happened was fresh in my mind.

We took on a client around my age about that time, with kids my kids' ages, though I'd quit with two and she was working on her fourth. Jean passed me the reins for much of this family's prenatal and postpartum care, and I was excited and nervous to learn she planned for me to take more responsibility at the birth as well.

Renee began laboring a little after the New Year, after two or three-days' worth of on-again-off-again contractions, and for the first and only time of our lives, my entire family ended up at the birth.

Renee invited Hannah, then aged seven, to attend the birth for the sake of her daughter, and she asked Luanne Turner from our youth group—our chief babysitter, as well as my future client and apprentice—to videotape. I ran over for a quick visit in the early morning when Renee's waters broke to listen to the baby and run through our infection prevention instructions. I came back home hoping her labor would wait for Luanne to get out of school, but Renee was ready for us before lunchtime.

I planned to fish Luanne from her classes on my way back over to Renee's, but when Brent saw how frazzled I was, he offered to fetch her for me. So, Hannah and I went straight to the family's house and Brent went to Battle Creek Central High for Luanne. Brent and Paul came inside with Luanne when they arrived and Renee and Alan asked if Paul could stay for their boys' sakes, and that's how we all wound up together. Brent sat out on the sofa with Paul, while Renee's children, Luanne, Hannah, Jean, and I squeezed around the bed to welcome the nine-pound baby.

Some homebirths are quiet and some homebirths aren't. I once attended a birth with a midwife who complained about the "chaos" the presence of the family's children created. I remember thinking that particular birth *had* felt a little chaotic—there were flailing arms and legs, tousled heads, and clamoring voices all over the place—but I also understood what the two of us experienced as chaotic was the essence, the beating heart of the family's life, and they loved their life.

The only thing that matters about those sorts of details at a birth is whether they're true to the soul of the family. It's the family's birth, after all, not ours.

So, Renee and Alan's birth was a busy, noisy, joyous event. Because each child was issued a disposable camera, the scene was bathed—in addition to limbs, heads, and voices—with stuttery flashes of light and shutter clicks, and when Renee's groaning, shifting efforts at last brought May forth, her wails joined the clamor.

Almost before the placenta was born, a birthday cake was brought from the kitchen and the bed was turned into a party table. Jean went home and Brent went for pizza.

Six mornings after May's bedside birthday party, Jean and I flew out the door to help usher in a family's eighth child. We arrived at five, the eight-pound, fifteen-ounce girl arrived shortly after seven, and we took off out of there at ten o'clock sharp for another birth in Kalamazoo. We were in such a flurry to go, while I was in the bathroom washing up and re-packaging Jean's hemostats and scissors and metal clamps, I also washed up and packed a curtain hook sitting on the bathroom countertop. Jean called the next day to ask me about it, nearly incoherent with laughter.

As it turned out, we could have taken our time and left the family with a full set of curtain hooks. We arrived in Kalamazoo to find Lucy, the forty-three-year-old mother of four, in labor, but in a very relaxed labor.

I've noticed through the years since this birth that often when a woman's birthed a number of times already, especially an older woman, her body will hem and haw and dilly dally at the edge of active labor a while. You can almost hear it say, "What? This again? Uh, yeah—no, I'd rather not." The midwives and the woman are left to find some way to cajole the unimpressed, disinterested uterus into doing its job. Hours, even days can be spent teasing and pleading and trying bribes. Till all at once, her petulant womb will harrumph and say, "Fine!" And with a rush of sinewy strength, will move to evict the child while we, often having retreated to the far side of a partly-closed door in order to watch and wait, find ourselves scarcely able to beat the baby into the room.

And so it was with Lucy. Lucy was more than willing to complete her labor, but her body elected to drag its feet and pitch little fits. Among the things we used to try to coax a whole-hearted effort out of it were nursing sessions for the toddler and a little swing dancing demo. Lucy and her husband Hugo were dedicated swing dancers and we three—Annie (Lucy's doula)[1] Jean, and I—sat open-mouthed on the polished wooden floors as the big-bellied woman and her adoring man, in a sort of slow-motion, effortless perfection, executed one fun move after another.

---

1   A doula is a nonmedical person who assists a woman before, during, and/or after childbirth, as well as her spouse and/or family, by providing physical assistance and emotional support.

The dancing was amazing to watch, but it was the nursing that did the trick. I remember watching this unique woman cradle her two or three-year-old son tenderly to her breast, patiently breathing through the potent contractions his contented suckling produced, feeling certain I'd not have been able to tolerate nursing a child through either one of my labors. But she just lay there so still, stroking his soft cheek and allowing it. She also allowed her three older children, finished with that day's home-school lessons, to begin practicing their instruments, strings and piano. Watching her lie stretched out on her side, breathing and breathing and breathing as her contractions ebbed and flowed, nursing one child while her others filled the house with music, I was filled with awe.

Then, right around three o'clock in the afternoon, she detached herself from her boy, set him aside, and, grunting with effort, brought another lovely child into the light. A nine-pound, eight-ounce son with his right hand wrapped snugly about his head.

Joy erupted! Another birthday cake was produced. A bottle of champagne was popped open. Even Jean and Annie and I, once the bulk of our work was finished, partook. We really had only a sip or two of the bubbly, but I possess just a fragment of memory after that of us three ladies shut up in a bathroom together, giggling like schoolgirls over something now long forgotten.

And so, it was a busy season, filled with activity and growth. Brent was great through all of it. Once a week he'd wave me out the door so I could go see our moms and their babies, so I could hammer away at the mounds of paperwork, so I could bury my nose in some textbook in the corner of a kid-less coffee shop. He sacrificed time he could have spent doing things that would have pleased and refreshed him—heaven knows he deserved a measure of pleasure and refreshment for how hard he worked—in order to take care of our kids. He taught them and played with them—oh, how he played with them! He took them on errands and hauled them along to youth group meetings. He fed them and bathed them, he made up crazy stories for them, he read to them and sang to them and he put them to bed. Once, I heard him say to a friend over the telephone, "Nope, can't come, but thanks. Yeah, yep, I've got the kids. No, I'm not *babysitting*—they're *my* kids!" That one went right to my heart.

He did ask me once, "So, whatever happened to a birth a month?"

"Kinda looks like I'm doing a little more than that, doesn't it?"

That earned me a set of raised eyebrows, but he didn't ask me to slow it down, so that earned him a kiss.

As great as Brent was with the children, the condition of the house generally fared otherwise. One of the first times I was gone a long stretch and came home to a find my nest a disaster area, he intercepted my reaction to it with a wave of his hand and a hasty, "Babe, I don't know how you do it. You're Wonder Woman. But, I kept 'em alive, didn't I?"

What could I say to that? He was one wise man.

Chapter

TWENTY-THREE

BESIDES ATTENDING BIRTHS, WE SPENT THE springtime preparing for another trip to Mexico, as well as dealing with a problem that had been looming for months, if not years.

Between the births of Hannah and Paul, I developed a slight cough. By the time Paul was a year old, a measure of extra work to breathe joined the cough. Brent was worried and insisted I go to the doctor. Dutifully I went and after describing what I was experiencing was offered a course of antibiotics.

"Antibiotics?" I said. "But I'm not sick."

"If you won't take the antibiotics, we can't help you."

"Ahh, I see."

When Brent asked how it went, I explained I was told I couldn't be helped.

The years passed and the difficulties waxed and waned without a discernible pattern, but through the months before that summer's trip, the trouble worsened until it was difficult to function. I couldn't talk while moving, I had to hold my breath when taking blood pressures and listening to hearts and lungs, and I'd begun sleeping ten to twelve hours per night. It was just plain hard work to breathe and I was starting to wear out.

I did my best to shield others from the issue, mostly because I found their concern stressful; plus, it took a good deal of the energy I needed for breathing to calm folks down and assure them that, no, I didn't need an ambulance.

A couple weeks before we were scheduled to leave for Mexico, Jean expressed her concern about me going on the trip in such a condition, and her concern seemed to shake Brent awake. We were so busy getting ready to go and I worked so hard to minimize what was going on, he'd been lulled out of noticing it. But Jean woke him up and he insisted I go back to the doctor.

I went and with only a cursory examination was told I had asthma. Now, I hadn't spent the previous seven annoying, uncomfortable years just wishing I could breathe better. I read all I could about throats and lungs and breathing issues, including asthma, and I was confident I didn't have that. I explained that and, mentioning I felt as though I had a hand squeezing my throat, asked if there was a way to look down into it. My idea was dismissed with scarcely an acknowledgment and I was sent from the office with prescriptions for Prednisone and an albuterol inhaler.

I went home without filling them, assured Jean and Brent I'd be fine, climbed into the front seat of the Chevy Astro we borrowed from friends, and off we went to Mexico.

It was a good trip, but hard. Hard from the word go, too. I was breathing like a freight train. The kids and I rode along in the bad boys' van with Brent. Before we made it a hundred miles down the road, we had to bring Hannah and Paul into the front seat (a single seat) with me just to preserve them from the boys. Five hundred and nine miles down the road, in the stifling heat of a Bourbon, Missouri gas station, the Astro conked out. Six hours later, we were back on the road. Don't ask me how Brent managed it. I can't even remember what exactly went wrong. All he had to say about it was he learned a lot from the string of intoxicated mechanics who stopped over to take a look, four in all, as they came and went through the hot and elongated afternoon.

We pulled onto the YWAM base around three in the morning, twenty-four hours after we left Battle Creek. The staff emerged from their quarters, squirreled the group away, and disappeared. After a minute or two, we four Woodards realized we weren't going to be squirreled away. We glanced at our sleepy children, exchanged looks bleary-eyed with fatigue, shrugged our shoulders, and tucked ourselves back into the smelly, grimy vehicle, grateful that at least the night was cooler than the day was. Somewhere on that trip filled with misadventures, the kids and I spent part of a night sleeping out on a Texan sidewalk, too, one snuggled up under each of my arms.

Our group of sixteen merged into a group of about two hundred and, three days later, we were rumbling south in a caravan of old street buses. The trouble I was having with one of the more basic functions of daily living was, by then, not disguisable and, soon after we arrived in Monterrey, I was struck down with a ferocious case of bronchitis.

Initially, I was embarrassed, but over the numberless days I spent ill and struggling, the waves of young folk coming around the clock to lay hands on me and say the most earnest prayers touched my heart and chased my pride away. And, amazingly, I rose from my sick bed one morning, thin and weak, but breathing without effort. It appeared my scorching fever and those heartfelt petitions burned away the affliction. I remained trouble-free through the rest of the summer. I was thankful to the point of tears and Brent was, too. We completed the trip and returned home encouraged by my return to health and my steadily-increasing strength.

And how I needed strength and health, as from almost the moment we stepped from the van, I was sucked into a perfect vortex of ten birthing mamas.

The first of those ten moms was a thirty-six-year-old former obstetrical nurse, Colleen, and her husband, Darren. Colleen had us out to her home early in the morning, ten days past her dates. Things started the day before with a rupturing of her waters at bedtime. She had rather a long labor for a repeat mom, this being her fifth child, and she showed us by how she labored that her baby's head wasn't flexed so well as could be desired.

Colleen spent more than two hours pushing, straining in all manner of positions to get the thing tucked and traveling through her pelvis. She moved from chest and knees to an exaggerated side-lie, from a supported squat to McRoberts. We offered her a bite of this and taste of that as her energy dwindled with every contraction.

Nothing sounded good to her, but at last I scrounged up a protein bar called "creamy peanut" and told her just to take it like medicine. She ate about half of it, glancing at the wrapper and muttering that the thing was anything but "creamy." Some while later, after exerting an incredible aggregate of exertion, she produced a yowling nine-pound, ten-ounce baby girl. A moment or two after that, she spotted the remains of the protein bar and consumed it with relish. "Oh!" She gushed. "That's delicious! What *is* that?"

Later, basking together in the ethereal afterglow of the beautiful baby's birth, we reclined upon the family bed talking over this part and laughing over that part and oohing over the rest, and I mentioned I hadn't been to many births yet. Colleen's doula said, "Really? I'd have thought you'd been to lots of births. How many have you attended?"

I told her Colleen's baby was my forty-sixth. She looked at Jean and said, "Wow. She's a natural."

On the drive home Jean remarked upon the exchange, laughed, and said, "I think you're getting better than me."

I returned home both surprised and glowing with pleasure, especially in light of how unnatural I felt through the last six years of birth attendance. I wrote about it the next morning in my journal, then finished with a prayer. "Lord, You and I both know, if I'm any good at midwifing, it's because You've purposed for me to be and have provided for Your purpose to come to pass. You're the Author and the Finisher, the Beginning and the End of every good thing in my life."

Exactly two weeks later, we slipped over to a little apartment in Marshall just before dawn to tend Anne and Kevin, in labor with their first baby, and right on Anne's due date.

Things moved along nicely through the morning and early afternoon, if on the slow side, until Jean had another woman begin to labor. Anne was around six centimeters dilated and the second woman had a history of quick births, so Jean flew to attend her.

Jean returned about the time Anne reached nine centimeters and we all were excited, thinking we were close to meeting her baby. I honestly can't remember what the time was at that point, but I do know she stayed right where she was for ages. Anne's labor was much like Colleen's a few days before. The baby was sizable, and its head was ill-flexed, but the difference was Anne was a first-time mom—and what a difference that can make.

We tried everything we knew—holding that last brim of stubborn cervix back while Anne shifted into every position a laboring woman has been known to assume, to no avail. Around half past midnight of the next day, the demoralized mother and her exhausted husband were ready to go to the hospital.

We arrived thirty minutes later and as the doctor felt she had a good chance at a vaginal delivery, things were arranged accordingly, including placement of an internal electronic fetal heart monitor. That's where an electrode gets screwed into the baby's scalp. And that's when I lost it. Nearly twenty-four hours with this family, combined with my tendency toward squeamishness over instruments of tampering, sent me right over the edge.

Sightless, I slipped into the hall, felt my way to an uninhabited waiting room, and collapsed on a loveseat. Toward morning, Jean came to tell me a cesarean section was underway. I sat up, hollow-eyed, deathly white, having drooled all over the pillow I laid my head on. Anne and Darrell's pretty little baby was born soon after, and I was happy, I was relieved, but I was also heartbroken.

The next birth was a heartbreaker, too. Fanny Wickey, a young Amish woman from the north, was preparing for her second attempt at a homebirth out of two pregnancies. Her first attempt culminated in a cesarean two years prior, though I can't recall why, as we weren't her attendants then.

Her body began to toy with the idea of laboring at thirty-nine weeks of pregnancy, two weeks after she was rolled and kicked about by an angry heifer in her barnyard. We came and spent eleven hours with her, amazed to find her legs and buttocks still covered with yellowing bruises. By suppertime, Fanny progressed to an encouraging six centimeters, but, soon after, her contractions spaced out until they disappeared entirely.

We went home and everyone managed to sleep until she called for us to come back around four o'clock the next morning. We were dismayed to notice this birth was progressing much like the last two we attended, including (like the second of the two births) an essentially first-time mother's pelvis. Fanny reached nine centimeters halfway to noon, then went no further.

We took walks and took baths and took car rides, we put her here and put her there and put her everywhere while we tried and tried to get that cervix to melt away. Then, on yet another slow walk along her tranquil, wild rose-lined dirt road, she confessed she really didn't think she'd be able to birth her baby vaginally after all.

There's such a fine line to walk with that in midwifery. Many times, a mother says a thing like that at some point in her labor. One of the most important things we do at births is encourage the tired and weary woman to see she actually is birthing her baby vaginally, and she has everything she needs to persevere and finish what she started. We say that, and then she digs deep and presses on. Almost without fail, she's rewarded with a gooey, squalling baby to clasp against her pounding heart.

But you never can truly know what the outcome will be. When the ordeal ends with a mind-blowing birth, all the work and pain it took to achieve it seem worth it. But when a grueling labor ends with surgery, the feelings often flow otherwise.

Jean and I encouraged Fanny to hang in there with her labor, and her mom and husband did, too. She allowed us to encourage her, and she agreed to stay home and keep trying, but later, after all was said and done, I heard her tell a visitor the experience was just awful and it cut me to the heart. I hurt for her and suffered doubt and regrets for a long while afterward.

Around a quarter to five in the evening, the baby let us know she'd had enough labor with some flitting dips in her heart tones. We packed up and she was born by cesarean soon after we arrived at the hospital. She was only two ounces past seven pounds, but the doctor said he'd never seen a baby so inextricably tangled in an umbilical cord before. We wondered ever after if the incident with the cow was at all to blame for her misfortune.

The shine cast over me by the compliments I'd received for my budding skills at Colleen's birth was sufficiently scuffed in the aftermath of Anne and Fanny's experiences.

And that's midwifery.

Just when you start to think you're all right at what you do, you get one or another stern reminders of how little you personally have to do with the miracles you're privileged to witness.

Birth usually works. Period.

Six days after Fanny's birth, we were blessed with a better experience that restored our souls, our faith, and a bit of that sheen, if not all of our mangled pride.

A fun couple living at the edge of Battle Creek found themselves in a hard and hasty labor one muggy evening. Jean called me to come as she scuttled out her door, and I arrived just behind her, a mere twenty minutes before the baby.

Sally was groaning through a contraction on her hands and knees next to the bed when I slipped into the room. Jean had already managed to get things set up. Tim, Sally's husband, obviously thrilled by everything going on, was on his knees beside her, providing a constant stream of praise and encouragement.

With the next contraction, Sally stood up and leaned over the bed; with the next, she crawled up to her knees on the bed; and, with the next, she stood bolt upright on the bed. I think if there had been a ladder hanging down from the ceiling, she'd have scrambled right up it.

Jean climbed onto the bed and knelt before her, taking Sally's hands in hers and grounding her with kind words and such a gentle touch. With the very next contraction, the baby's head began to show a bit.

"Tim, do you want to catch?" I said.

Tim looked at me, the pupils of his eyes dilated so wide only a slight band of hazel remained visible. "Yes! Yes, I do!"

We scrambled onto the bed as the baby was born to the chin.

I took Tim's hands in mine, acutely aware I'd never caught a baby without Jean immediately handy. "Put your hands on either side of the baby's head." I shifted his hands a little. "One on top, and one on bottom. Yes, there. Like that."

"Now what?" Tim asked, glancing at me. His onyx eyes were swimming in unspilled tears.

"Now just wait for Sally's next contraction."

"Okay," he whispered, his voice husky.

Sally's next contraction began to build and as she and Jean reestablished their grasp on one another's forearms, I covered Tim's hands with mine and helped him gingerly press the baby's head toward Sally's bottom. The movement released the first shoulder. I helped Tim press the baby's head then toward Sally's belly until the second shoulder was released.

The rest of the baby slipped easily into her father's hands amid a shower of waters.

"Oh! Ooohhh!!! Ooooooohhhhhhhh!!!!!!!" Tim cried, and burst into both tears and peals of laughter.

Sweet redemption.

And further redemption came crowding upon the heels of that birth when a first-timer brought her nine-pound, six-ounce son earth-side. The woman, though a graduate of The Bradley Method Childbirth Course, a course that advocates taking it easy on the pushing, did have to push with every ounce of her strength for the better part of three hours. Once, in the quiet between a set of contractions, she said, "If my childbirth educator were here right now, I'd whop her on the head with a skillet."

Seven days after that, we ushered another nine-pound, six-ounce baby into life. It was the family's seventh child, and the result of the forty-one-year-old mother's tubal ligation reversal. She birthed on Jean's stool, nice and easy. Several years later I ran into that woman, Kristina, at a midwifery conference in Grand Rapids. We talked a minute or two, then she said, "But, Kim, whatever happened to your blue eyes?"

"What blue eyes?" I asked. "My mom tells me my eyes haven't been blue since I was a two-year-old."

"Oh, no!" Kristina gasped and clasped her hands over her heart. "You had bright blue eyes when my baby was born! I know you did! It was your beautiful, ocean-blue eyes that got me through every single one of my contractions. I just looked at you through each one and lost myself in them."

I really didn't know what to say. I was sorry to disappoint her with my olive-green peepers.

Within twelve hours of our return from Kristina's birth, we were up and hustling to receive a young woman's first baby in Lake Odessa. He was born a heartbeat after our arrival and no sooner had he come when another laboring mom called to say she needed us.

Jean sent me flying out the door in a flash, as that second mom already felt like pushing.

I arrived to find the tiny, three-week-early baby already born. He seemed okay at first, but before long, he let me know he was struggling just a bit to keep his lungs fully inflated, so we whisked him off to the hospital.

We had an eleven-day break after that, then we were right back at it. Around seven in the morning, a man named William called to say his wife, Matilda, was surely and at last "doing it" one day shy of forty-three weeks gestation.

The family of soon-to-be-five lived in a very small, two-bedroom apartment in one of Kalamazoo's more congested areas. I arrived with Jean and an uncomfortably full bladder to discover Matilda was laboring in the only bathroom they had. I really couldn't go outside, it being such a busy neighborhood, and Matilda was obviously so close to birthing I didn't dare go anywhere else.

I happened to be near the bathroom—I guess I could hardly keep myself away from it—when she called from the tub to say she thought she felt like she could push.

When I poked my head through the door, she asked, "Do you think I should I stay in here, or get out?"

Though my conscience twisted with my unadulterated self-ishness, I told her I imagined she'd be more comfortable in her bedroom. She flung herself from the tub, dashed across the hall, and plopped down upon the stool while I slipped into the bath-room and relieved myself.

Not too long after, Matilda and David's wee ray of sunshine lay nestled safely in Matilda's arms. Two or three years later, the couple had another baby and, once again, she was in the bathtub upon our arrival. That time, she opted to stay in it to give birth and I thought, with a flush of shame, how she certainly would have preferred to remain in the tub the previous time, too.

Nowadays I'm not above using the toilet while a mom's in the tub when the great outdoors provides no suitable alternative, though I do ask the dads to step out for just a second.

We attended this birth with Eve, Jean's former apprentice, and with Annie, the doula who'd attended the wintertime swing dancer's birth with us. We were ready to head for home by lunchtime and, as each of us was available and feeling rather celebratory, we decided to have a bite together at a nearby restaurant before we parted. We were merrily on our way when Annie realized she hadn't any shoes with her. "I was in such a hurry, I guess I ran from the house without them!"

We hesitated momentarily, then I suggested we just march right on into the restaurant as though she were properly shod. We did and, once we were safely seated, the giggles began rippling and wouldn't stop. I suppose it wasn't that funny, but we were filled with the special sort of joy that flows after witnessing a birth, a blessed euphoria that follows you and lingers awhile, making it easy to cry and so easy to laugh. Every birth seems to send me off with more love in my heart.

Bright and early the next morning, we were on the road again, this time heading toward Homer to help a couple birth their second child. Altogether, it was a nice birth, but the mom sustained a second-degree tear with a labial hematoma to boot and, as I'd been the one to suggest she use the birth stool to bring her little one forth, I was determined responsible for the damage.

Jean arranged for her repair, while I made her a batch of epsom salt packs to keep inside her pad a few days. Fortunately, the tear healed nicely, the hematoma resolved, and the family was happy with their homebirth, but I did carry a sick feeling away with me from that one that was difficult to shake.

I'd just attended ten births in seven weeks. You really can learn so much, attending births at that pace. You're able to settle into a rhythm where you can see to the regular parts of attending births almost without thinking about them, leaving you freer to focus on and absorb the more notable elements. It remains that way even beyond student-hood, especially, for some reason, in regard to gear and supply set-up. Too often, when I attend a birth after a bit of a break, I find myself standing next to the supplies and my bags, scratching my head and trying to remember what all the stuff is for, and where I last saw my watch.

But the pace of that summer took a toll on my family. I asked Brent the weekend after the last of those births, "So—how do you like midwifery now?" I was fully prepared for him to tell me he hated it and wanted me to quit.

"I like it fine," he said, unruffled. "It isn't this way all the time."

Chapter

TWENTY-FOUR

AT THE END OF THAT SPRING AND SUMMER I looked over the calendar and wrote in my journal with a smile and big, bold lettering, "NOTHING BIG IS HAPPENING FOR A LONG TIME."

We settled back into our homeschooling routine soon after the births of early September, and prepared to enjoy the slower pace of another glorious autumn. But, at first only by scarcely perceptible degrees, I began struggling to breathe again.

I closed my eyes to it as long as I could. Brent seemed to as well. We effectively kept our eyes closed until, as before, Jean finally mentioned it. By the second week of October, it was worse than before and breathing became the focus of my life. I spent my days working to live my life and breathe at the same time. The coughing worsened, too, until once or twice daily I'd have a fit so severe I'd wonder if I'd survive it, hoping for my kids' sake I would; usually they were somewhere nearby, watching me with their fathomless brown eyes. The fits left me sweaty, teary-eyed, wiped out from my efforts, and with astounding headaches. It became impossible to move and talk simultaneously and I began sleeping unconscionable lengths of time, though I'd often wake with a jolt after ceasing to breathe altogether. The days were long and laborious, the nights interminable and increasingly restless. I was exhausted, demoralized, concerned. I guess we both were.

Not knowing what else to do, I returned to our doctor's office. I visited the office three times the last eight or ten days of October, and each trip proved just as frustrating as my previous visits. Every bit of information I provided, every question I asked, every comment I made was answered with, "Mrs. Woodard, you have asthma."

The doctor at my first visit back said she'd prove it to me. A peak flow meter was produced and explained. I was told that, normally, a woman my age and height could blow into that bit of plastic and expect to register a number between 400–430. The doctor said asthmatic women of my size and age suffering respiratory distress might register numbers as low as 200–215. She said those women would take a couple puffs on their inhalers and head to the nearest emergency room for breathing treatments. To prove I had asthma, I was to blow into the meter, take a breathing treatment, then blow into the meter again. The proof would be the substantial improvement in the numbers.

I said I was game and I blew a one hundred. I took the breathing treatment, waited a little while, and blew again. One hundred.

"Hmm," said the doctor, "try again."

One hundred.

"Try again, Mrs. Woodard. This time, really try."

Sixty.

"Okay, let's try one more time."

I told her I couldn't, I was all out of energy and breath. I asked if I might have something besides asthma. I mentioned I felt like I had a hand squeezing my throat most of the time.

"Mrs. Woodard," the doctor said with a sigh, "you have asthma."

"Should I get a CT scan?" I asked.

"Mrs. Woodard, you have asthma."

"Should somebody take a look down my windpipe?"

"Mrs. Woodard, you have asthma. If you won't allow us to treat you for asthma, we'll see you in here next year with emphysema."

It was like talking to a fence post. I went away with new prescriptions, an appointment for a chest x-ray, and an unhealthy dose of discouragement.

I spent the next few days thinking and praying. I really had, have yet for all I've experienced in life, a very simple view of life and God and the Bible. God says in the Bible He made me, He loves me, He's rescued and redeemed and healed me, He has good plans and amazing gifts for me, and He'll be with me all the time.

I decided then more fully than ever before I believed that. I went to a conference in the fall and had the opportunity to create a summary of my belief. Though I can't recall exactly what the point of the exercise was, I remember we were invited to write and share a statement with the group. With my struggles fresh on my mind, I wrote the following: "They say I'm ill with asthma. And, indeed, my body works hard to breathe.

"But I know I'm not ill. I know it's only a matter of time before the truth manifests, and my body comes into agreement with my soul and spirit. Until then, I can rest, and wait in peace."

Meanwhile, I had more and more trouble breathing and coughing. I felt like I was trying to suck my breath in through a soda straw, and my throat and ears ached constantly, the way they ache when you're trying to hold back tears. Luanne, our superlative babysitter, came to babysit *me*, since Brent wasn't comfortable leaving me alone anymore.

One evening in late October, we met a woman, Jane, in the church parking lot. Our teens, her sons, and some of the neighborhood youths got into a little scuffle after youth group. Once Brent sorted things out and settled things down, we had a nice talk with her.

As we turned to leave, Jane asked after my labored breathing. We told her what was going on, and she said I ought to try to get an appointment with her husband, Gregory Harrington, a pulmonologist and infectious disease specialist at The Lung Center.

I called his office first thing the next morning. I was told I'd need a referral, so I called our doctor's office to request one. I was told I'd have to come in for another visit to get it. I made my appointment and then, hoping to appear more cooperative, started with the Prednisone and tried the inhaler. I went to the doctor's office the next afternoon, jumpy and cranky from the pills and having abandoned the inhaler after my first puff when I found it magnified my difficulties. The steroids seemed to make things worse, too.

At that visit, I saw a young, new guy. He had me blow into the peak flow meter for him, and my blow registered sixty. He was instantly concerned. He told me he would double my dose of steroids, then hospitalize me if I showed no improvement after two days.

I told him the steroids made it harder for me to breathe.

"No, they don't," he said without looking up from his papers. "Have you tried the inhaler?"

I told him I had, but the inhaler made it harder to breathe, too.

"No, it doesn't," he said.

I told him it did indeed.

"No, it doesn't, Mrs. Woodard. Use your inhaler. Use your inhaler every single minute until you feel it working."

I was shocked and offended. Then I remembered I hadn't come to argue about my diagnosis or mode of treatment; I was there for a referral to Dr. Harrington's office.

"Mrs. Woodard," he said, heaving a heavy sigh, "you have asthma. If we send you to Dr. Harrington's now, he'll just treat you for asthma exactly the way we're trying to treat you for asthma."

I told him I really didn't think I had asthma. I reminded him how I hadn't responded at all to the breathing treatment, and I told him how I felt as though I had a hand squeezing my throat. He looked stricken and ready to burst into tears.

With Hannah and Paul sitting right there, absorbing every word, he asked, "Mrs. Woodard, don't you know people die from asthma? Do you want to die?"

Glancing at my little people I said of course I didn't want to die, but supposed I wouldn't die of asthma, as I just didn't believe I had it. I asked how my chest x-ray came out. He admitted my lungs appeared clear. My oxygen saturation levels were nearly one hundred percent as well. I told him I only wanted a referral. I told him that was the only reason I came in. He said he preferred to wait until I was on the medications seven to nine days before contemplating a referral. I left with an appointment to see him the next week.

The next day, it occurred to me to call another doctor in town, a friendly, more naturally-oriented MD I'd recently met, and ask if I could switch to his practice in order to obtain a referral to Dr. Harrington's office. The doctor asked a series of questions, including whether or not I'd eaten any fish recently. I answered his questions, and said I hadn't had any fish. We talked a bit more and, finally, I asked outright if he'd take me and refer me or not. He asked if I thought I might have inhaled a fish bone. I reminded him I'd said I hadn't had any fish. He said I'd certainly be welcome in his practice, but he likely wouldn't refer me to Dr. Harrington either. Disappointed and more than a little incredulous, I said I thought I'd just stay put.

"Okay!" He said. "Feel better soon!"

I can't even describe how dispiriting that conversation was. Feel better soon? I felt like I was dangling at the edge of death with those best equipped to help me just hanging out and watching the show.

I woke the next morning, tired, in pain, and simmering with anger. I called my physician's office and absolutely insisted they refer me to the specialist. Dr. Harrington's office even advised me to say I'd sue if I didn't get that referral and wound up with permanent damage, but I couldn't bring myself to do it because I knew I wouldn't sue. I just dug in my heels, and *insisted*.

An hour later, the office called to say I could come for another appointment Saturday morning. I bit back a smart remark about not being able to afford three fruitless visits in one week and said I'd be there.

So, up and off I went that pretty autumn morning. Not surprisingly, I was greeted with more of the same from a third doctor, technically, our actual family doctor and the senior man in the practice. But I was prepared for that and determined to stay in his office until I got what I wanted.

"Mrs. Woodard, I know you don't want to hear this, but you have asthma. I don't blame you for not wanting to have asthma. I have asthma and don't want it either, but you're going to have to accept facts and take the medications we've prescribed for you."

I took a deep breath—the deepest I could, anyway—and repeated everything I'd said to everybody before. I didn't think I had asthma, I suspected I had something in my throat as I felt I was getting choked. The drugs made it worse. I just wanted to see Dr. Harrington.

"You know, Kim," the doctor said, "people like you—people who want more control over their healthcare—really don't fit very well into our practice. You come in here in rough shape, then refuse to be helped! What are we supposed to think about that? The drugs don't make it worse—you just don't like drugs and you don't want to take them. If I send you over to Dr. Harrington, he'll only offer you drugs, too."

I told him I hoped Dr. Harrington would also offer an opportunity to better explore my condition and, therefore, my options.

The man sighed, kissed me on the forehead, and wrote out my referral.

Three days later, I was in Dr. Harrington's office. I couldn't help but wonder while I waited in my stiff paper robe if I really might have asthma and was about to find I'd kicked up a giant fuss over nothing, but as the doctor walked through the exam room door, he paused, listened to me draw in a single raspy breath, and, with his hand still on the knob, said, "Yeah, you don't have asthma, you have an airway obstruction. We'll do a CT scan tomorrow, then I'll look down your throat first thing Friday."

It was that simple and that quick. I laughed all the way home. Breathlessly.

I woke at three o'clock Friday morning, too nervous to stay any longer in bed. I read my Bible. I prayed. I exercised. My friend

Anita took me to the hospital because Brent was finishing a night shift. I wrote a letter to my family doctor the night before and I delivered it to him on the way. I felt it was important for him to know that what he'd called "wanting more control," was me taking seriously the responsibility to properly steward the gift of my life. I wanted him to wonder what might have happened had I relinquished control and submitted to an inaccurate diagnosis and treatment protocol. I wanted to offer him the opportunity to learn from the experience with me. I wanted him to see the fantastic possibilities embedded in working with clientele willing to read and think and communicate and work and take their health by the horns.

I signed off with, "I'm writing to encourage you and your staff to look for the chance to work cooperatively with clients who 'want more control,' to listen carefully to them and be pleasantly surprised at what you may learn from and with them. They'll be the clients who get better or die without blaming you for being human. Rather, they'll get better or die thanking you for your sincere best efforts to help."

Remembering that bit all these years later, I can say striving to be such a healthcare provider myself has proven a rich and rewarding experience, as well as an essential one. So much of what I know as a midwife I've learned from my patient, gracious clients.

A few days hence, I received a very nice, brief note in which the senior doctor wrote, "The news of your problem hit us hard, and everyone is aware and doing inward looking to see how we could have handled this differently."

I returned to consciousness after the flexible bronchoscopy to learn I was about to be transferred to the University of Michigan Health System by helicopter. A normal female trachea is generally twenty-one to twenty-two millimeters in diameter, though a diameter as narrow as ten millimeters is still considered within normal limits. My trachea measured a mere three millimeters. It would seem I really had been sucking my breaths through a straw, and a narrow straw, at that.

Post-procedure, Dr. Harrington was worried on many levels, from not knowing the cause of the stricture, to not knowing how the bronchoscopy would affect it, and wanted me at U of M as soon as possible.

I was disoriented from the sedatives I received, but I begged Brent not to let them fly me there, as I didn't think our insurance policy covered life-flights. "I feel the same as ever, Brent. Ann Arbor's not that far away, just drive me over yourself. I'm fine. I can tell."

But Brent was worried, too, so off I went, thundering east through the dusky skies of evening. I was stashed in the intensive care unit, also, I was sure, unnecessarily, but decided not to argue. I was going to get the care I needed and I was grateful.

The next thing I knew I was perched on the end of a bed in a room made of glass, wrapped in a peek-a-boo hospital gown with EKG wires plastered against my chest, oxygen tubing snaking from my nostrils, IV lines taped on my forearm, my hair standing on end, and some kind of goo smeared and dried across one of my cheeks, while the nurse who settled me in drilled me with an assortment of questions.

We finally neared the end of the interview. "And when was the last time you exercised?"

"This morning."

He looked up at me. "Really?" He asked.

"Really," I answered. "I'm not sick. I'm just having a little trouble breathing."

"Well," he said with a smile and a wink. "Don't you let us make you sick, then, okay?"

From there, a team of doctors examined me, poked me, tested me, scanned me, talked to me, and puzzled over me for nearly a week. One afternoon, I had a group of five students with stethoscopes crowding around me, each in turn, listening to me breathe. Another afternoon, while they all were still puzzling, someone brought my children up for a visit.

Hannah trotted in, hopped up onto my lap, and said, "Mom, listen, I've been thinking and I know what to do to fix you. It'll hurt, but I'm sure it'll work. If somebody would just get me a butter knife, I could do it for you right now. You'll just have to tilt your head back and open your mouth. I'll stick the knife down your throat and clean it out in there for you."

By the next morning, I was provided the diagnosis of idiopathic laryngotracheal stenosis, and was told I'd either undergo a reconstruction of my trachea, or, ironically, what my seven-year-old had suggested, a cleaning and stretching of it with a series of dilator rods. The surgical event, whichever it would wind up being—and the surgeon placed his bets on the reconstruction—was scheduled for the end of the week.

That afternoon, a frightened nurse laid out a supply of epinephrine syringes, airway catheters, tracheostomy tubes, and other bits of lifesaving equipment. When Mark Iannettoni, the chief of thoracic surgery, came in that evening to talk things over with us, he noticed all the items the nurse scrounged up and spread around my room and said, "Whoa! I'm sorry! That stuff would scare the hell out of me."

The big day arrived, and I was nervous, but ready. I sounded like Darth Vader, I had to go to bed every night breathing some mixture of gas that would allow the air to slip more easily past the crimp in my throat, I coughed until my headaches were untouchable, my oxygen saturations were dipping, and my normally low blood pressures were bouncing all over the place.

I reached for my Bible and felt inspired to turn to Isaiah fifty-two. I laughed out loud when I read it.

"Awake...Clothe yourself with strength...Shake off the dust...Rise up...*Free yourself from the chains about your neck.*"

I was wheeled into the operating room, prepared to wake with a reconstructed trachea, but I woke instead to find I'd skimmed by with only a dilatation.

When I came to after the surgery, the tremendous rush of air filling my lungs disoriented me, and my efforts to breathe were ridiculously uncoordinated. Things got even worse as the grogginess wore away and the gratitude kicked in. I began sobbing and saying, "Oh, thank you! Oh, thank you! Oh, thank you!" until I nearly passed out. My throat and ears were on fire and my sobs only fanned the flames, but I was so thankful, I couldn't stop. Finally, the nurses calmed me down, but it was a challenge to stay calm as every moment I breathed so easily made the tears gush afresh.

The prognosis was periodic dilatations and, eventually, a reconstruction. I said okay, but I inwardly rejected that according to my view of supernatural healing.

It must be stated here that medical interventions don't fit my view of God and life very well, though I'm aware there's a lot in life I don't fully understand. But my default is to expect miracles. I truly expected a miraculous healing and, despite requiring surgery, I still expected to be miraculously fine from then onward. So, I said okay and thank you, and the next day I went home. My throat and my neck and my shoulders, and even my ribs hurt, but I was thrilled and filled with energy, and I re-entered my life with vigor. Incredibly, I missed only one birth.

Chapter

TWENTY-FIVE

WE CLOSED OUT THE YEAR WITH THANKSGIVING, Christmas, and four beautiful births beginning with that of a darling baby boy born to a sweetheart, her husband, and their eight-year-old daughter in Kalamazoo.

And I learned a very important lesson at that birth.

By that time in my apprenticeship, the reality of attending births in untidy homes was not novel. Therefore, I wasn't surprised or bothered to find Amy's home a less than tidy one. I'd actually expected it to be less than tidy. My first clue to the state things might be in at the birth was dropped at one of her prenatals about a month before.

"Come in, come in!" she said as she swung the door as wide as her smile. "Come in and look what I've done! I got all my supplies, *and* I cleaned the bathroom and the kitchen!"

She showed us around with palpable pride, glowing brightly as Jean praised her. And, as Jean praised her, I wondered how long it might have been since she'd cleaned those places and whether she realized she ought to try to keep them clean through the weeks while she waited for her baby to come.

It took only a cursory glance upon our arrival to realize the thought had failed to enter her mind. None of the living spaces appeared inhabitable; every square inch of counter in the kitchen, plus both sides of the sink and the stovetop, were occupied by precarious towers of dirty dishes, and the bathroom was just plain gruesome.

Without a second thought, I set to cleaning. I finished in the bathroom and was preparing to tackle the kitchen when Amy, noticing my efforts in spite of the incessant waves of pain undulating over and about her slight frame, made an awkward apology, and a gleam of illumination dawned in my brain.

I'd embarrassed her. There, in the very throes of her vulnerability, on one of the most special days of her life, a person she was counting on to accept and support her unwittingly sent an unaccepting, unsupportive message, and it stung.

The unfortunate experience revealed to me that, without realizing it, somewhere along the line, I decided *my* standard of cleanliness and order was *the* standard of cleanliness and order, and I saw in an instant how arrogant that decision was. I came away from that chilly winter's evening chastened, repentant, and determined never to repeat the error. Not to say I'd never tidy an untidy home again. Many, many times since I've entered homes that demand I clear a workable space. The difference was learning to work discretely, doing only what I needed to do—only what the mother would appreciate I do—while abstaining from making assessments or judgments. It was learning to respect and appreciate the woman and her way of life for what it was: hers, and not at all mine. It was an even more powerful lesson when I considered its scope of applicability beyond my career, and one vital for me to learn.

A fat, nine-pound beauty was born after that, also in Kalama-zoo, and then a handsome boy right on Christmas Eve near Char-lotte to a woman who spent her early labor making a batch of chocolate cream pies almost as delightful as her son, lined up as they were beneath the gingham-curtained windows of her kitchen.

Another handsome baby boy was born then, three weeks early to a set of first-time Amish parents in Vermontville, a day or two before the turn of the year.

We drove through a magical swirl of thick snowflakes right around twelve o'clock, and passed the remaining hours of the night warmed by a fire crackling in the woodstove and charmed by the way the mother and dad labored together.

I was allowed to help the spellbound father receive his baby girl and, then, with the mother crying, "Dad, we did it! Dad, we did it!" I gently rubbed the child's breath into her.

I carry the holiness of these moments everywhere I go. They live within me, pooling into an ever-deepening reservoir of won-derment. The mothers, unbelievably strong—the fathers, visibly moved by their wives and tiny babies, looking at them like they're the sun, the moon, and the stars—the tears, the laughter, the outpouring of love, the "Oh! Ooohhhh!! Oooohhhhh!!!"

The fact I'm invited into those matchless moments, invited in to be touched and to be changed by them, is among the pro-foundest of life's gifts.

It was a good birth, yes. But the mom sustained an impres-sive tear and, again, my handling of the birth was determined the reason for it. Between the knowledge of my failings and the way my mistakes caused the new mother to suffer, it was all I could do to maintain consciousness as we secured the care she required. During her repair, I had to run to the bathroom, tear off my sweater, and splash myself all over with cold water in order to regain my head. Fortunately, the tear healed nicely.

On the last day of December, I went through my records for the year and was pleased to see I'd attended twenty-two births, making for a total of nearly sixty. I crossed over into the New Year, the new century, the new millennium much the same way we observed Thanksgiving and Christmas that season—quietly, almost wearily, but deeply grateful, and even in awe.

After all we went through, I felt ready for a fresh year, though I'm not sure I'd have felt so ready had I seen what the year would hold.

We were mildly disappointed to launch into it with a second dilatation of my trachea, but it proved a simple affair I was able to put behind me in only a few days.

Soon afterward a most yummy baby boy was born to an Amish family near Charlotte. It was a nice birth, but the mom had a hemorrhage that took a bit of doing to resolve and, though the child was the family's third, she suffered a significant tear. I don't recall the tear being due to any fault of my own that time, but, again, I hovered at the brink of sensibility over it. The night was long, the room was hot, the air was thick with fumes from the kerosene lamp, and I was tired. I hung on by my fingernails till we were back in the car, where I promptly conked out. It wasn't until many years later that I realized the victory I scored that night by staying conscious and completing my tasks.

The next baby born was a hefty nine-pound, eight-ounce boy, "born to mommy and dad and sister," I wrote in my journal the next morning. "Juicy and sweet with just a mite of dark hair. He looks like his daddy. The birth was painful, but it went well. Mama suffered only a tiny split of a tear that we were able to leave alone. The placenta was enormous, weighing in at two and a half pounds. The child is loved and celebrated! The joy radiating from the family made the work feel easy and we left with light hearts."

It was around that time Brent and I had a serious talk about whether or not we wanted to spend a year or more at YWAM ourselves. We talked about it on and off since the first life-altering trip four years before and by then had sent a good many of our graduated teens there. Though we loved our jobs and our life in Battle Creek, the idea tugged continuously at our hearts. But, as we considered, we realized it would mean a substantial sacrifice of home, possessions, ministry, policing, midwifery, homeschooling, and financial security. We decided to stay put.

I was disappointed, but resigned myself to it and settled in to Michigan life in a way I hadn't allowed myself to before. We did a bit of work on the house, got a dog, planted some blueberry shrubs, and bought a car. The car wasn't by any means new—it was an eight-year-old Plymouth Voyager—but we paid cash for it and it was the first truly trouble-free vehicle we were able to buy since the gently-used Honda we purchased when Hannah was a baby. And, mercy, what a streak of vehicle troubles we had through the years.

We started with a beat-up Ford truck that nearly took Brent's finger off the year Hannah was born. One afternoon he shoved a thousand dollars into his pocket, rode his bicycle some four or five miles across town, purchased the truck, tossed his bike in the back, drove home, and proceeded to spend the next year working on it.

We bought the Honda after that, but it was accidentally totaled by a friend. Our replacement Honda was totaled by an uninsured drunk driver. We had an old Bronco II for a couple years that had so many electrical issues it appeared possessed.

Then we had what the teenagers dubbed "The Land Barge." I don't even remember what exact brand that monstrosity was, possibly a Dodge. It was a great big, brownish-yellow conversion van with a fin on top and curtains at the windows. Brent sold a much better car to get it, but he did it because the church wouldn't purchase the bus we needed for hauling the teenagers around.

One afternoon while I was out and about, he called me and said, "Kim! You won't believe this! I just bought a van for $785.00! It's beautiful!" And in his practical mind, it *was* beautiful. He went to all the junkyards in town and scrounged up a couple extra seats and, before we knew it, we could get eleven or twelve kids into it.

And then there was the Honda Civic Wagon we purchased out in Arizona. It was cute, rust-free, and a lemon. Ron got it to Michigan for us the summer after Emily was born. I fetched it from Mt. Pleasant and it was overheating before I was halfway home. Brent fixed it, and it overheated. He fixed it again, and it overheated again. He fixed it one more time, and it blew a head gasket.

When it blew the head gasket, he purchased another old Honda Civic Wagon from a salvage yard, one with a ruined body but solid engine. He spent the better part of a summer switching out the engines, often using the kids to help him, as his hands were too big to squeeze into all the nooks and crannies and crevices of the foreign-constructed machine. At last, he had the thing up and running again and then I nearly ruined it. It actually happened the Saturday I went to the family doctor for my referral to the specialist. Luanne was staying with us at the time. I described the incident in my journal.

I left the doctor's office to drive home. Now, Brent usually leaves the key in the ignition all the time and I had a feeling I ought to leave it in when I pulled into the doctor's that morning, but then I thought, "Don't be foolish," and I removed it.

I noticed it came out in something of an odd way and, when I opened the door, a buzzer sounded. I checked the lights, then checked everything else I could think to check, paused, shrugged, shut the door, and went inside.

When I got back out to the car, I couldn't get the key in all the way. I turned it over and tried again. I fiddled with it, jiggled it, coaxed it, sat flummoxed a few minutes, tried to start it though the key would only go part way in, and—bingo—it started! I drove home without another thought until I tried to shut the car off.

Yes. So. I tried to shut the car off. I pushed, I pulled, I wiggled, I pleaded—all to no avail. Then the key came out, but the car stayed on. I ran inside and called Brent at work. He told me to keep an eye on the heat gauge and hung up. I went back out to look at the gauge and noticed it was getting hot. Assuming Brent was on his way, I hoped he was hurrying. I went back inside and, not too long after I got in there, began to hear a hissing noise. I looked out the window and saw clouds of steam billowing up from under the hood!

I called Brent again, in a panic. You know, I think this was the first time in my life I'd ever really panicked. I mean, I was freaked out! I didn't know what would happen! Would the car explode? Would it shatter the living room windows? I made the kids run down to the bedroom and, learning Brent was not on the way home due to making an arrest, I tried hard to do everything he told me to do while every nerve in my body screamed, "DANGER! GET AWAY!!"

But I went out, popped the hood, propped it up, then danced about it in fright as Brent tried to explain how to disconnect the spark plugs and distributor cap. What Brent said was unclear to me. I could hardly see anything he was describing. All I could see was this heaving, shuddering, boiling, hissing, belching cauldron of imminent death by fire and shrapnel. Brent said he was on his way and hung up. Luanne came out with me and was excited but calm as she bent over and looked into the engine—from the dangerous side—and tried to get me to tell her what Brent had said to do. But I couldn't let her touch it! Oh, my heart was breaking over all Brent's hard work on that blasted engine! I desperately wanted to reach in and yank at the cords he'd tried to describe!

Then something popped, and the horrible noises surged and swelled, and Luanne and I ran like a couple of jack rabbits into the house and down the hall where we crouched with the kids in the corner of their bedroom, waiting in dread for an explosion.

After a moment or two without an explosion, my heart forced me back into the garage. Then my brains chased me back into the kitchen. I plunged my shaking hands into my yellow rubber gloves and dashed again to the churning, blowing, menace, hopped about like a maniac, then skittered back indoors. I hovered behind the kitchen door, flapping and fluttering and begging God to help me, berating myself and bewailing my cowardice.

At that moment, Brent roared into the driveway in his patrol car, leapt from it, dashed to the Honda, fearlessly leaned over the convulsing, sputtering thing, and with one deft motion of his hand within its fulminating depths, did something, and all went silent but the sorrowful, dying sigh of the radiator.

Brent straightened, looking grim. I stood trembling with both anguish and relief, my gloved hands clutched at my throat. Without a word, he turned and returned to work. I released Luanne and the kids from the bedroom and went and slept like the dead for two hours.

Thankfully, the car survived and we sold it to a mechanic for four hundred dollars the next spring.

Chapter

TWENTY-SIX

SPRING EXPLODED UPON THE SCENE IN RIOTOUS life. The dazzling white bracts of the dogwoods and the half-filled wine-goblet blossoms of the magnolias; the fine sprays of lavender redbud and the generous, matronly blooms of the lilacs; the vibrant melodies of robins and cardinals and orioles; the choruses of spring peepers rising and falling upon the balmy, snow-melting breezes all went to work to lift our spirits and invigorate our winter-weary senses.

That arresting vernal equinox brought, besides the delights of regeneration, the excitement of a meeting with Jean. Jean wanted to talk with Nan and me about "The Next Level."

"The Next Level?" I asked. "What Next Level?"

Yeah, Nan wanted to know, too.

Jean shook her head, laughed, and said, "The Next Level in midwifery! What did you think? You two have been to more than fifty births and it's time you began preparing to complete your apprenticeships. It's time you both do more appointments on your own and time I start rating your performances at births."

I was surprised, pleased, and terrified to learn Jean was thinking this way, and it marked the first time it occurred to me since before the genesis of my apprenticeship that I might really and truly be able to become a midwife.

I went home and told Brent, then dove into my studies with renewed energy and enthusiasm.

And the very next birth I attended was the very first birth I attended by myself. It wasn't planned, I didn't personally know the family, and I was only barely aware they even existed. It happened on Brent's thirtieth birthday. At half past midnight, we climbed into bed musing how thirty years before Brent's mom would have been starting labor for him, when the telephone rang.

Brent answered, listened, and said, "Yes, she's right here."

"Hello?"

"Are you Kim?"

"Yes."

"Okay, good. I'm Rod. Listen, my wife's in labor and Jean Balm's at another birth, but she says you'll come on out and deliver our baby. Where do you live?"

I blinked as my pulse rocketed into outer space. "Uhhhh—I live on Kirby Road."

"Great. We'll see you in about ten minutes."

"Wait—what?" I heard him, but his words failed to register.

"Ten minutes. I figure that's as long as it should take for you to get here, eh?"

"Oh! Sure! Yeah! Er—well, but do I have time to get dressed?"

"I guess so, but you'd better make it snappy. This baby's gonna come any sec."

I threw my clothes on, though I've gone to more than one birth in my pjs since—I even took a mom to an Indiana hospital in my pajamas once—ditched teeth brushing for a stick of gum, and dashed out the door with my woefully inadequate bag of gear. All I had was a blood pressure cuff and stethoscope, a fetoscope, a measuring tape, a watch, a sandwich baggie of gloves, a jar of urine dipsticks, and a baby scale.

"You're gonna do great, Hon!" Brent called as I dove into the car. "I'm so proud of you! I'll be praying for you!"

I flew along the back roads between our houses beneath a splash of twinkling stars, but all I really noticed was the bolt of adrenaline coursing down my spine and clenching my buttocks and thighs into a mind-numbing vice, while every other cell in my body quivered and my age-old cycle of prayers thrummed to life.

God! Oh, my God! Please! Oh, please! God! Oh, my God! Please—

I pulled into the family's driveway around one o'clock and noticed someone was dumping buckets of water out of an upstairs window.

Okay. Waterbirth. Guess they let the hot water heater run cold.

I bounded up to the house, banged on the door, and Rod let me in. Out of breath and with my heart hammering so hard I could hardly hear, I asked him if the baby had come yet.

"Not yet!" He said, pointing me to the stairway. "But any minute!"

I took the stairs two at a time and found the man's wife, Gwen, on her hands and knees.

She was a forty-year-old nurse, about a week past her dates, calmly blowing through the powerful workings of her body while her friend, Kelly Ordway—also an aspiring midwife—worked to fill the fish-bedecked kiddie pool with water warm enough to birth in. I nodded to her and she nodded back, though I thought she looked a little alarmed to see only me.

Things were moving along, but, glancing at the laboring woman, I relaxed. I'd have a little bit of time before the child made his appearance.

"Hey there, Gwen. I'm Kim."

Gwen smiled and lifted her hand. "Hi, Kim. Thanks for coming."

I pulled my meager things from my bag and listened to the baby's heartbeat and took his mama's blood pressure. I measured Gwen's contractions while I found and set out the things we needed for the birth: the under pads and blankets, the paper towels, and squares of gauze. I had to ask for a length of string and a pair of scissors to boil for cutting the cord though, as well as a sheet of paper and a pen to write my notes, grimacing at my glaring lack of professionalism and thinking Kelly looked even more alarmed.

I finished my preparations and settled in to wait, but I didn't have to wait for long. Though her labor began at midnight, Gwen was feeling like she could push by two o'clock. I checked her, and found she had just a smidgen of cervix yet at the front.

She decided to climb into the pool. She sighed as her heavy body slipped beneath the surface of the warm water. She laid her head against its rim and shut her eyes. A minute ticked by and she said, tapping the pink polka-dotted sunfish beside her left ear, "Ah ha! I found where the cat pricked the pool."

Rod stood beside me, looking down at Gwen's immense belly with obvious admiration. He hitched up his shorts, swiped the back of his hand across his nose, nodded his head, and said, "Yep, this one's gonna be a twelve-pounder!"

A twelve pounder? Oh, yes, I'm sure. And I can get to you in ten minutes, and the baby's going to burst out of your wife in mere seconds, too. Who is this guy?

Inwardly, I rolled my eyes. I didn't even consider twelve pounds a possibility. It was better I didn't. I was nervous enough to be the only attendant as it was.

With most of her contractions, Gwen pushed gently. By twenty after two, I felt we ought to be seeing something of the baby. It was her fourth, after all. Gwen said I could check her, so I leaned over the decidedly deflated edge of the pool and a wave flowed out and soaked me from the shoulders down.

I halted, surprised, but as there was nothing else to do but go on, I examined her. I could still feel that bit of cervix, so I stroked it away as Gwen pushed. With the next contraction, I put a little pressure at the rear wall of her vagina, and the baby's head slipped right down into the space.

Then I felt around a little more and noticed for the first time the size of the child's head. It was enormous, with the molding—evidenced by the wrinkles in the skin that form as the bones of the baby's head slip over one another while squeezing through the pelvis—so exaggerated I thought with a start I was feeling his umbilical cord.

I could feel Kelly's eyes on me, trying to read me, but I avoided them and, doing my best to keep my cool, felt and felt until I was confident what I felt was only a thick wrinkle. A few minutes later Gwen eased that huge head out. It took a little extra work for her to bring his body out, but bring it out she did and, as his face cleared the water, he coughed twice and the pink swept from his chest to the tips of his stubby fingers and toes. The hefty placenta followed without incident, Gwen had a normal bleed, her tissues were intact, and the baby nursed long and deep. She did struggle with air hunger and dizziness on the trip to and from the bathroom, but Kelly and I soon had her tucked snug into her bed.

And, by golly, wouldn't you know it. That baby boy—born in a mere two hours and twenty-eight minutes—was, indeed, twelve pounds. He was twelve-pounds, three-ounces with a fifteen-inch head.

I shook hands with Rod, hugged Gwen, gave Kelly a squeeze oozing with relief, and drove home in a state of pure euphoria, unable to believe I just attended a birth by myself—and such a fantastic birth, too. That child still holds the record for size in my practice these many years later.

What a great start to "The Next Level of Midwifery!" Oh, Jesus! Thank you with all of my heart!

And, through that second drive of the night, I did see the beautiful wash of starlight overhead. I thought I even saw a shooting star streak across the endless vault of obsidian sky.

I rode the froth-flecked crest of the wave that was Gwen and Rod's birth as it curled and rolled through every glittering nuance of turquoise and sapphire and emerald in the brilliant sea of my hopes and dreams.

Until the wave, like all waves are destined to, dwindled into whorls of foam with fine fingers of fog rising to shroud its surface.

In other words, such a maelstrom of misfortunate events, mistakes, and mortifications were in the forecast that, by the time I made it through, the angst I'd suffered over my blunders through the year previous was more akin to light spring showers than the downpour I thought it had been.

TWENTY-SEVEN

A VIVACIOUS, NEWLYWED COUPLE WAS DUE TO give birth next and, as with many of the couples I served that year, I was allowed the privilege of overseeing much of their care. Viola and Amos Troyer, ebullient with expectation, were a joy to work with. They lived off the beaten path in a crumbling American foursquare brick back-dropped by a dilapidated barn and trimmed with rambunctious beds of bright orange day lilies and blinding white hydrangeas. The faithful Standard Bred stood in the pasture, shoulder-to-shoulder with a brown cow and pair of tawny goats, while a copse of hoary sugar maples stood guard at the entranceway of the homestead and hordes of insurrection-ary chickens challenged my approach to the rear door. The place was undeniably a work in progress, but the pair took obvious delight in the task of its rejuvenation, just as they clearly delighted in one another and in the child blossoming in Viola's depths. Though Viola and the child within her were a-bloom with health, my week-by-week inspection of her belly and its underlying support systems cast a bit of a shadow over my anticipation of her birth.

I decided against mentioning my concerns to Viola and Amos—you never could know what wonders a woman's body might work through a labor and I wanted her to enter her time of travail filled with the excitement and faith she overflowed with at each of our visits—but I reported my findings to Jean.

Viola's fundal height, a measurement from the upper ridge of a woman's pubic bone to the topmost point of the steadily expanding uterus, was alarming to me. Forty centimeters at thirty-eight weeks; forty-one centimeters at thirty-nine weeks; forty-two centimeters at forty-one weeks. While fundal heights usually follow weeks' gestation, they tend to top off in the upper thirties and, in a first-time mom, generally even dip a bit when the baby drops before its birth.

The baby appeared to be positioned well, with its spine following the curve of Viola's round abdomen, but its head wasn't flexed very well, and it was remaining markedly high.

And then, when at forty-one weeks, a week past her dates, Jean instructed me to check Viola's cervix, I noticed the baby's head was, indeed, very high, and that Viola's pubic arch appeared to be mildly flattened.

Jean shared my view it would be better not to voice our apprehensions to the two. There wasn't much we could do to alter my findings besides encourage her to keep on with the exercises and herbs we suggested she employ, as we hadn't yet discovered the value of chiropractors for positioning and Gail Tully was many years from creating her wonderful resource, Spinning Babies®.

Still, with that flattened arch, I don't know that things would have gone differently even with access to such tools. Viola's labor would determine its own outcome and, though we'd do all we could to entice the child to make the passage and to inveigle Viola's body to allow it, ultimately, we'd be forced to submit to its lead.

Roseanna Grace initiated her journey by kicking her waters loose one sunshiny morning, and by the time the warmth of the summer day began to subside, her mother was in active labor.

We arrived to find Viola and Amos glowing both with the work and with excitement, and we were pleased to find Viola's cervix thinning and opening and the baby descending well. Hope flickered to flame and carried us through the hours of the night, but by noon of the next day it began to splutter. Viola, like the mothers from the summers before, reached nine centimeters by sunrise, only to remain at nine centimeters *ad infinitum.*

When finally toward suppertime we recommended a transfer to the hospital, Viola and Amos melted into a flood of tears. Our tears mingled with theirs as Amos cradled his wife in his arms and rocked her. They'd worked so hard to birth their new baby into the love and life and laughter of their close and cozy home, and I believe they would have worked harder still, but Viola's body was talking to us, and demanded to be heard.

Their exquisite, nine-pound daughter was born by cesarean just before bedtime and we rejoiced to meet her. But our joy was touched with sorrow, too. While we all were very, very happy Roseanna Grace was healthy, we were also very, very, very sad she had to be surgically removed, and I learned the two, the happiness and the sadness, were well able to be experienced together.

To heal well, Viola and Amos, and even Jean and I, needed the coexistence of that joy and sorrow to be acknowledged and honored, so we spent many weeks talking and listening and healing.

And the first of the storm clouds began to gather upon the horizon.

Chapter

TWENTY-EIGHT

I STUMBLED HOME FROM THAT BIRTH AND STRAIGHT into the truly horrific experience of offending a client.

I was sent to examine a newly born babe who was struggling to gain weight and, upon investigation of the child, wondered if it might have Down Syndrome. I said as much, suggesting she be examined more thoroughly by a doctor, and I spent a good deal of time and effort afterward attempting to make amends for my indiscretion.

I slipped around the next bend and thought I caught a glimpse of the sun. One of my dear friends was poised to give birth to her fifth child and she asked me to be her midwife. But days doomed to darkness often start out as light and innocent as nearly every other day.

Julia called to tell me she thought she might, at last, be starting with her labor. She hoped so, at least, and I hoped so, too. Being my friend, Julia knew I'd begun working more seriously toward the completion of my apprenticeship. She knew, too, I wanted to earn the North American Registry of Midwives (NARM) Certified Professional Midwife (CPM) credential, and part of earning that credential involved attending a quantity of births as a primary midwife under the supervision of a preceptor.

Knowing all this, Julia invited me to be the primary midwife under supervision at her birth. I had taken similar roles a handful of times already, but this was the first time I was given the opportunity by a client, and I was unspeakably honored and excited. I'd taken the lead in her prenatal care with all the relish of a novice, and now was about as eager as she was for her to have her baby.

Julia called to put me on alert that morning and, after her body fiddled about with the idea of having the baby throughout the day, began to labor in earnest around bedtime.

As I prepared to head over, I called Jean only to learn she was with a laboring mom in another city. I was disappointed to miss my chance to be supervised, but Jean said she thought she could secure the services of another midwife.

She had trouble finding an available midwife that night, however, until she thought to call an old friend. Pam was retired, but still occasionally attended births. I'd never met her and was surprised and grateful to learn she was willing to help me. I was excited for the excuse to meet her, too.

And then a third family in yet a third city started labor as well with no one else to call.

The first hour I was with Julia and her husband, Troy, was spent on the telephone. Jean and I wracked our brains on behalf of that third family. I suggested Pam, the midwife coming to help me, go on down there instead. Alternately, I volunteered to go down myself, once Pam reached us. Neither option was considered viable, possibly because of the distance. Finally, Jean, realizing I needed to focus on the family I was already with, told me to get to work. She'd take care of things.

Whispering prayers for the other moms, babies, and midwives, I busied myself with Julia and Troy. Kelly, the woman who'd helped me with Gwen and Rod, was with us as well, and I was glad to have her there.

Toward midnight, Pam arrived. We were happy to see her, but instantly everything changed. She came in like a stiff breeze, making it clear she had no intention of "just watching me work." She meant to take charge, get the job done, and get back out of there.

Her manner took me by surprise, and I reeled a bit as I took it in, but then I took a deep breath and pulled myself together.

Okay, okay. This'll be okay. Just, whatever ideas you had about Julia's birth, let them go. This isn't about you, this is about Julia and Troy and their family.

I didn't like it, but I recognized the sacrifice Pam made to come serve a family she didn't even know and understood my obligation to respectfully step aside.

The family I was serving, however, felt differently. When this midwife, mere minutes after her arrival, said while literally snapping on a glove, "Okay, let's see where you're at," Julia hopped up, said she had to pee, and dashed into the bathroom, nearly slamming the door behind her.

Julia and Troy were seasoned parents and seasoned homebirthers. Julia had a history of birthing quickly once she got started, and she knew what she wanted and what she didn't want.

I myself am not the sort of midwife who automatically works to hurry a birth and, for the most part, when a mom's birthed before, I wait to check her cervix until she requests it or starts to feel like she could push.

A minute after her escape to the toilet, the bathroom door cracked open and Troy peeked his head through to ask if I'd please come in there with them. I could feel my pulse quicken and my face flush under Pam's glare, but decided against looking at her directly as I stood to comply.

When I closed the door behind me, Julia, perched on the toilet, said, "Kim, we want to have this baby the way we've planned! We want you to be the midwife! Can't you check me if I need to be checked?"

I was touched, but my heart sank into my guts. I knew the chances I'd be able to explain what this family wanted without offending Pam were slim. I also knew to do what Julia wanted would violate both Pam's position of authority over me—should she prove offended—as well as Jean's, and that there would be some serious consequences further down the line.

But most of all, I understood the one and only moment Julia and Troy would ever birth their new baby was that very night and, before God, as much as it depended on me, I'd see to it they'd have it the way they wanted it, whatever the consequences.

I eased myself back into the hallway and approached Pam like a cringing hound. I cleared my throat, smiled, and began. "Hey, Pam? Um, Julia really had this birth planned out—I mean, you know, she'd planned for me to be the one to do her checks and—"

Pam's eyes blazed as she snapped the glove back off her hand. "Fine!" And she turned and stalked down the stairs.

Kelly and I looked at one another and Kelly mouthed, "Oh, my gosh! Where's she going?"

I wondered that myself. For a minute, I thought she might be leaving, but then I heard her plop onto Julia's sofa with an angry mutter.

A wave of nausea spooled over me and the heat flushing my face seemed to ooze from my fingertips and toes. But then I remembered my resolve, braced myself, and went back to care for my friend.

It still was a lovely birth. Amidst the robust exertions of her marvelous body, Julia regaled us with the impromptu performance of an African Warrior Dance she learned in her youth and, when she felt the birth of her baby was imminent, sent us to rouse her four other children to come witness the incomparable, unrepeatable event. More than once, when Pam appeared on the point of taking over, entreated by subtle cues from Julia, I held firm my spot as her caregiver.

At ten minutes after two in the morning, bathed in the oohs and aahs of his curious siblings, a glorious nine-pound baby boy was welcomed to life by his own father's gentle hands, and right on his grandfather's birthday, too.

Things were a bit on the exciting side for a spell after that. I felt Julia was bleeding too heavily. Pam did not. Pam left, and I spent fully thirty minutes providing external bi-manual compression, expressing big, juicy clots from time to time and trying desperately to think only charitable thoughts.

Things settled down by degrees and all four children were able to cut the cord—yes, in four separate places—and examine the placenta with me before heading back to their beds, and I was back in my bed before too long afterward, though I doubt I need mention I failed to fall asleep.

A couple weeks later, I was summoned to discuss Julia's birth with Jean and Pam.

"The meeting was a trial by fire," I wrote in my journal. "Intense and painful. By the Grace of God, I accepted all that was said. I explained I knew I'd erred and understood why they were upset with me. I described what I'd been thinking, not to excuse myself, but to ease the way my errors stung and offended both of them. I apologized. I received corrections and warnings. We smiled, we hugged, I said thank you, and I went to the car and cried until I had no more tears to cry."

I received a dreadful written rating from Pam comprised of "fairs" and "poors," but she wrote in the comments, "Kim and I had issues with her not wanting my input or suggestions. I feel these issues were resolved in a meeting after the birth. I look forward to attending another birth with her." I was grateful for the comment, but prayed earnestly to God I'd be spared another encounter with the woman.

A good deal more occurred that summer and fall than I'll ever be able to tell. Many of the things that happened are more the stories of others than my own, and we'll leave it at that.

Life is challenging. When challenges manifest themselves, we're stretched. Sometimes we're stretched until we struggle just to survive the stretch. And nobody looks very good while they're struggling to survive. Proverbs 17:9 tells us, "He who covers an offense promotes love, but he who repeats the matter separates friends." And, so, the most I'll say is, the year 2000 was a dark, stretching, surviving year. It seemed one exacting obstacle led to another that led to yet another. It was the worst season for per-plexities and self-doubt I'd experienced to that point. The saving grace of it was I learned how to keep from the pits of depression and, though I did teeter at the edges of it, I managed to stay clear and functioning.

It was a significant time in one important respect. I came to understand with an unvarnished clarity I'll not be able to please others all or even most of the time, nor is it my job to do so. Sometimes I'll get credit I deserve; other times I'll get credit I don't deserve. Sometimes I'll get unwarranted blame; other times I'll have earned blame I don't get. My best will often do, but will never be enough. My job is to do the best I can, to apologize and mend things if possible when I fail, and to not get too caught up in regard or opinion.

The question I learned to use to examine myself is this: before the Almighty, is my conscience clear? That's what ultimately matters. "But You have seen," says the Psalmist. "Lord, You Know," writes Paul in Corinthians.

It was a painful but essential lesson to learn. "But, you know what?" I wrote in my journal. "God is the salvager of bruised dreams, broken hearts, and busted bodies. I'm thankful for that. God, please do that for me. And strengthen me for what lies ahead."

Another lesson I learned through that trial-laden season I also jotted into my journal. "Every single person will at some point let you down. If it's people you're counting on, you'll be devastated. I'll not hold it against the hurting people around me when, out of their hurt, they unwittingly hurt me. When someone is kind, when someone fulfills a promise, when someone loves me and treats me well, I'll receive it like a wonderful surprise, like an unexpected gift."

Though I toyed with the temptation to quit my apprenticeship, fortunately, midwifery isn't a thing you can quit on the spot. I had a whole string of friends counting on me to take part in their care and, as is often the case, as I pressed on in service to them, the mostly beautiful births I witnessed—for, after all, most births really are beautiful—renewed my heart and my strength to carry on.

Chapter

Twenty-Nine

I DIDN'T QUIT AND WAS SOON BACK TO WORK AND with another particularly demanding birth. From Monday morning until Wednesday night, Jean and I traveled 475 miles through three trips to and from Lansing. We were up for a thirty-seven hour stretch over the course of those trips, with one disjointed nap snatched amidst times. On the second trip up, the first-time family was rewarded with the birth of a big baby boy. The ordeal lasted mere minutes shy of thirty hours and was topped off with a hearty postpartum hemorrhage, but the mom recovered well through the weeks after and was proud and pleased she'd managed to stay at home and accomplish that birth.

The fact several of our clients were friends and pregnant-again clients really went a long way toward brightening those grim times, and the challenge of reaching toward the goal of certification worked to solidify my dedication to the work before me as well. Having begun finding myself alone at births from time to time, I furthered my commitment to the completion of my apprenticeship by investing in a full stock of gear.

That autumn, I snuck away for another dilatation of my airway, and this time came home in severe pain. Doctor Iannettoni said it was a more difficult one to perform and asked me not to let it get so bad again. I was so miserable by the morning afterward, I decided to take the narcotic he sent me home with, but, no sooner had I swallowed it than Jean called to say she was at a birth and a second client thought her labor was stirring. I leapt up and downed eight activated charcoal tablets, then spent the next several hours in misery, waiting for the woman to call me to come. Three weeks passed before she did. Ouch.

We were unbelievably busy from then through the rest of the year. The first morning of October dawned with three women contracting. We canceled our plans for the day, but closed it without being summoned by any of them.

The next week, one of the three women who teased us began her labor. It was yet another supremely long first birth, but this young woman was one of the most determined and confident I ever worked with, and I can't say I've seen the likes of her since.

Her waters broke on the fifth of October, her labor began the morning of the eighth, and she was ready for us to come by the early hours of the ninth. She was completely dilated at noon, but didn't birth her baby until eight hours later.

When she began to push, she would work for some twenty or thirty minutes in a position of her choosing, then announce she needed a break and proceed to shut herself into the bathroom for a soak in the tub. She did that every hour from noon until she finally birthed her scrumptious baby girl a minute or two after eight that night. Then we waited nearly an hour for her placenta to come.

When she noticed we were getting antsy about that, she said, "You know, it took a long time to get the baby out, why should the placenta be any different? I'm fine. Don't worry. I'll have it soon."

A few days later we were called away to Charlotte to help a husband and wife birth their fourth baby. Mama was nearly a week past her due date and just gigantic, but she had a quick birth with a labor lasting less than five hours. When her waters ruptured partway through, I'm sure more than a gallon of fluids rushed from her. It took almost every towel she owned to mop the living room carpet. We got those towels washed, dried, and folded again just before the ten-pound, four-ounce, twenty-three-inch-long baby boy made his entrance. He got a little hung up on the way and arrived with an apgar score of only five, but he responded readily to our efforts to resuscitate him. The placenta came easily and with no extra bleeding, and the mom sustained just a slight tear. I was back home by morning.

Jean and I rose from our beds five mornings later, again with multiple ladies contracting. Plans again were canceled and, again, we did nothing but stay home.

Two days later, the first of the two ladies welcomed her seventh son into the world, a hefty nine-pound, ten-ounce chunk of cute, and two days after that, Emily and Dan, the second family in question, gave birth.

Emily threatened preterm labor throughout her pregnancy, and it was a tough go for her. She was a homeschooling mother of four and we spent many hours both with her in person and over the telephone throughout the ordeal of her bedridden state. At last, she made it to term and, as contractions began rolling over her, she relaxed and let them roll.

She had an odd labor, though. It took some time for us to notice it, but Emily's labor really only stayed steady if she remained in her bed, alone with her man and the candles glowing along her dresser-tops.

Emily could scarcely feel her contractions as it was. If we asked if she was having one, she had to feel her belly to see and, after a bit of time on her feet, they'd just space out until they disappeared altogether.

Finally, we realized what was happening. We decided Emily and Dan would go on to bed while Jean and I waited on the downstairs sofas for Emily to feel she could push. Three times we were called to the bedroom because Emily felt the urge, but each time except for the third time, we arrived to find her standing and the sensations passing.

She wanted to birth on Jean's stool and to catch her baby herself while I took pictures, but every time she got up, there went the contractions. The third time she called us to her, she remained in her bed.

I knelt beside her and she asked, "What should I do?"

"Why don't you stay there in bed till you feel the baby begin to slide out. Then you can just quick hop over to the stool."

"Okay, that sounds like a good plan."

We set everything up and tucked ourselves away into the corners of her room to await the magical moment. Of a sudden, it came.

Moving rapidly to the stool, Emily said, "Okay! Here it comes!"

And she reached her two arms, encircled with a graceful network of veins, down to receive the tiny girl, delicate as a rosebud, as she slipped from her mother's body. The room resounded with her wails and the candlelight flickered and danced as if in the wake of her emergent spirit.

An evening later, Jean called me to come help her with a first-time Amish family in the south.

Though I didn't know it then, by the time I moved away in 2014, I'd serve Grace and Owen Ray Coblentz through all their pregnancies, all their losses, all their close calls, and most of their births. Over the years, this woman and her husband would become treasured friends who stood beside me through my own string of losses and life changes.

But on the night of Grace's first birth, I'd only seen her once and she didn't seem too impressed with me. I went on to further tarnish her opinion of me by getting lost on my attempt to reach her home.

Jean called around eleven o'clock, asking if I'd please come. I said I would, scribbled my directions, and started out. The family lived in the heart of St. Joseph County, but I, missing a key turn, wound up in Three Rivers. It was a pretty foggy night and I like to think that's what happened with the turn, but I don't know. My skill at getting to new places was in its infancy then.

I arrived at a quarter after one, relieved to find I hadn't missed the birth, though Jean's arched eyebrows revealed her thoughts about my misadventure and I'm certain Grace would have preferred to already have "had it passed," as the Amish say. Sadly for her, the baby remained within another three and a half hours.

There really isn't a whole lot to do while waiting for babies to come. We arrive, we sneak in and get vitals and assess the progress of labor, we discretely set up the supplies and our gear, we go to a distant corner with a flashlight and do all we can with the paperwork, then we settle in and wait. Birth at home isn't like birth in the hospital, and it isn't even recognizable when compared to Hollywood's version of the event.

While diverse in detail, the families who choose to have their babies in the privacy of their homes are alike in the way they experience their births. Birth in the home is usually a quiet, intimate affair. The lights are kept low, voices are hushed, footfalls are on tip-toe.

We midwives spend most of our time preparing the bodies, minds, and spirits of families for birthing before the event and, therefore, at the event itself find we're minimally required. We're ready and willing to help, but mostly we monitor, set up, wait, then support. We support the process that's occurring. We don't oversee labors, we don't deliver babies, we don't manage third stages, we don't take charge of newborns.

We watch, we wait, we support, we serve—but we only support and serve to the degree our support and service is needed or desired. So, with our ears ever attuned to sounds issuing from the next room, slipping in from time to time to auscultate a heartbeat or measure a blood pressure or to whisper a suggestion, we do a lot of reading, knitting, writing, and napping. I've been known to grade papers and balance checkbooks at births, too.

At any rate, I finally arrived at the Coblentz home where I settled into the wait with Jean. About an hour later, Grace began pushing, and a little more than two hours after that, her brand-new daughter filled the house with her lifesong.

Grace didn't tear and didn't bleed, the baby nursed like a champ, and I was home and in bed by morning. We were amused to learn later that Grace told Owen Ray at some point during her labor she didn't think we were especially helpful and they certainly were "never having them again!" Owen Ray told us. To this day, Grace refuses to validate the story, but, remembering the birth pretty well myself, I believe it.

Then, two of our best friends birthed their first baby.

Allow me to say, it's impossible to describe what it means to be asked to attend the births of family and friends, the births of

those who mean the whole world to me. I can never really believe
I've actually been asked, not for all the years passing thereafter.
I can't believe I'm that trusted, can't wrap my head around the
fact I've been invited to take part in such a special event. The gift
of that trust and experience infuses my life with an incomparable
energy and engraves the names and faces of those priceless people onto my heart. They become a part of me.

And this family was just so incredibly special to us already.
The father, Nate, had been in our youth group. He was, in fact,
the young man Brent prayed over all those years back before our
first adventure.

Through the early years of our association, the relationship
was a bit one-sided. We invested a lot of time and resources into
him—not always pleasant times—and we went a fair piece without seeing much in the way of returns. But the years steadily
shifted things until not only did we see a ripening of our invest-
ments, we were rewarded with a deeply faithful friend.

Nate married Natalie upon their graduation from Youth
With A Mission's School of Evangelism, and he brought her
home to Michigan. Natalie burrowed immediately into my heart
with her effervescent spirit and when, some months after their
wedding, she called to say she was expecting and wanted to birth
at home with Jean and me, I was beside myself with joy.

We went to them late one night, three days before Thanksgiving and, through the early morning hours of the season's first
snowfall, I had the privilege of helping that boy-turned-man
receive his daughter from the secret places of his beautiful soul
mate.

I attended two more births for the family through the course
of years—the last of which would be Hannah's first time attending a birth as my helper.

We had three pregnant moms in Kalamazoo at the time and each week, the kids and I would make the rounds of them together. It was an especially snowy season and, for all that snow and our many misadventures in it, the three appointments would often take us eight hours or more to complete.

One of the Kalamazoo ladies was a friend of mine, Helen, due mid-December. On Helen's visit two weeks before her due date I felt her belly and found the baby was breech. When I told her so, she said, "Oh, no. No. Nope, Kim, it isn't breech."

I asked if I could do a vaginal exam to double check. She said sure, and I was positive I could feel not only a little bottom, but a little foot, too. "No," my friend said. "It's head down."

I didn't know what to say. I didn't know what to do. I called Jean on the way home and she said there wasn't anything to do if Helen insisted the baby was head down. Jean told me just to go the next week, see how things felt, and see what Helen said then.

That next Wednesday I made the eight-hour tour of Kalamazoo again and I decided I was more sure than ever Helen was carrying a breech baby. The visit went exactly like the previous visit, only this time I felt what I thought were *two* tiny feet in her pelvis. "Kim, no," Helen said. "The baby isn't breech!"

I asked if she'd be willing to get an ultrasound to see for sure, but she said an emphatic no to that, too. I left and called Jean again and she said the same thing as before.

The next morning Helen called me in a panic. "Kim! I think I'm starting labor! I'm starting labor and I know the baby's breech! I'm gonna call our family doctor!"

I suggested we call our back-up doctor, but she wanted to talk to the man she knew. A half hour later she called again to say her family doctor wanted to get her in for a cesarean. We called our back-up.

Our back-up said he would meet Helen at the hospital and see if he could do an external version for her. Helen and her husband went straight in, but the nurses in labor and delivery told her they didn't have a bed available. Helen told the nurses she was in labor, but they shook their heads and sent her away. She went to a relative's home nearby to wait for a bed. The doctor said he'd do what he could to get a spot for her, but, until he did or until her labor really kicked in, all she could do was wait.

When Helen called to update me and tell me how frightened she was, I did my best to calm her down and to think practically. I told her a breech labor is often mild for a long time, then can get serious quickly. I told her when a breech labor strengthens and the cervix begins to open, the baby's body will often slide into the vagina before the cervix is fully open, making a woman feel like she has to push before it's safe to push.

"Just lie down while you wait for a bed to open for you," I said to her, "and if something changes—if the labor gets strong and you feel like pushing—don't. Don't push. Go straight to the hospital, and *do not push* until the doctor tells you it's okay."

So, she laid herself down in her sister's home and relaxed the best she could until her waters broke and a tremendous urge to push swept over her. Her husband rushed her to the hospital and she told me later she chanted all the way, "Don't push! Don't push! Kim said don't push!"

By the time they reached the hospital, Helen was eight centimeters dilated and had a little leg dangling from her vagina. Soon after that, the doctor noticed a tiny knee presenting.

Back at home, I was in agony! Helen's mom and dad, also dear friends, were keeping me abreast of the situation and I was desperate to go be with her, but Jean told me not to go until Helen specifically asked for me.

Brent, watching me struggle, finally said, "Kim, just go! She *already* asked you to be her midwife! What more do you need?"

I sprinted out the door.

The drive to the hospital lasted an eternity and when I finally burst into her room, the baby had just come. The child's wails filled my ears and Helen's cries joined them as she reached her hand toward me. "Kim! Kim! Where were you? I needed you!"

We really were all so happy. The baby—a footling-kneeling breech, as it turned out, an incredibly rare combination—birthed with ease some thirty minutes after Helen arrived at the hospital.

Before I left, I heard the charge nurse say to the midwife who worked with our doctor, "Well, that never should've happened. Should've been a section."

The midwife answered that she thought a birth as smooth as Helen's was always better than surgery.

I agreed, feeling grateful for the safe and natural birth of the baby. Though some midwives and a few doctors are willing to help families birth breech babies, most only are if a number of favorability factors are met. Those factors are determined by the number of babies the mom's already had, her weeks gestation, and the estimated size of the baby—but the most important determinant is the sort of breech the baby is. The most favorable breech for an uncomplicated vaginal birth is a frank breech, where the baby's bottom clearly presents and the baby's feet are up next to its head. A complete breech, where the baby's bottom presents, but where its legs are folded and crossed next to its bottom, isn't so favorable. To have a baby present with even one foot or one knee foremost is even less favorable.

My friend wrote me the nicest letter after her daughter was born.

Dear Kim, thank you doesn't even begin to tell you how grateful we are for everything you've done. Had you not been there the day our baby was born, I probably would have had a c-section. But God knew <u>all</u> of this and He gave you the knowledge to know what to say at just the right time. I'm just very thankful to have had you for advice and support through my pregnancy. You may not have physically been there when our baby was born, but you were in my heart and mind, and for that I'm <u>very</u> grateful.

Chapter

THIRTY

HER LETTER WAS A SALVE TO MY SOUL DURING A difficult spell when, at every turn, I appeared inadequate.

The year drew to a close. I wrote in my journal on New Year's Eve, "When people birth their babies, you see utter reality. A birthing woman never pretends. You can't live in birthing moment intensity every day, but I've gotten a taste for the melding of spirits that happens at a birthing when people come to the end of themselves. They're in such a vulnerable place. They need to be able to trust you; to entrust themselves to you. It's sobering. It's a privilege. It's an honor to be so trusted and called upon to help. Birthing is one of the most intense things a person will ever experience. Its heights and depths are extreme, often with only the barest of differences separating the two. It's empowering and humiliating, impossible and exhilarating, all at the same time, with no room for fantasies or charades or ideals."

I realized that's true of learning and practicing midwifery, too.

"I'm really beginning to appreciate the challenging array of facets this call on my life presents—it keeps my perspective broad and balanced, keeps me stable and flexible, keeps me humbly aware of my limitations. I understand the more responsibility I hold, the more important it is I keep a close eye on my ambitions and motivations."

Rounding the corner into 2001 found Brent and me taking a serious second look at the possibility of going to Youth With A Mission. Again, we compiled and evaluated the upsides and downsides to going, considering and reconsidering the ostensible deal breakers. Many nights in bed, holding hands in the dark, we talked until well past prudent hours, drawing from the depths of our hearts our secret hopes and nascent dreams and smoldering passions.

Where I was inclined by nature to plunge head-first into a pretty good idea, Brent had a maddening bent toward waiting for inward resonance—that unseen yet sturdy assurance he was hearing from God. I say maddening, but I admired that quality in him. He was every bit as adventurous as I, but his adventurous side was tempered with an eerily accurate sixth sense and almost obstinate patience that enabled him to watch and wait and trust his guts through every measure of clamor and pressure, well beyond all comfort.

Together we committed to further examination, further talk, further prayer.

The immediate next bend in our road—another point to be considered in light of our desire to spend a year as missionaries—was the fact I continued to have difficulty breathing and continued to need regular medical attention. This, despite my spiritual beliefs, revealed one by one the subtle ways I misunderstood God and His heart for me. As these misunderstandings surfaced, they were resolved, but it was a process requiring the catalyst of specific events, plus an insulated space of time to be accomplished.

At the dilatation in the fall, Dr. Iannettoni said he felt the next step would be to attempt a reconstruction of my trachea. We left with him expecting me to call and get the thing scheduled. I said I would, but I didn't want or intend to do it. As grateful as I was to have been properly diagnosed and treated, it went against the grain of both my temperament and ideology to submit even to the serial dilatations. To agree to reconstructive surgery seemed a whole other thing altogether. According to my understanding of God and His Word, I shouldn't need any of it. At times, a disquieting series of thoughts rippled through the back of my mind.

"I stand in this place and I think. I think, 'If You are willing—' I think, 'If You were willing—' I think, 'If You had been willing—'"

I decided afresh to believe God accomplished my healing two thousand years before like it says He did in the Bible and, anytime I noticed I was struggling to breathe, I used the struggle to remind me of that and to say, "Thanks, God, for healing me."

After all, Jesus said to ask, to believe, to receive. If I ask and, after asking, truly believe I've received what I've asked for, even if I don't see what I've asked for quite yet, the appropriate response would be to say thank you, rather than to keep on asking and asking.

Part of reaffirming my beliefs seemed simply to eschew making an appointment for the reconstruction. I felt to make that appointment would be both a declaration of unbelief as well as an ultimatum. I wanted to trust what God promised would appear in its own time. I told Brent I'd go get the thing done if God came down from Heaven and said, "Hey, Kim? Yeah, I fixed

258 A Midwife in Amish Country

it so healing is for everybody, but I actually want *you* to get surgery instead."

Brent hardly knew how to respond and, like many others, really couldn't understand my insistence on a seemingly remote and ambiguous divine intervention at the rejection of readily available and competent medical help. But I can be tough to argue with sometimes. We didn't come to an agreement, but he didn't insist I call, so I just didn't, and I ejected the topic of reconstruction from my mind.

Early one Saturday morning in January, a term client in Lansing called to say she started labor the evening before, then, realizing her baby was out of position, stopped it with a glass of wine.

We ran up there to examine her and, sure enough, the child had shifted itself transverse—head right, bottom left—exactly crosswise to her body. We called our trusty back-up doctor and he said he could see her Sunday morning for an external version.

Sunday morning, we met our client, Lucinda, and her husband Will, in Kalamazoo for her version. The doctor got the baby head down again and we skedaddled to our respective homes to prepare for the birth as Lucinda could now quit her efforts to forestall labor.

Cramps and contractions flirted with Lucinda through the morning and afternoon before settling into a nice rhythm. She and Will had us out and driving to them beneath a spectacle of bright stars by ten. The couple had two children about the ages of my own, nine and seven, and they lived in a teensy house between Lansing and DeWitt with a narrow, winding walk coated in a layer of ice. A cheerful friend was present, the children were bright-eyed with anticipation, Will was attentive, Lucinda was laboring beautifully, and the atmosphere was cozy and quietly festive as we made assessments and set up our gear and supplies.

THIRTY-ONE

SUNDAY PASSED INTO MONDAY, 12:30 CAME AND went, 1:00 and 1:15 slipped by, and then at 1:30, both children yawned, stretched, announced they were sleepy, and conked out together on the sofa.

At 1:45 a.m., the woman's water sack ruptured. Jean crouched on the floor to listen to the baby's heartbeat and it was then we discovered the baby's umbilical cord had prolapsed.

A prolapsed cord is a true emergency. When a cord comes through a cervix ahead of the baby, the contracting uterus pinches it between the baby's hard head and its mother's hard pelvis, cutting off the baby's supply of oxygen. Jean immediately got the mom moving forward, onto the floor and into a knee-chest position while instructing the father to call 911. Jean reached inside the mother and pressed the baby's head up and away from the unyielding bones while I snatched up the Doppler and listened to the baby's heart. Thankfully, it recovered a steady rhythm.

I listened to the baby's heart after every contraction, even as I scurried about in preparation for a trip to the hospital by ambulance. First to arrive in response to our call for help was a stocky guy with a shock of white hair crackling in every direction out from under a baseball cap. He plowed his way into the bedroom with a wooden box labeled "birth kit" in one of his meaty hands and announced he'd come to deliver the baby.

I swung him aft and herded him back into the living room, explaining as we went.

"This baby can't come vaginally," I said. "It has a prolapsed cord and will need to come by c-section in the hospital. We intend to get there by ambulance. Can you go outside and flag down the ambulance for us when it gets here?"

Out the door he went and I zipped back into the bedroom to check heart tones again. The little house began to get crowded as fire fighters, police officers, and other first responders arrived. It was standing room only by the time the EMTs made it, stamping the snow from their boots as they entered. Amazingly, the two children on the sofa snoozed on.

Between heart tone checks, I ushered the EMTs into the bedroom saying, "This baby can't come vaginally. It has a prolapsed cord and will have to come by c-section. We need to get this woman to the hospital immediately and in this exact position, with this midwife doing exactly what she's doing."

They said they didn't know if they'd be able to do that.

I said, "Of course you can."

So, they did.

As we headed toward the door, the EMTs said they didn't know if they'd be able to get the stretcher outside and down the slick path.

I said, "Of course you can."

So, they did.

When we reached the ambulance, Jean whispered to me she didn't think they'd let us get in with Lucinda.

I said, "Of course they will, just climb inside."

So, we climbed inside.

Once we were rolling, I advised the EMT riding in the back with us to call ahead to the hospital and let them know we were coming. She picked up the telephone and said she was on her way with a laboring woman, and the baby was crowning.

I told her, "Tell them we have a prolapsed cord. Tell them to set up for a c-section and meet us at the door with a gurney."

I was still listening to heart tones after every contraction and they were still strong and solid. Lucinda was amazing, kneeling there on that bouncing bed, her backside waving about in the air, breathing through her contractions and a steadily increasing urge to push. The EMT held the woman's hand and we worked together to soothe and encourage her until we reached the hospital. As we pulled toward the entrance, the EMT said she didn't think anybody would be there to meet us.

I said, "Of course they will."

And they were.

I told the man who met us, "This woman needs to get on that gurney in this exact position, with this midwife doing exactly what she's doing."

He said he didn't know if he could do that.

I said, "Of course you can."

So, he did.

When we reached the elevator, Jean whispered she didn't think they'd let us go up, too.

I said, "Of course they will, just go on in there."

So, in we went.

As we approached the operating room, a nurse flew out, switched spots with Jean, and Lucinda was whisked through the doors. Within ten or twelve minutes her child was out and screaming.

The doctor exited the room a while later, found Jean, shook her hand and, turning to disappear down the hall, said, "Great teamwork."

I took a taxi back to the house to fetch our things and the car, reflecting as I went. What a wild night! It seemed as though I sprouted a pair of big, black, feathery wings when that fella with the birth kit box burst into the family's bedroom, and I unfurled those wings and spread them over Jean and Lucinda and Lucinda's unborn baby until the nurse took Jean's place at the OR door. Big, black, feathery wings, smeared with blobs of blue Doppler gel.

We made it back to our homes Monday morning around six or seven o'clock and I crashed. Tuesday morning dawned threatening snow and saw us running out the door for a birth in Tekonsha.

We arrived to find Jammi and Ben Pace—clients at the time, who would later become dear friends (and for a season, Jammi would apprentice with me)—in an active but leisurely first stage of labor. Joshua, their second child, didn't arrive until suppertime that evening. It's interesting to note that each of Jammi's future babies came fast—so fast, we had to rush to make it—but this time, we had a short cord wrapped tightly around the baby's neck.

It isn't unusual at all to have a cord wrapped once or twice around a baby's neck (one in three babies generally do), but something many midwives have noticed is, when you have an unexpectedly, uncharacteristically lengthy labor, a short or tightly wrapped cord will often eventually show itself. Even midwives are subject to either the urge or the pressure or both to get labors going and over with quicker. But I've learned, unless some sort of identifiable challenge is holding things up, it's better, as long as mom and baby are doing well, to take a step back and trust even those surprisingly longer births. It's like the slower, gentler labors give the cord a chance to stretch a bit without causing problems for the baby.

This isn't always the case, though, as the birth that followed demonstrated.

The next evening, we were called out again and drove to Kalamazoo through a blur of snow, arriving at an unusual, octagon-shaped house nestled a ways back in the woods at a quarter till seven.

We were startled to find the first-time mom already pushing. I began to set up while Jean listened to the baby. We were further startled and concerned, too, when Jean clocked the baby's heart rate at 80–90 beats per minute (120–160 is the normal range for an unborn baby).

Jean checked her. She was complete and making good progress, so we put her on the birth stool, hooked her up to the oxygen, and got her pushing with all her might.

A tiny, five-pound, nine-ounce dew drop was born at four minutes past seven with her umbilical cord wound snug around her neck two times. Regardless, she was in great condition and proved a most uncommon child.

She nursed right away and for a nice, long time while we tidied up and knocked out the paperwork. When it was time to examine the baby some hours later, we were enchanted to find her just as intent on examining each one of us. Every person in the room was subject to a serious, thoughtful gaze, and when we finished looking her over and returned her to her mother's arms, the wee thing rewarded us with a broad smile. We were wonder-struck and, tired though we were after the turbulent week, the time we spent there with that timeless soul refreshed our spirits.

I think about that baby girl from time to time. I guess she'd be in her teens by now. Is she still as curious and musing now as she was then? Just as mysterious and magical? I wonder.

We headed home toward midnight and Jean got stuck in the driveway when she backed up into a heap of snow. I hopped out to push and set us laughing until our sides cramped when I went down and nearly disappeared beneath the car.

Chapter

THIRTY-TWO

A WEEK LATER, I RECEIVED A LETTER IN THE MAIL from Ann Arbor informing me my tracheal resection was scheduled for Valentine's Day.

I couldn't believe it. I felt violated and planned to call and cancel the next Monday. I went to church in an ugly mood and listened to the message, ironically one about supernatural healing, with soured attention. At the close of the message the pastor invited anyone hoping for a supernatural healing to come forward for prayer. I didn't want to go up, but felt compelled to.

It was a small church at the time, and everybody knew us and was aware I was dealing with a breathing issue, so, as I went up, I found I was followed and surrounded by a group of friends desiring to pray with me. A forest of loving hands rested on my head and shoulders and back as the pastor prayed. When he said amen and we moved to return to our seats, one of those friends said, "Kim, I feel like Jesus is wanting to know, can you just trust Him?"

When she said that, an image flashed through my mind of Jesus taking me by the hand and leading me away to the hospital, and I knew in an instant that's what He wanted to do. It was as if, as I'd told Brent would have to happen, God had indeed come down from Heaven and told me in person He wanted me to go for surgery.

The emotions rushed in like a flood. I was surprised; I was hurt; I was offended; I couldn't understand. I was furious.

Uncharacteristically, especially since I was in public, I began to cry. I cried and cried and cried as a train of thoughts looped so continuously through my head I thought I'd go crazy. *If You loved me, if You valued me, if Your Word were True, You wouldn't make me go this way!*

My friends, one by one, unsure why I was crying and too polite to ask, hugged me as we gathered ourselves to leave. I was quieter by the time we reached the car. After some minutes driving toward home, Brent asked what was going on. I told him as the tears began to flow afresh.

He absorbed what I told him, then said, "Honey, I don't think you understand about the Love of God—"

His statement reignited my anger and I cut him off, right in front of the wide-eyed and wide-eared children in the back seat. "Well, if I didn't understand about the Love of God, I guess I wouldn't be a Christian, now would I?"

We finished the drive in strained silence, and I spent the rest of the day wrestling with those simple words. The truth of them worked their way into my burning heart and I realized no, maybe I didn't understand His Love like I thought I did. I absolutely could not understand His decision, not one single tiniest bit, that was for sure. I seethed with anger, but by bedtime came to terms with the events of the day and when Monday dawned, I didn't call to cancel my appointment.

With an odd, peaceful regret and one client still pregnant, Brent and I hit the road for the hospital in the early hours of Valentine's Day and by one o'clock in the afternoon I had a shorter trachea and a wickedly grinning gash of dried blood and superglue on my neck.

During the surgery, Dr. Iannettoni discovered, instead of a single narrowed ring of tracheal cartilage hidden beneath the surface of my throat, I had four narrowed rings, with the foremost of those rings being the cricoid cartilage of the larynx or, in other words, my voice box.

Naturally, he was hesitant to touch that. He performed a dilatation, then removed rings two, three, and four. I recovered quickly and was on my way home in only two days, but the prognosis for my future was I'd need one or two dilatations of that top ring every year for the rest of my life.

Though I'd have to submit to eight additional dilatations over the next three years, I eventually would heal past requiring further medical treatment for my throat. But I couldn't know that then, and in the moment, I was deeply disappointed by those words.

Through the following weeks, I had a lot of time to think about all that had gone on in my body, as well as about everything going on in my head and in my heart. I thought about all the surgeries. I thought about my faith and my beliefs. I thought about all my thoughts in spite of my faith and beliefs and in spite of all those surgeries. I was frustrated and angry and increasingly bitter.

I talked about it all with God, even though I was hurt and mad as blazes at Him. I went through those weeks as though I were suspended, on hold, like the pause button on the music of my life was pressed.

One evening while I was recovering, Brent brought a movie home for the kids to watch. It was an animated version of the

Easter story, a story I'd been exposed to in numberless ways and numberless times over the years of my life. We settled in to watch it together, though I was anything but interested.

And then, as we watched the story unfold, I saw it as though it were my first time.

I watched as the most perfect Person lived a most perfect life filled with compassion and love for regular folk. I watched as that most perfect Person wrestled with fear and with a powerful aversion to pain and suffering and death when He realized those regular folk intended to brutalize and destroy Him despite the love He'd shown them. I watched as that most perfectly lovely Person surrendered, even embraced His fear and aversion and allowed those regular folk to brutalize and destroy Him—for the sake of those regular folk.

Somehow, I saw it with fresh eyes, and the understanding began to spread over me, though I would never fully understand all the events of this life, I could forever and always trust the love and good will of that most perfectly lovely Person—that most perfectly lovely God of mine.

It wasn't a new thought, but, for the first time, that thought slipped past my mind, slipped past my soul, and slipped into my heart where it began to germinate. I can honestly say I've never doubted His love or good will toward me since, though I've gone on to face far greater trials than a narrow airway and surgical procedures.

The words of R. C. Sproul sum it up best. "Why do bad things happen to good people? That only happened once, and He volunteered."

Thirty-Three

MARCH TRUNDLED IN AND WE MADE THE DECISION
to sell the house and go to YWAM. Brent turned the youth group
over to Todd Bradfield, a man who began serving with us
through the winter. We decided to take the teens on a final trip
to Mexico mid-summer, then make the leadership transition
before the new school year began.

We also decided it was time for me to make the push toward
certification. I ordered the necessary materials from NARM, and
we began preparing the house for sale.

There was much to do. We'd kept the house sound and functional, but, because we decided when we purchased it to forgo
cosmetic improvements until we cleared away our debts, the darn
thing was still just really ugly. We squeezed opportunities to
scrape and scrub and paint and replace into every available crev-
ice of time—days, nights, and weekends. An entry from my
journal during that season reads, "we're working like farm animals around here." And we were.

The certification packet from NARM arrived mid-March. My heart gave a lurch when I saw it in the mailbox. I took it straight to the office and tore it open, but my nervous excitement dissipated as I began to scan the contents.

I ordered the materials feeling fairly certain I was close to meeting the requirements only to discover, because most of the hands-on work I did after passing from the assistant or "active participant" stage of my apprenticeship was done on my own rather than under Jean's direct supervision, it was inadmissible. Then I leafed through the forty-five pages of "Comprehensive Skills, Knowledge, and Abilities Essential for Competent Midwifery Practice" and, seriously underestimating my personal collection of skills, knowledge, and abilities, true discouragement set in.

At that time, an applicant needed to attend twenty births as an active participant, then, as a primary midwife under supervision, attend twenty additional births, twenty initial prenatal exams, fifty-five regular prenatal exams, and forty postpartum visits. Up to that point, I'd attended seventy births as an active participant and eleven births as primary under supervision—not too bad—but ninety-three prenatal visits and fifty-four postpartum visits were conducted entirely by myself and I had scarcely attended any visits with Jean in any role besides assistant.

After I finished making the painstaking account of my seven and three-quarter years' worth of work, I took a yellow highlighter to the forty-five pages of essential skills, knowledge, and abilities. I left white the items I felt I'd mastered up to that point, then colored every item—there were anywhere from ten to twenty items per page, maybe even more—in which I felt I lacked adequacy.

I'd venture to say eighty percent of the items glowed an accusatory yellow by the time I was through. It appeared as if I knew nothing and nothing I did counted for anything. Disheartened, demoralized, and dismayed, I put that blasted packet on the rearest rear shelf of my closet, and that's where it stayed until the next year.

When I told Jean I didn't think I'd be able to fulfill the requirements, describing the impermissible nature of my hands-on experience, and explaining the remedy required was that she spend the entire next year watching me work, Jean agreed I'd not be getting certified anytime soon.

A few weeks later, however, she asked to look over the requirements versus my experience and, doing so, said she was willing to spend the next year allowing me to serve as primary midwife at the births we attended and would attend prenatals and postpartums with me functioning in the primary role after all. Those forty-five pages of "Comprehensive Skills, Knowledge, and Abilities Essential for Competent Midwifery Practice" stayed on the shelf, but I returned to work filled with gratitude and a cautious measure of renewed hope.

In April, we attended a first-time Amish family in Vermontville as they welcomed a seven-pound son into their family. It took a while for the placenta to come and when it finally did come, mama started up with a brisk bleed. But we got it stopped so quickly it was almost as though it hadn't happened.

Six days later we attended another first-time family, this time up in Lansing, right on my Grandpa Banfield's last birthday. This baby was also a boy, though much bigger at eight-and-a-half pounds, and after a much longer labor.

On Father's Day, we helped a young Amish family welcome their ten-pound son to life, even as they said good-bye to the baby's great-grandfather. Then, on my thirty-first birthday, we attended another first-time family. A nineteen-year-old woman brought her baby boy into the light five short days after her father passed from it, drawn away from her by cancer.

Oh, poignant life!

Two days later, we took off for a fourth trip to Mexico. We spent the night before our departure tearing the carpeting off the floors, then we packed the group into I can't remember what and left.

I was exhausted. I'm sure Brent was, too. I don't know what he did, but I fell asleep every time I sat down through the first four days we were away from home. I wrote in my journal, "Boarded the buses at a quarter till five in the morning. Slept till eight o'clock on a three-person seat with Paul, a cooler, and two cardboard boxes. Now I'm sitting with Hannah and three coolers on the same three-seater. Gonna fall asleep again."

Hannah and Paul, at nine-and-a-half and nearly seven, were excited and very much a part of things on this trip, which made it fresh and fun. They dressed up as clowns, complete with face paint and boisterous hair, made balloon animals, took part in the skits, passed out a little stack of books they'd spent the winter making about Jesus welcoming the children, and talked to everybody who breathed.

"Hannah had a balloon pop in her hands today," an entry in my journal says. "I hate popping balloons! I asked if it scared her. She said, 'No, it's a surprise—a sudden sorrow—a sorrowful surprise—but it isn't scary.'"

On this trip, Hannah and Paul drank the one and only Coca Cola of their littlehood when one of the families we visited offered to share. I was torn over that, but recognized how rude it would be to refuse. I admit it was Brent's elbow in my ribs that did the most to help me recognize that. The kids were in bliss.

We stayed at a school nestled in a groove of the mountains on the outskirts of Monterrey. It was peaceful and pretty in there, but overrun with cockroaches. And they were huge critters, too—three, four, five inches long. One ran right across my face while I was in bed and I killed another that was perched on our bedroom wall with my shoe in the dark on the way to the bathroom. I went and found it later to make sure I hadn't imagined the incident.

In one single evening, we wound up with five people either ill or wounded in our room, and one of them moved in to stay until the end of the trip.

We went immediately back to work upon our return home. We attended our final youth group on August fifteenth, both a sad and happy evening. For eight years, we'd served a jaded and suspicious demographic according to the idea that while it's important to share the truth of the Bible, our primary job, rather than preaching a lot about dos and don'ts, was to create a space conducive to encounters with the Living God. We held that people couldn't be browbeaten or manipulated or coerced into faith in God, that faith in God is the response of hearts and minds seeing Him for Who and all He is.

For all the work and heartbreaks and mishaps of those years, we made a difference and we really loved the kids we worked with and the people who helped us; most of our helpers were kids who grew up within the group, or parents of those kids. We treasured the time we spent with them and we knew we'd miss it. I still do treasure those times. They made a difference in us, too.

The house was listed according to plan at the end of August and, though we were still scrambling with a few loose ends, it showed immediately and was sold nine days later.

We'd been so busy getting it ready we nearly forgot we'd need to move when it sold. We hadn't even called our folks to tell them it was on the market yet. We went to bed the night we accepted the buyer's offer, realizing we had to get busy looking for a rental, but first thing the next day, my Aunt Kathy happened to call. She asked what was going on with us and I told her we'd just sold our home.

She didn't miss a beat. She said she and T. R. wanted to sell T. R.'s old house, but wanted to improve it before putting it on the market. She suggested we rent it from them and help them get it spruced up a bit while we were there. We said we'd love to and began to pack.

I ran off to Ann Arbor for a tracheal dilatation, spent the day after that digging holes all over our back yard so the septic tank could be inspected, and then went to help welcome another baby into another Amish family. The child was his mama's second son. He came easily, but his entrance was marked with tears. The woman was losing her father to an illness that spanned the length of her pregnancy, and her hope was her dad would have the chance to hold her newest child before he died. The little guy arrived just in time to meet his grandpa and to soothe his mother's aching heart.

And then came September 11, 2001.

I'll never forget halting my work to answer Brent's phone call that morning. He told me to go switch on the television. The first airplane hit the first tower and, as we were talking about how in the world a thing like that could have happened, the second airplane roared into the second tower before my eyes. I watched the horrifying footage of people leaping from the inferno, then was dumbstruck to witness those buildings collapse into clouds of dust. News of further atrocities rolled in hour by hour and, by the end of the day, we learned more than three thousand souls were lost.

Birth, death, calamity—I've always been amazed at the way life insists on moving forward regardless of these occurrences. I remember feeling amazed to discover regular life hadn't halted in awe after I attended my first birth eight years before the events of that autumn. A mere six years after them, I was shocked to find it had the gall to carry on when we laid Brent to rest in a frozen field one brutally cold morning in January. Just like the baby who crossed paths with his great-grandpa on Father's Day morning, and the baby in July who just missed meeting his granddad, and the newest babe reclining in the arms of a grand-father who would soon pass from life.

The second to third week in October was filled with our closing, the completion of our move, a surprise thank you party from the youth group, a quick trip to Lake Michigan to celebrate our anniversary that we basically slept through, and a mad dash for the birth of a nine-plus-pound baby in Lansing.

I topped the month off by hitting a deer with my Voyager, the second car-deer incident out of what would eventually be six.

And then we crossed into November.

Chapter

THIRTY-FOUR

TWO WEEKS WERE PASSED ON THE QUIET SIDE AND then off I went for another dilatation of my airway.

The morning after, Jean rustled me out around five for a first-time mom having a swift labor in Olivet. She went straight over and barely made it. My throat felt like it was on fire and I could hardly haul myself from my bed. The woman had a handsome little man-child in three-and-a-half hours with scarcely a tear. I dragged myself back home, crawled back into bed, slept the day away, then was out the door again at nine that night to aid a family birthing their seventh child in Nashville. We arrived toward ten and the ten-pound, one-ounce boy was born a couple hours later. It took a bit of doing to dislodge his broad shoulders, but his mom and Jean managed it.

Some months after he was born, his mother, noting a change in his personality, took him to the doctor. The doctor did a head-to-toe examination of him and proclaimed him a healthy specimen. His mom begged to differ. The doctor tried to reassure her, but she'd have none of it. "Something's wrong with my baby," she told him, "and I need you to find out what it is."

A battery of tests was ordered and a tumor growing at the base of his spine called a sacrococcygeal teratoma was discovered. It was surgically removed soon after, and the baby's personality returned to normal. That story provided another profound lesson in the necessity of listening to and trusting parents.

We celebrated Thanksgiving and Hannah's birthday, and then learned the YWAM base we planned to move to closed its doors almost the minute we sold our house. We were certainly surprised at the news and it ushered us into a very quiet, very thoughtful season that would carry us well into the New Year.

Then Renee and Alan, a family from a couple winters before—the family with the birthday cake and pizza, whose birth my whole family attended—gave birth to a great big boy a few days before Christmas. That time around Renee's pregnancy and birth plans included a whole heap of variables. Renee was due the week before Jean was scheduled to leave the state for Christmas. Jean's trip was planned before the couple came to care and, though Renee usually birthed her babies a couple weeks past due, they still wanted to try for a homebirth with us. Our trusty back-up doctor and midwife team in Kalamazoo agreed to pitch-hit should the need arise, and we all four were satisfied enough to move forward with care.

Around the baby's due date, Renee went for a prenatal visit with Jean and presented with a borderline high blood pressure. Jean also gave her cervix a nice stretching, as we all hoped she'd give birth before Jean was slated to leave town.

Jean sent Renee home with instructions to come by my place the next day for a blood pressure check and repeat stretch, so she and Alan appeared on my doorstep around three in the afternoon.

I took her blood pressure first. It was good and we exhaled a collective, relieved sigh. "I guess I just really do need my protein. I'll be sure to get it in better till I have the baby," Renee said, climbing on my bed and arranging herself on the pillows. "Oooh! Comfy!" She smiled at Alan. "Just leave me here. I could take a nap!"

We laughed as she pulled up her shirt.

I planned to give her cervix that stretch, but wanted to feel how the baby was positioned first. I placed my hands on the great orb of her belly and they were so small in comparison, they looked like they belonged to a child.

Good night! How big is this child?

Renee's first baby was born by cesarean section, and the doctor who performed the surgery warned her she'd never be able to birth a baby bigger than seven pounds naturally. Renee, however, wasn't the sort to accept a judgment without evaluating it, and she went on to give birth to three children vaginally. Each of them weighed in at well over eight pounds. The third weighed more than nine.

This one's gotta be pushing ten.

With my right hand pressed lightly into the flesh above Renee's navel and my left hand spread over the space just above her pubic bone, I began the gentle rolling, rocking movement midwives use to gain access to the depths of bellies filled with babies.

I asked Renee's body with my rolling, rocking hands, for permission to press further, further, further, until the outline of a form was revealed beneath my fingertips.

The baby stretched beneath the pressure, and rewarded me with a thump.

"Hello, Sweetie."

I was thumped again, and then again as I began to search for signs of a head above the brim of Renee's pelvis.

Thump. Thump.

I shifted a bit in order to examine the area with both hands.

Thump. Flutter-flutter-thump!

I did my best to keep my face expressionless, but those thumps were pretty low for a head-down baby. I returned my right hand to the space beneath Renee's ribs and began to rock and roll, rock and roll in exploration, until my palm filled with the smooth, firm edges I'd been looking for.

I wiggled it gently and it bobbled like a ball on a string—or, rather, like a head on a neck.

I took a breath. "Um, guys, I think I'm feeling a head up here."

Renee and Alan, who'd been chatting to me about this and that while I felt around, instantly stopped talking and craned their necks to look at my hands.

"It can't be," Alan said.

"No," Renee agreed, "it can't be. The head wasn't up there when Jean checked yesterday."

I looked at Renee and, taking her hands in mine, pressed them over the spot. "Feel this, Renee. Can you feel that hardness? Can you feel the way it bobs back and forth?"

Renee's eyes filled with tears. "Oh, no. Oh, my goodness. But are you sure?"

"Yes, are you sure, Kim?" Alan asked.

"Feel it for yourself, Alan. It'll be easier for you to feel than it is for Renee. It's hard to feel your own belly. It's pretty awkward."

I laid his hands on Renee's ovoid middle. "Press from side to side. Press one side at a time. See how that makes the shape of the baby appear?"

"Oh!"

"Now, see? See how it moves down here?" I moved his hands to Renee's lower abdomen. "See how, when you move it—when you rock it a little—the whole form shifts back and forth?"

Alan nodded, while a tear escaped Renee's lashes and splashed onto her cheek.

"It moves like that because of the way the baby's bottom joins with its back. Now," and I placed his hands over his baby's head, "see how the head moves? See how, when you rock it—gently, gently—it just sort of bounces between your hands? See how it moves, but no other part of the baby's body moves?"

"Oh, yeah—"

"The head moves that way because the neck is so flexible—"

"So, it's breech?"

"Yeah. It's breech."

"But it wasn't breech yesterday!"

"I know—"

I called Jean from the kitchen.

"Jean, Renee's baby's breech."

"What? It wasn't breech yesterday!"

"Well, it is today. Please come over here."

Jean came over and, sure enough, the baby was breech.

We began talking through options. Jean had her hands on the baby—on Renee's belly—just feeling it in there as we talked and, suddenly, it flipped right back over.

I ran and fetched a binder from Jean's car. We strapped Renee into it and Jean suggested she repeat the cervical stretch. Renee and Alan agreed.

Jean found Renee's cervix to be eight centimeters dilated.

Naturally, we expected her to have her baby practically that moment, but one day passed, then another, and then another, with no signs of labor whatsoever. Jean consulted with the doctor and he said, "Just break her water." But homebirth midwives don't often do that. A couple more days passed without labor until, with only one day to spare before Jean was scheduled to leave, the doctor repeated his advice.

The next day, Jean's final day in Michigan, we relayed the doctor's recommendation to Renee and Alan. We reviewed the various risks, from the probability of a prolapsed cord, to the potential to transmit infection, to the possibility labor would fail to start. They said they understood the risks, and wanted to try.

So, at 6:04 that evening, with my hands on Renee's belly, holding the baby's head firmly over the brim of his mama's pubic bone, Jean reached inside and pricked the water sack. Clear waters trickled from Renee while the baby's head settled even more nicely into his mama's pelvis while his heart continued to patter steadily along like nothing happened.

Renee's contractions began a rhythmic squeezing almost immediately.

By 10:13, Renee began to feel the urge to push and at 10:27 p.m., Renee's ten-pound, seven-ounce son, with one thick hand clamped against his fifteen-and-a-half-inch head, was born on the living room floor right beside the Christmas tree at 10:27 p.m.

"Oh! Oh, God, thank You!" Renee wailed. "Thank You! And, hey! Where's that doctor who said I couldn't have a baby bigger than seven pounds? He should've seen this!"

The kids' disposable cameras clicked away madly, the birthday cake was fetched from the kitchen, the pizza was ordered, and Jean boarded her airplane the next morning.

THIRTY-FIVE

WHEN THE YOUTH WITH A MISSION BASE WE planned to go to in Arkansas closed, we didn't let that hinder our plans to enter the mission field until I spent a month calling around to other YWAM bases. The issue was the children. We understood we were unable to homeschool them while we were in training, and it stretched us to consider even a temporary departure from teaching Hannah and Paul ourselves. But in Arkansas, there was a private school right there on the grounds. It had very few students, it utilized a curriculum similar to ours, it would only be for a year, and it was almost next door to our classrooms.

We came to terms with that compromise, but, as I made the rounds of calls to other bases, it became clear what was available in Arkansas was an anomaly. To enroll in any other YWAM program, we had to put the kids in the nearest public school, and we weren't at all willing to do that.

It was an interesting time. From start to finish and all the way through, we knew we did what we were supposed to do in selling the house and discharging our debts, but it apparently was for a purpose other than the one we supposed.

So, as I mentioned, we entered a season of quiet contemplation. With Brent working weekdays, we had every evening and each weekend to spend together for the first time in our married lives. He came home for supper, then we went for walks around the elementary school across the street from us. The kids ran and played as we walked and, as we walked we talked and prayed about our future.

Usually the talking would be as simple as asking if the other had any ideas or sense about what we ought to do. For weeks on end, the answer was we didn't, so, we committed our lives afresh to God and walked on. Brent's dad was nearly beside himself over the uncertainty, but we trusted the way would become clear and were able just to enjoy all those quiet nights together.

That winter, Hannah came along with me on a day's worth of visits. That wasn't so unusual by itself, as I often towed the kids along with me on appointments, but that day, Hannah served as my helper.

She'd already attended a couple births—both of Renee and Alan's birthday cake and pizza births, actually—and though she enjoyed them, she seemed to regard the experiences as ordinary as any other. She also appeared to view the day-in, day-out parade of big bellies and squishy babies through our lives as pretty ordinary.

People asked Hannah from time to time, "So, do you want to be a midwife like your mama?"

Her answer was always, "Oh, no!"

"Oh no!" remained her answer until she helped me with Nate and Natalie's third birth, and I left it at that, feeling very firmly people are "called" to their life endeavors, not persuaded to them. But on that day, Hannah expressed an interest in helping and I was more than pleased to indulge it. The mothers we served were downright delighted. She felt and measured bellies, listened to heartbeats, weighed babies, and even helped me perform a newborn screen.

And that day shimmers like a gem in my memory. The hours we passed in the mellow countryside mark the beginning of the gradual shift in our relationship from parent and daughter to friends, and was the first hint of the partnership we would come to enjoy as Hannah ripened into womanhood.

She was only ten then, but what a remarkable person she was already. Somewhere that winter, I wrote about her in my journal, "Hannah's so interesting! She really thinks and she asks good questions. She desires to understand. I try to open things for her, to show her where to look for insight, to teach her to listen to her conscience and to the voice of God, and she's so quick to get it."

My relationship with the kids was a thing that kept me on my knees before the Lord. It refined my character. It stripped away the remnants of self-preservation. It stretched the limits of my compassion and deepened the sense I was born to support, encourage, and bless those around me. And it forced me to learn what it means to truly "lay your life down" for others.

That metamorphosis equipped me with a reservoir of courage and insight, strength and love I'd draw on many times as I walked within my callings as wife, mother, friend, and as an attendant at life's crossings—mostly comings, thankfully, but a surprising number of goings as well.

One of the most wondrous experiences of my lifetime has been witnessing the transformation of my children from secrets in my womb to noteworthy adults—from responsibilities that sometimes overwhelmed me, to two of my closest friends.

———

In the spring, I went for another dilatation then ran off to attend a smattering of interesting births.

A young Amish mom and dad birthed a hefty eight-pound, nine-ounce son who, through all the time his head was visible, spun and twisted and turned as though he were hunting for the best fit for his exit. The first couple times he turned his head, his mama, thinking we were doing something to her cried out, "Oh! Please stop!" She could hardly believe we weren't touching her.

Then it took her an hour and twenty-one minutes to expel her placenta and, though in those years I experienced a good number of delayed third stages, that one is yet the record holder.

A couple nights later, we met out in Jean's neighborhood for a birth. I got myself into a bit of trouble with the couple we were serving that evening when I did one of their prenatals for Jean a few days before. I was feeling the woman's belly when she asked me to estimate the size of the baby. I told her I guessed he was about eight pounds—seven-and-a-half or eight. Pretty normal. Pretty okay. Jean called that evening to tell me the mom was upset I'd thought the child would be so huge, but then she went on to birth her seven-pound, twelve-ounce daughter in just under three hours.

Two weeks passed and a family living toward Hastings had their sixth child. The baby was a tiny thing, only six pounds, nine ounces. It took some suctioning—a thing we very rarely do—and a good bit of rubbing to get her breathing, then a half hour of free flow oxygen to keep her pink. Her mother had a heavy bleed, too, but we left everybody healthy and happy at our departure.

Eleven days after that, and another Vermontville Amish first-timer had a fat baby boy after a fairly quick labor. The child came with both his hands grabbing his ears.

The next morning we were called out to catch a baby girl who was all wrapped up in her umbilical cord, including a tight loop around her neck. We decided to try the somersault maneuver, or pressing the child's head toward the mother's pubic bone, allowing the body to slip out without further tightening the cord.

March burst upon the scene, and I was encouraged by both Brent and Jean to dig out the NARM packet. I'd moved it with us to T. R. and Kathy's house, and stuffed it straight into the depths of the new office closet. But I climbed in there and pulled it out, tallied my experience and felt further encouraged, then glanced over those forty-five highlighted pages and felt my heart sink.

Jean asked to look at them with me and, as she flipped the pages and scanned the items, said, "Kim, you know *that*, and you know *that*, and you know *that* and *that* and *that* and *that*. Kim! You know these things!"

I told her, while I might know and be able to do many of the things listed on those papers, I didn't think I could honestly say I knew the concepts well, nor was I able to perform many of the skills gracefully. I certainly wasn't able to execute them like Jean.

"This is entry level midwifery, Kim, not midwifery mastery. The question is, do you have the knowledge and experience necessary to get the job done? The purpose of the certification process is to allow you to see if your knowledge and experience is equal to the practice of safe midwifery. If it isn't, the process will reveal that. You might not be a great midwife now, but you'll get better as you go. That's the only way you *can* get better."

That's what I needed to hear. I sat down and looked again at those intimidating, interminable items, this time with a green highlighter in hand, and I only marked the lines I felt I truly needed to work on. Jean still rolled her eyes at me when I showed her the adjusted pages, but I begged her to just accept I'd marked the items according to the dictates of my conscience, and made her promise to help me with them. I crafted a study plan and set to work. I taught myself the skills I still needed to learn and demonstrated them for Jean, using my friends and family and a select few clients as supremely gracious models.

Then, I studied and studied and studied and studied and studied. Every spare minute I studied. Being on the thorough side of things, I accumulated scores of fascinating, though minor details about moms and babies and birthing with which I drove Jean to distraction and alternately bored and horrified my loved ones. At one point, at one birth, when I suggested the pain the laboring mother was experiencing might be due to annular detachment of the cervix, Jean banned me from making any further observations at any births until *after* I took my exam.

The weeks of that springtime were filled with Woodard walks and talks and prayers about the future, with the kids' schoolwork and soccer games, with home and yard renovations for my aunt and uncle, with study and skills demonstrations, with births and appointments.

One day we enjoyed an especially nice set of appointments, and I wrote about it in my journal. "We visited five moms and five babies today, all healthy, all beautiful, all totally different. When we asked one of the mothers, a first-timer, how she liked motherhood she said, 'Sometimes it's disgusting, sometimes it's beautiful.' And anybody who's been a mom for any length of time will know just what she meant."

THIRTY-SIX

SOME NIGHTS LATER, CINDY, A THIRTY-NINE-YEAR-OLD woman in Kalamazoo, called for us to come over. She had a history of quick births and this one was no different, running its entire course over a mere seventy-seven minutes.

Once we arrived and got things set up, Cindy, reclining on her bed said, "Hmm—I think I need to pee."

We told her to go on to the bathroom and pee then. She said, "Well, you know, since I have my babies so fast, maybe you should check me first. I really don't want to have my baby on the toilet."

Jean checked her and said she ought to be okay, as she was just five centimeters.

Cindy waited through another contraction, stood up, then said, "Oh! It's coming!"

She flung herself back onto the bed and the first thing we knew, her son was in her arms. He was Cindy's seventh son, but she was so thrilled over that baby you'd have thought it was her first. She melted my heart. Cindy had been pregnant a heart-breaking total of eighteen times in her life, suffering more miscarriages than she rejoiced in births.

Eleven nights later, an Amish couple in Vermontville celebrated their seventh wedding anniversary with the birth of their fifth child.

On April Fool's Day, we ran over to U of M for my seventh dilatation and, a few mornings later, our church's new pastor, James Sunnock, invited Brent to breakfast and asked him to consider accepting a full-time youth/associate pastor position at the church. Brent was surprised and pleased, though we both were initially disinclined to accept his offer. We continued in our pattern of walking, talking, and praying, only now with a bit of a new focus.

A week or so later, Jean called to tell me Miriam and John Yoder, a first-time Amish family up in Vermontville, were in labor. Miriam was a wispy little thing and John was an oak tree. I remember wondering for just a split-second the first time I saw John what Miriam was thinking to marry such a giant, worrying just a mite about her birth. But then I relaxed. Women are amazing. They can almost always get the babies they grow out of them, even when they're big. And Miriam really was amazing, too.

In the weeks before her birth, we noticed her baby was in some sort of off-kilter position. Head down, but off. We'd just begun hearing about the Webster Technique from Dr. Cooper in Battle Creek around that time, so we suggested she pay him a visit, but she had a chiropractor she liked already right in her area and preferred to stick with him.

A few nights later, Miriam began a quirky, seemingly unproductive labor. The contractions were irregular and short; enough to keep her from being able to rest, while not nearly strong enough to get the job done. We arrived an hour before midnight. After three hours of uncomfortable restlessness, we decided a stiff drink for Miriam and a nap were in order.

Jean and I headed to the nearest twenty-four-hour grocery to pick up a bottle of wine, where we were embarrassed to learn Michigan law prohibits alcohol sales after two in the morning.

I can only imagine what the lady at the counter must have thought about the pair of women going through her checkout lane at that hour with a sack of pears and a bottle of red Moscato. As our items swept their way along the conveyor belt, she reached over, snatched up the bottle, and whisked it behind the counter, saying, "You can't have that!"

Dumbfounded, we asked why, and she explained the law. When Jean protested the wine was for medicine, I blushed to my toes.

We returned to the little home with its windows glowing warm against the velvety black sky without the "medicine." We did what we could to get Miriam comfortable and resting, then Jean and I fitted ourselves the best we could end-to-end on their only piece of furniture, a microscopic loveseat.

Every so often one of us would tiptoe in to listen to the baby's heartbeat and see how Miriam was holding up. We could hear her whispering to John through the night.

"*Ich bin hes.*" "I'm hot."

"Ooohh, *ich bin kult.*" "I'm cold."

"*Ich btach zu da toilet geh.*" "I need to go to the toilet."

"*Ich btach un* drink, please."

"Please *rebb meh bukal!*" "Rub my back!"

"Oh, no, *rebb doh.*"

"No, John, *doh.*"

"Ahhhhhh, Johnny. *Ya. Dengi.*"

John met every need with tenderness and the solicitousness of a boy head-over-heels in love, once he managed to figure out exactly what those needs actually were.

Toward dawn, Miriam's labor began to pick up a bit. Jean decided to check the woman and was busy doing that while I puttered around in the kitchen with a pan of oatmeal.

Suddenly, Jean was beside me. "Why don't you check her, Kim."

I glanced at Jean's face. I was curious, but unable to read what I saw there.

I went to check with Jean hovering at my elbow. What I felt was a puzzle and I've only felt it two times since. I was confident I was feeling a head, but that head was marked with some weird depressions and a very odd knob. I nodded at Miriam and John, smiled, and said, "Yes, yes, good! Feels like five centimeters," as I eased my fingers from her.

Seconds later, Jean and I were back in the kitchen, whispering furiously. What on earth were we feeling? Neither of us could guess, except I feared it was some dreadful deformity. Miriam's labor steadily intensified and both Miriam and her baby's vitals remained strong and regular. We felt cautiously optimistic with the progress they were making.

Within a couple hours, Miriam began to feel like she could push, and we encouraged her to do so as she felt the urge. She reclined quietly on her side on the bed, while John stood looking down on her with awe engraved on his face. Jean and I knelt here and there on the floor, waiting in watchful silence as the woman grunted and breathed and grunted and breathed her child steadily toward the day.

The hush of holiness unique to homebirth began to steal over the room and soon we noticed the woman's efforts were affecting a swelling, then a bulging, then a subtle opening of her tissues. I leaned in to dribble a little oil over the stretching, spreading surface and—and—

And what in the world is that?

I leaned a little closer and saw again what I thought I saw. Within my mind, the enchantment shattered. I identified a tiny nose and pair of swollen lips. I motioned to Jean and breathed in her ear, "Why don't you take a look with the next push."

With the next push we each looked, our cheeks fairly touching as that nose and those lips peeked out at us. When the grip of Miriam's uterus relaxed its hold on her, Jean straightened and clasped her hands. "Okay," she said, "It's not a head. It's a butt."

My mind detonated and twisted away in all directions as Jean went on to make a little speech about breech birth.

My gosh! Oh, my gosh! A butt? It's a butt? I can't be a midwife! I can't even tell the difference between a face and a butt!

A statement directed my way drew me back to the bedside and I scrambled to retrieve the scattered shards of my brain.

"Because it *is* breech, isn't it?" Jean said, looking at me.

Before I could stop myself, I said, "Is it?" Then, instantly realizing my mistake, added, "Because I don't know a thing about breech babies."

I would have jabbered on, had not another contraction begun to squeeze the slender, silent woman. Jean and I leaned in for a second look and, by golly, there they were again, that nose and those lips!

Jean stood and said, "We'll be right back!"

She dragged me from the room and right out the front door. The life of my apprenticeship and future as a midwife flashed before my mind's eyes, and I opened my mouth to stammer out an apology for questioning her judgment before her clients, but Jean cut me off. "Let's pray!"

She said some simple prayer and, as she did, a profound sense of peace settled over me. When Jean finished, she asked what I thought. I told her I thought we were seeing a face.

She said, nearly hopping up and down, "A face? Oh, my gosh! I just really can't be your teacher anymore! I can't even tell the difference between a butt and a face! Oh! Oh! What do we do?"

I remarked that since it was positioned properly for a face presentation birth—chin poised to pivot Miriam's pubic bone— and seemed to be coming nicely, I thought we should go back inside, set up for a resuscitation, and receive the baby. Fortunately, I'd just studied the section in my third edition of *Varney's Midwifery* dealing with face presentation.

And that's exactly what we did.

Eleven or twelve minutes later the tiny baby girl, with a long-fingered hand squashed over one of her eyes, slipped with amazing ease into the world. She was dreadfully swollen and needed to be resuscitated, but she responded readily to our efforts. She also astonished us by exhibiting a perfect harlequin effect; for the space of at least thirty minutes, she was red on one side of her body and perfectly white on the other. The placenta came soon after the baby, sporting an accessory lobe and an impressive thirty-seven-inch-long cord.

When we arrived for her week-one visit, John said, "Well, little Neva's a cutie now, I'm glad to say. I hadn't realized she was only puffy. I just thought we'd had a real ugly little girl. I pitied her, though, still, I loved her."

Amidst all this, Brent and I continued to walk and talk and pray about our future.

On a gorgeous Sunday afternoon, a family of horse-breeders in Nashville birthed their fifth child as three spindly-legged foals danced about their dames through the couple's bedroom window.

Back at home, Brent and I walked and talked and prayed.

Five days after that, our friend and one of our pastors, Mike Lutz, died.

Brent and I walked and talked and prayed.

Eight days after that, a first-time mom and daddy birthed a glorious, seven-pound, fourteen-ounce girl in the veil, or yet within her waters.

Still, Brent and I walked and talked and prayed.

Day in and day out, we walked and talked and prayed without feeling we were getting any closer to an answer until one balmy afternoon, Brent walked into Pastor James's office and told him he'd take the job.

The kids and I were out visiting moms and babies the afternoon he did that. We were driving along one of those timeless country roads so old and narrow and seldom used the branches of the trees standing along its sides had grown together, stretching up and spreading out overhead to form a fluttery green ceiling. As we passed beneath the flutter of green, with the sparkling sunlight shifting and flickering around us like a fine spray of fairy dust, I knew we were supposed to stay in Battle Creek and take that job.

The very moment I knew that, Brent called to tell me what he'd done.

Chapter

THIRTY-
SEVEN

JEAN TACKLED THE ARDUOUS TASK OF SIGNING
every single item on the endless, formerly highlighted "Comprehensive Skills, Knowledge, and Abilities Essential for Competent
Midwifery Practice," pages, complete with the litany of my experience attending and conducting all manner of births and visits
and exams, in the presence of a notary. I then solicited six letters
of reference from professionals, clients, and friends personally
acquainted with my performance as midwife and, with my
insides nearly strangled with fear, obtained my cashier's check
for an unmentionably substantial amount of money for our single
income family, photocopied every last sheet of paper, whispered
a desperate prayer, and entrusted the whole kit and caboodle to
the United States Postal Service.

Then I took a deep, shuddery breath and hurdled into the
summer.

Brent turned in his resignation and, since he'd gone back to
road patrol when the schools let out, I rode along with him one

last time. I always loved to ride with him. It was really something to see him at work. Each time I went, I returned home imbued with fresh respect and appreciation for him, as well as with a renewed heart to support him so he'd be able to function at his safest and best.

That last ride confirmed to me he made the right decision to move on to full-time work with children. We rolled along the streets of the Post Addition, a troubled neighborhood he often worked and, as those over-used police cruiser brakes squealed, the area's children banged open the doors of their homes and flocked to the car.

I sat back and watched with tears stinging my eyes as he climbed from the car to crouch down eye-level with those masses of kids. Soon his arms and his lap were filled with them. They patted his bulletproof chest and examined his night stick, then begged him to sound the sirens and flash the lights. Each child got a turn, wrapping little arms around Brent's neck and squeezing till I thought my heart would burst.

When Brent returned me home, Hannah and Paul were summoned outdoors by the trademark squeal of those brakes and he was rushed once again.

Brent's final day at the Battle Creek Police Department was punctuated by a party, and it was such a bittersweet parting. We were excited to move forward into the new things God was calling us to, but still, the tears continually pressed against the backs of our eyes. Brent loved his job as a police officer. We all four loved it and we would miss it.

And he would be sorely missed. He was awarded Teacher of the Year that spring by the Battle Creek Public School System for his outstanding work as liaison officer and Lieutenant Reed, spokesperson of the party, made a very moving speech. The last thing he said was, "One thing I know for sure is, every kid in the Post Addition knew Officer Woodard. We all see Brent has a gift with these kids and we're going to miss having a man like him around."

Once again, I was struck by how well-loved Brent was. His secret was the way he made every soul he encountered feel like he or she was the most important soul on earth.

Brent was to be brought before the church the next Sunday, anointed and prayed over, and officially installed as a pastor. I was invited to stand up with him and I was so excited about it, I bought a new skirt to wear for the event.

That Saturday night, however, a fellow midwife called to say she was ready for me to come help her with a set of twin girls in Homer.

Jean and I had agreed some months before to help her with the birth, but never expected the woman to carry on so long with her pregnancy. She was five days past her due date, and a first-time mom, too. The first baby was born at twenty minutes after two o'clock Sunday morning, but the second wasn't born for another two hours and forty-two minutes.

Secretly, I spent the night fretting over the likelihood I'd miss Brent's induction into the ministry. When it was time for us to head out however, I realized although I'd have to drive straight from the birth to the church, I could just make it. I was rumpled and blood-stained from the long night as opposed to showered and donned in my lovely new skirt, but thankfully Brent cared little about things like appearances. He was just glad I was there. And he was proud of me, too, bloodstains and all.

About that time, NARM sent word my paperwork was acceptable, so I was cleared to take the Skills Assessment, a performance examination of sorts conducted with living, breathing pregnant moms and newborn babies. If I could pass that, I'd be eligible to take the written exam in the fall.

I scheduled the exam with a midwife on the Michigan Midwives Association Board, Patrice Bobier, for the end of July. She was excited and told me we were sure to have a wonderful time. I hung up feeling queasy.

I studied all I could while working like a mad woman to finish the improvements we were making on T. R.'s house and yard so it could be put up for sale, and I was rewarded with a raging, head-to-toe case of poison ivy. Between the paperwork, my studies, the births, myriad appointments—I attended the births of ten babies that summer—career changes, home improvements, and the poison ivy, I approached the Skills Assessment nearly worn out.

Still, on the thirtieth of July, the whole family piled in the car to drive me up to Patrice's. We arrived with my head throbbing, my insides roiling, my hands shaking, my knees failing, and with a dad (who was also a pediatrician) looking high and low for Jean. He told me his wife, due any day, was bleeding.

I found Jean for the man, squeezed my family, and knocked on Patrice's door.

I'm happy to say, once I got going, I was okay. I showed Patrice how I wash my hands, how I set up my oxygen, how I administer intramuscular injections, how I examine pregnant moms and newly-born babies.

I showed her how I do my job. And I loved my job.

I did still leave feeling a bit sick for not knowing if I passed— the evaluators didn't grade the assessments, they just watched the candidates work and recorded their findings—but Patrice was kind enough to tell me she thought I did all right.

The morning after the exam, Jean called to see if I would come to Kalamazoo to help her with a birth. It was the pediatrician's wife; it turned out the bleeding was only her bloody show.

She started with her contractions while I was taking my test. Jean was over there when I called to tell her it was over and I'd survived. We were hours away and, it being the woman's third baby, I went to bed supposing I missed it. So I was surprised and a little alarmed when Jean called to say the woman was still in labor.

I headed over and was happy to find the woman in transition, but I shouldn't have been. She'd been in active labor since the evening before and had stood literally the entire day; then she spent a good three hours with a lip of cervix that refused to resolve. By bedtime, she was fading rapidly.

Finally, the last of her cervix disappeared and the exhausted woman began to bear down with her contractions, but she was piteously ineffective, standing there in the middle of her living room. I suggested she lie on her bed to push.

She said she couldn't, because lying down hurt her legs too badly. I wasn't sure how she could know that, as it had been almost a whole day since she did anything other than stand, but I just said, "Yes, I know. I know it hurts. But no matter what you do, something's going to hurt until the baby's born. Right? Why don't you just surrender to all the hurt, lie down, grab your knees, and push your baby out."

So, she climbed up on her bed and had him out in about twenty minutes. The baby surprised us by opening his eyes and looking around the moment his head was free, and he continued to surprise us by being one of the quietest babies we ever tended. We resuscitated him—his one-minute apgar was only four—and he came around, but he continued to be quiet.

Jean and I were concerned, but the father of the baby assured us he was fine. Another pediatrician and wife, friends of the couple, were there for the birth as well, and that doctor also thought the baby was okay.

We relaxed and enjoyed the victory with them, and we leaned in to our opportunity to learn from the men. The little guy was just a peanut at seven pounds, four ounces and, despite his dawdling start at breathing, he nursed beautifully.

The next day a woman in Dowling gave birth to her baby after spending nearly twenty-seven hours with broken waters, and a few days after that, we attended the birth of a tenth child in Kalamazoo with a prolapse of the umbilical cord.

When we realized what we were dealing with was a prolapsed cord, the dad called for an ambulance while the mother shifted to her chest and knees. Jean went to work, intending to press the baby's head up and away from the cord, but she was actually able to push the bit of pinched loop out of the way. I checked and re-checked the baby's heart tones and they recovered nicely, but none of us had the courage to proceed with the birth at home after that.

The paramedic arrived, ready to load mom up and take off, but the couple opted to transport by car when they were told neither the father of the baby nor even one midwife would be allowed along in the ambulance.

The trip to the hospital was uneventful, and the nine-pound baby boy arrived in excellent condition soon after.

Baby after baby after baby came. Then one afternoon, I opened the mail and discovered I'd passed the Skills Assessment and was authorized to schedule my exam. In those days, an applicant could only take the exam at a location within her region in February or August, or at the annual Midwives Alliance of North America (MANA) conference held every autumn.

I decided to take the exam that fall at the conference in Boston, and Jean decided she would come with me.

Chapter

THIRTY-
EIGHT

ON SEPTEMBER 27, 2002, NINE YEARS, TWO
months, and twenty-four days after I attended the first birth of
my apprenticeship, I attended the last.

Ring!

Off I went.

There it is! Oh, God, thank you.

I found the stone farmhouse easily enough. It was the only
one along that isolated stretch of gravel.

But it was the isolated stretch of gravel I had troubling finding
in the gloom of the rain-splattered night.

My nerves and stomach were coiled into a knot so tight I
found it hard to think clearly, and then, just as I reached the
intersection of what I thought ought to be Hacker and M-66, a
semi-truck roared past me, rocking my minivan like a rowboat
on rough waters and sending a spray of mud across my windshield, obliterating my view of the minuscule green sign marking
the corner.

The paper scrap with scribbled directions I'd crushed against the steering wheel fluttered to the floor as I skimmed through the intersection, and my already-quickened pulse surged in my chest and thundered into my head.

Ah! Gosh! I know that's it. I gotta go back! But what if it isn't? Oh, Lord! Oh, Lord God! What am I doing out here? Please help me! Please help me get there! Please help me get there and please help me do a good job and please, please help me not faint or throw up!

I swung the vehicle around and roared back. I slowed when I approached the intersection again, squinting past the swish of wiper blades to read the sign.

Who makes these things so tiny? Hacker! Yes!

I skittered around the corner, then crunched and rumbled along the washboard of sandy dirt as rapidly as I felt I safely could.

I shrugged my shoulders, shook my head, and relaxed my grip on the steering wheel a mite, taking a measure of comfort in the fact I'd found the laboring mother's road, though only a very little comfort. The evening's foray into solo practice was thrust on me of a sudden. I'd attended but one birth alone through my nine years catching babies and I was still twenty-nine days from taking my midwifery examination.

The outline of a house rose from the darkness and sea of wet, windswept fields, interrupting the train of my thoughts. My heart tripled its pace, but as I rolled into the driveway, the four sturdy feet of a rusting windmill standing before the weather-beaten, whitewashed barn and long, low row of rickety fencing illumined by the sweeping fan of my headlights helped to smooth the disheveled edges of my soul. The place was new to me, but the landscape was as familiar as home, looking, as it did, like most

Amish farms, like my own grandfather's farm—even like my lifetime.

I released the breath I'd been holding and glanced toward the house. The glimmering light beckoning to me from the borders of a window shade further eased my anxious spirit.

I climbed from the warmth of my van into an icy breeze laced with raindrops, gathered my bags, and picked my way among the puddles scattered between me and the front door.

I let myself into a narrow mudroom and my nostrils filled with the pungent crosshatching of odors singular to Amish entryways. The aroma of rich soil and that which springs from the soil. A whiff of grease, oils, and well-worn leather. The tang of harsh soaps. The musk of workhorse flanks, of udders bulging with warm milk, of guard dogs, of barn cats. The acridity of hens and the funk of swine. Scents that cling to boots and coats, fraying straw hats and bonnets lining the wall. Smells rubbed into the very floorboards and windowpanes and doorjambs of the room by generations of folk who'd spent their lives close to earth.

I tapped lightly at the kitchen door, but turned its knob without waiting for a response. Midwives never wait before the doors of the laboring.

"Hello?" I said, and I stepped inside.

Three smiles shone in the mellow light of an oil lamp as I squeezed myself into the room and, at once, I had work-worn hands moving to ease my bags from my shoulders and a rivulet of *Deutsch*-seasoned talk filling my ears.

A splash and a groan awakened me and brought my surroundings back into focus.

Goodness! What's going on? Where am I?

I blinked and saw Ruthann and David Ray Detweiler. I was with them in their bathroom.

Oh, yes! I'm at a birth! I'm at a birth for Jean! I'm at a birth without Jean!

There was shy Ruthann, afloat in her bath, her hand-stitched nightgown waving about and caressing her form like undulations of seaweed. She was blowing through the crush of her womb's embrace while David Ray, still reclining along the ledge that lined the tub, kneaded his wife's slender neck between his thumb and fingers.

Ruthann relaxed and turned her cheek into the meat of his palm with a long, low sigh.

I turned my head, and there were the two mothers, capped and aproned—care-worn hands clasped into the laps of their plain dresses, one set of warm brown eyes hidden by two perfect circles of glass shining in the lamp light, simple, stout, hard-working, deeply devoted wives, mothers, grandmothers.

I glanced about the room and took in again the hissing lamp that bathed the room in a dulcet glow, the green window shade, the hand pump standing over the chipped porcelain sink, the claw-footed iron tub, the saw blade painted with the couple's wedding date—trappings from another time, the markings, the imprint of things Old-World and Amish—things that once represented obstacles to me, now representing objects of my affections and respect.

I glanced at my wristwatch. I'd gotten lost in memories—in nine years of trial and triumph.

Hopefully triumph. That test is still ahead...

Still, nine years and there I was, walking fully in my calling.

Oh, Father, thank You. And, oh, Father! Help!

I crossed the room with my Doppler and knelt beside Ruthann, and we all smiled at the sound of the sturdy-hearted child tucked within his mother. I recorded its measure on my slip of paper and returned to my chair.

The minutes ticked by, Ruthann's contractions lengthened and strengthened, she breathed her way through one particularly long and strong contraction—and my heart jumped into my throat.

Oh, dear God...

A gush of blood was swirling about her in the bathwater.

Elizabeth, seated near my elbow, leaned forward and nudged me. "Do you see that, Kim?"

"I do."

When the contraction began to fade, I stood up. "Ruthann, can you come on out of the tub? I need to see what's going on with you and the baby."

David sat up.

Ruthann looked down at the scarlet waters. "Oh!" And she laughed. "That's only my pillow!"

I glanced doubtfully at the sodden wad of black and blue material between her shoulder blades. She noted my glance. "No—no, really! It's the pillow." She dislodged it and pulled a clump of scarlet velvet from the quilted covering.

Nora let out a sigh and Elizabeth laughed, though weakly.

David Ray looked rather bewildered.

"Oh, my gosh." I put my hand over my heart and exhaled. "Okay."

I looked up at David Ray's creased brow. "Everything's okay. But..." I reached for one of the towels hanging on the back of the bathroom door. "Ruthann, we still should get you out of there. I'm not sure you ought to soak in a vat of dye while birthing your baby."

Elizabeth and Nora agreed and stood as well. Nora spread a bathmat on the floor and Elizabeth stretched a beckoning hand toward Ruthann. "*Kom*, Ruth."

David Ray helped Ruthann to her feet just as another contraction began.

"Oh, no—ooohhhhh." She wrapped her arms around his thick neck and clung to him as she rocked her hips back and forth, back and forth, back and forth. The hem of her once-white nightie, now a lovely shade of pink, swished and teased at the surface of the stained waters. "Ooooooooohhhhhhhhh. Oh, David. *Ich kon net des du.*"

"What did she say?" I asked.

David looked at me. "She says she can't do it."

"Oh! Oh, Ruthann, you can do it!"

"Yes!" Elizabeth and Nora chimed in. "You surely can, Ruth!"

"*Ya, Mamm*," David crooned into her ear. "*Du konshts du.*"

The contraction released her and she scrambled from the tub and sprinted from the bathroom. She only just made it to the sofa bed when another powerful wave rose to consume her. "Oh, dear! Oh, my goodness!" She threw herself across the sheets. "Ooooooohhhh! Ogghhhrrrrr..." And, like that, her squeals became throaty groans.

"Oh, my!" Nora said. "Is she pushing?"

I smiled. "It sure sounds like it."

I pulled on a pair of gloves and peeled her soggy nightie from her thighs, then smothered another giggle. "Ruthann, may I take off your panties?"

"Oh!" She said, even as she grunted and groaned and shifted her hips. "Ought they come off, then?"

Um, yes, you adorable thing. The panties ought to come off.

"Yes—"

I helped her slip out of them just as a new surge of strength swept through her and there was the top of little Joshua's head, his black hair slicked into a single shining curl by his mama's birthing nectar. I squeezed a dribble of oil over him and his mother's spreading tissues. The contraction subsided and Joshua retreated till only the curl was visible.

David Ray was sitting at Ruthann's head and she had hold of both his hands. I glanced up to look at them. Ruthann's eyes were closed, but David's had a sparkle of tears in the corners.

I smiled at him and nodded. He smiled back.

Ruthann stirred, let David's hands go, grabbed her knees and drew them to her chest, and grunted.

And again and again and again, like the sun appearing over the edge of the horizon, the soft, black orb advanced in one single smooth motion. He paused as he crowned, the widest point of his head, released from the limits of his mother's pelvis, smoothed and stretched and spread his mother's opening to the full.

"Oh, oh, oh, oh, oh, oh, oh." Ruthann panted.

"Good, Ruthann." I whispered. "Easy. Gentle."

"Ooooohhhhhhhhhhhhhhhhhhhh."

And Joshua spun free of his mother's body in a perfect, graceful arch, and I helped him complete it by bringing him up and over and into his mother's outstretched arms.

"The baby! Oh, the baby!" The grandmothers burst into joyful, tear-splattered song as they hovered over my shoulders.

Ruthann burst into tears and her cries joined her baby's cries. "Oh, David! Oh, David Ray! We've a new baby!"

"Oh, Ruth! *Miawh hen un nei baby*!" And David burst into tears, too.

Chapter

THIRTY-NINE

A FEW DAYS AFTER JOSHUA'S BIRTH, I SPENT A DAY working in the south with Jean. The next morning, I wrote a few lines about it in my journal.

Jean intends for me to begin taking more responsibility for the clients down south once I pass—Ah! If I pass—my exam, and she feels the birth I just did is a good way to reacquaint myself with the community.

It was an odd day. It felt like the closing of a circle. Nine years before, I'd started working with Jean down there. I was only twenty-three then, amazed to be attending appointments and births at all, and feeling a strange mixture of both gratitude and apology as I did.

Truthfully, every time I still feel thankful for having been invited, as well as a bit apologetic, though I feel more confident now that my help-to-hinder ratio has risen to greater parts help. Anyway, nine years, three hundred fifty-one prenatals, one hundred twenty-three babies, and one hundred sixty-three postpartums later, I found myself following along with my dear friend again, visiting the daughters of the women I visited back at the start, and that feeling swept over me—that closing circle feeling, the feel of a coil sweeping both close to and far from its origins as it winds its way through the years of my life.

It makes the next ten years seem nearer, and so real.

That autumn was overflowing. We started back to home-schooling. We realized we'd need a home of our own again and, as we thought we'd like to build one, started looking for property. I constantly cleaned the house in order to keep it ready for its multitude of showings. I ran off for yet another tracheal dilatation and missed a birth. We purchased a parcel of land. T. R. and Kathy's house sold. I found us an apartment to rent and began to pack.

And all the while, my upcoming exam loomed larger and ever larger before me, but I could find no time to study.

The night before Jean and I were scheduled to fly to Boston was filled with last minute packing and streams of distressing news. The tenuous health of my failing grandmother took a turn for the worse and my sister-in-law's labor induction out in Texas deteriorated into an emergency cesarean section.

Morning dawned overcast and cool and I realized with gratitude I'd managed to snatch a few hours of sleep. I scrambled to shower and dress while the phone jangled continuously with updates.

By the time Jean picked me up, I knew my nephew was safely born and both he and his mother were doing well, but I also learned my grandmother had slipped off to heaven while I slept.

Jean and I made it to the airport with scarcely a second to spare. After getting hung up at security because of the safety pin I used to keep my jeans zipped, we made a movie-style dash through the airport, barely making it onto the plane.

We reached the conference center around suppertime, and I was a mess of jangled nerves. I had a boiling headache, I could hardly eat, and, once we hit the pillows, found I couldn't fall sleep.

In the morning, a full-blown case of test anxiety accompanied me to the examination site where I joined a group of similarly suffering souls.

It was a strictly conducted exam. We gained entrance via photo ID and were allowed food, drink, a pencil, and not one thing else. Fairly shaking with trepidation, I took a seat by a woman armed with a bottle of Bach Flower Rescue Remedy and a sack of marshmallows. We tried to smile at one another. We didn't even try to squeak out a greeting.

The test was comprised of 350 questions and we were allotted two four-hour blocks of time to answer them, separated by a break for lunch. We were instructed to turn in our tests if we needed to use the bathroom and advised only one of us would be excused to the bathroom at a time.

We turned our answer sheets over, opened our booklets, and began. When I finished and looked up, I noticed I finished first, and wondered if I ought to re-examine my answers. I decided against it. I did the best I could and felt intuitively that fiddling with things couldn't possibly help.

I took my test to the woman watching over us, and she whispered, "Have you got to use the restroom?"

"No," I said, "I'm finished."

She hesitated, then said, "Are you sure? It's only been ninety minutes." A wave of nausea fizzed at the back of my throat and my vision dimmed, but I swallowed and said I was sure, and stumbled from the room.

I spent the first fifteen minutes of my lunch hour calculating—yes, with a calculator—exactly how many questions I thought I'd missed compared to the number of questions I was allowed to miss and, then, feeling much, much worse, spent the rest of my break chugging up and down the building's four flights of stairs. I knew I should eat something, but could choke nothing down.

I returned to the testing site, lay on my back in agony before the door while the interminable minutes to one o'clock crawled past, steeled myself to slow down and really take my time, then took my seat with my fellow ashen-faced females.

And the afternoon session mirrored the morning session exactly, right down to our lines. "Have you got to use the restroom? Are you sure? But it's only been ninety minutes."

Brent spent that entire afternoon finagling the rearrangement of our airline tickets so I'd be able to attend my grandmother's funeral, slated for the next day. Before I knew it, I was back and we were driving toward her home in Drayton Plains.

We spent the three days after laying her to rest clearing our things from my uncle's house and getting settled into our apartment, then Brent took off for a ten-day ministry trip to the Philippines.

Such wild times! But I suspect it was a mercy we were so busy. It took two to three weeks in those days to learn the results of the exam and, even with all that wildness, I was sick with waiting.

Daniel 5:27 kept running through my head. "*Tekel:* You've been weighed on the scales and found wanting."

I wanted to know how I did, but if I failed—Oh! I could scarcely contemplate it! So many years were on the line, so many hours of work, so many of our hard-earned dollars invested.

What would I say to Brent if I failed?

What would I say to myself?

I spent a week haunting our mailbox until one afternoon I found an envelope from NARM inside it.

The sight of it sent a fresh wave of nausea over me.

"You've been weighed on the scales—"

I lifted it between my fingertips and, feeling I might faint, returned to our apartment.

"You've been weighed on the scales—"

I stood at the kitchen counter and felt my knees wobble and set to trembling as I eyed it.

"You've been weighed on the scales—"

I stood looking at it for an eternity, quaking, swallowing, sweating, listening to the children playing at some game in their tiny bedroom, wishing Brent were home to open it for me. Finally, I slit the envelope open and drew out the slip of paper within.

"You've been weighed—"

I unfolded the paper.

"You've been—"

"You've been—"

"You've—"

Passed.

EPILOGUE

THE SUMMER I TURNED FORTY-TWO, I SOLD THE
home Brent and the children and I built together and moved into
a house in town with Hannah. Paul was off to the Army. Brent
was gone, five years buried.

I unpacked a boxful of old journals onto a bookshelf and
stood back to regard it, marveling that the record of my entire
life up to that point fit so neatly into such a small space. Now I
marvel I managed to fit a third of my adult life into a single book.

Partway through the writing of this tale, I realized I'd forgotten to relate the story of the first birth I actually attended. It
happened May 28, 1986, about four months after I felt the call
to midwifery tingle in my soul. My sister Kris and I were at a
party with friends. I don't remember how we were reached, for
there were no cell phones in those days, but word came to us that
Karen—that wonderful woman who'd introduced me to midwifery and homebirth—was looking for me.

Somehow we managed to connect, and she told me she was on her way to a homebirth in Mt. Pleasant, only it was really a hotel birth. The birthing family was remodeling their house with the aim of finishing the project before the arrival of their newest family member, but the mom went into labor a mite earlier than anticipated. Apparently, the house was in a state less than ideal for birthing, so they decided to shift things to the Best Western out on Pickard Road. The family, midwives, apprentices, and doulas were en route to the hotel, and a goodly number of children were in tow as well. Would Kris and I be willing to come watch the troop of little squirmies in a second room? With hearts beating madly, we gave a resounding yes and made our way there as quickly as we could in my one hundred-dollar, 1973 Toyota Corolla.

My memory of the event is vague, which isn't like me at all. Possibly the fact I was close to a real homebirth and real midwives put me in some other state of mind.

I remember a dark room and two beds full of sleeping and nearly-sleeping children. A variety of women stole in and out of the room all through the night, hair and faces illumined by the hallway lights till they looked to me like angels with halos.

At some diminutive hour, Karen came and woke us, telling us the baby had been born, but wasn't breathing. She said the midwives were providing resuscitation and an ambulance was on the way, and she asked us to please pray. Kris and I rolled to our knees next to the bed and prayed with all our beings. We could hear commotion outside our door, but understood enough to stay put with our petitions and ponderings.

Finally, Karen returned to say the baby was revived and well. The only remaining concern I remember was that a worrisome spot of blood had besmirched the carpeting.

I have a remote memory, too, of Karen wondering if the experience would dissuade me from my pursuit of homebirth midwifery. I had a similar experience some twenty years later when my daughter, Hannah, attended a birth with me as a babysitter and wound up helping me handle a scary postpartum hemorrhage.

Hannah had been asked many times through her then fifteen years if she thought she might like to be a midwife, and though she'd always said no, I'd nurtured a furtive hope she'd find herself called to follow in my footsteps after all. Never once did I mention it, however. Homebirth midwifery is serious business, especially in our culture. A woman is either called to it or she isn't. If Hannah was so called, I'd need not ask her after it—she'd let me know.

In the wake of my nerve-rattling first birth, Karen worried I'd abandon homebirth midwifery. I felt Hannah's disinterest in homebirth midwifery would be sealed in the aftermath of helping me stem a torrential tide of blood. I surprised Karen by feeling more certain than ever in my calling, and Hannah amazed me nearly to tears when she told me on the way home from the birth, "Hey, Mom? Yeah, I'd like to be a midwife, too."

Today she's one of the finest midwives I know.

And so, I've told you the story of my labor and birthing into midwifery: a long, arduous journey, oft hilarious, occasionally grievous, generally joyful, incredibly beautiful; sprinkled and stained with tears and blood and waters and pee and sweat; costly, but costly because it's proven so precious.

I accomplished it, and immediately realized I was in the exact place I was before, only with letters after my name and a lot more responsibility. Earning the Certified Professional Midwife credential was and is something I treasure on many levels, but it merely marked a milestone in my journey.

I end this tale with the completion of my apprenticeship, and I plan to follow it with another book or two describing my first fifteen years of independent practice. But it must be said that every midwife I know possesses her own version of this story, with many of those versions worthier of finding their way into a book than mine.

I recently read a book about leadership called *Extreme Ownership*, by Jocko Willink and Leif Babin, a set of Navy Seal officers. They opened with the following statement which resonated deeply with me:

Who are we to write such a book? It may seem that anyone who believes they can write a book on leadership must think themselves the epitome of what every leader should aspire to be, but we are far from perfect. We continue to learn and grow as leaders every day, just as any leaders who are truly honest with themselves must. We were simply fortunate enough to experience an array of leadership challenges that taught us valuable lessons. This book is our best effort to pass those lessons on, not from a pedestal or a position of superiority, but from a humble place, where the scars of our failings still show.

I'm sure there are those who'd ask, "Kim, who are you to write such a book?"

I'm aware the world is home to a great many amazing midwives—midwives with more knowledge, more skill, and more experience than me.

Yet, though I'm "far from perfect," I have a story to share and I share it "from a humble place, where the scars of (my) failings still show."

I also consider my story a tribute to those great many amazing midwives I share this inimitable calling with. If any one of them weren't so busy fulfilling their call to serve, they'd have written this book themselves.

And so, this story is about so much more than one woman and her education.

It's a story about trust, respect, honor, and dignity. A story about uncommon communities of families who drew me into their lives and taught me their ways by allowing me to walk with them through some of the most intimate and powerful moments of their lives.

It's a story about love and life, beauty and strength, fulfillment and wholeness—a story of faith, discovery, temerity, grit, and overcoming challenges. It's a story about an ordinary woman who, by virtue of her surrender to Jesus Christ, managed to accomplish something extraordinary. It's a little picture of tending with care to God-given responsibilities while pursuing the entirety of divine purposes.

Yes, it's a story about the potential for each of us to be and do all God has created us to be and do, and to go on and use that to bless our world.

So You Want to Be a Midwife

A HOMEBIRTH MIDWIFERY APPRENTICESHIP IN modern America is truly a thing all its own. The following is the letter I give to those who request to apprentice with me. My hope is to awaken them to just what exactly they'll be getting themselves into if I take them on.

Homebirthing is first and forever about the vulnerabilities and incredible potentials of transforming families and their irreplaceable moments. The way these transforming families experience their incredible, irreplaceable moments irrevocably establishes the foundation and springboard for their physical, psychological, and even spiritual lives. Homebirth midwifery is about, is ever and always about, the reverent nurture and facilitation of these amazing transformations. There's nothing in all the world like homebirth, and nothing in all the world quite like the sacred calling and charge of homebirth midwifery.

Taking an apprentice tends to be a costly, exhausting, risky endeavor for a midwife, which is why so many gifted midwives choose to eschew it. It is, however, a necessary endeavor. I've spent a bit of time, therefore, in efforts to create an apprenticeship system that will preserve my strength, my effectiveness, my financial solvency, and my sanity as a midwife; that will rear up another generation of conscientious, competent midwives; and that will, most importantly, serve my clientele with excellence.

If I select you as my next apprentice, it'll be with the trust you're deadly serious in your desire to become a homebirth midwife, you're ready to serve my clients to the best of your ability, and you're ready—you and your family—for the work, for the study, for the strange and grueling hours, for the cost, for the sacrifice, and, yes, for the joy your apprenticeship most surely will be.

The first thing you're to know and to remember—always remember—is, in welcoming you within the circle of my practice, I'm trusting you with what I've been entrusted with—the priceless lives and moments of the families I'm honored to serve. Though you'll be welcomed with the aim to garner knowledge and experience and skill, the very second you enter the presence of any one of my clients, your primary task is to serve and bless— and to serve and bless according to my definition of serve and bless. Be mindful, initially, you'll likely have little to offer a birthing family I won't already be providing. This means your attendance at a woman's birth will benefit you far more than it will benefit her or her family. Keep that in the fore of your mind, and be so grateful.

I'm a Certified Professional Midwife (CPM). Certified Professional Midwifery is a limb upon one of two branches of the tree that is American midwifery. One branch of that tree is Certified Nurse Midwifery (CNM), a Registered Nurse's master's degree. The other is traditional or direct-entry midwifery. CPMs are direct-entry midwives who've submitted themselves to the scrutiny and standards of a body of fellow midwives for the purposes of personal accountability and quality assurance. In states that license midwives, the CPM is generally the criterion. At the time of this writing, there are just over three thousand CPMs actively practicing in the United States. I'm one of them. My daughter, Hannah Simmons, is another.

Though homebirth midwifery isn't currently legal in all fifty states, between one and six percent of the American populace living in each and every one of those states chooses to birth at home. The statistics of homebirth midwives shine with equal or better mortality rates than hospitals, with far better morbidity (disease and injury) rates than hospitals, as well as with well over ninety-seven percent of clients beyond satisfied with their experiences.

There are a handful of traditional midwifery schools in existence, but still, the general route into homebirth midwifery is private apprenticeship. Unfortunately, apprenticeships are notoriously difficult to secure. First, an aspiring midwife must find a homebirth midwife near her. Second, that aspirant must find a homebirth midwife with a nice, busy practice near her. Third, she must find a homebirth midwife with a nice, busy practice near her who's willing to train an apprentice. Fourth, she must find a homebirth midwife with a nice, busy practice near her who's willing for *her* to be the apprentice the midwife trains. I've received far more queries regarding apprenticeships than I could ever hope to facilitate in a lifetime of practice.

A homebirth midwifery apprenticeship is an apprenticeship to life. It's an apprenticeship to death. It's an apprenticeship to nuance and inconvenience and idiosyncrasy. It's an apprenticeship to wisdom and common sense. It's an apprenticeship to every single priceless dad and mom and baby you'll serve while striving to learn. It's an apprenticeship to each family's absolutely irreplaceable event. It's an apprenticeship to the depths of the apprentice's own heart and soul, where all her motivations and aspirations and desires and dreams, both noble and otherwise, will be dragged into the light and examined. A homebirth midwifery apprenticeship is a revelation.

Yes, a homebirth is one of the most significant, most intense, most gorgeous, most magical things a person will ever experience on earth, but a homebirth midwifery apprenticeship isn't for the romantic or the easy-going. Though a homebirth midwife radiates tenderness and embraces nature and unleashes passion, homebirth midwifery of itself isn't any of those things.

Homebirth midwifery is long drives at odd hours through inclement weather. Homebirth midwifery is sleeping under tables, or curled up on chairs, or along lonely roadsides while waiting for tow trucks—if sleep is to be had at all. Homebirth midwifery is feeding and watering, while neglecting to eat and drink. Homebirth midwifery is peeing in a back yard during an ice storm because Mama's been in the bathroom for eons and there isn't any sign she plans to come out. And then it's discovering the paper you used while relieving yourself—that was sitting right there on the kitchen counter next to the door—had been a recent casualty of a plugged and overflowing toilet. Why it was there on the kitchen counter, no one will ever know. Homebirth midwifery is unbrushed teeth and flyaway hair and grungy underwear attempting to appear professional during a transport. Homebirth midwifery is finding that delicate, essential place between necessary intervention and deleterious interference. Midwife Valerie El Halta once called it intercession. Homebirth midwifery is sharp wits and thick skin and ferociously gentle hearts and steely nerves. Homebirth midwifery is looking death right in the eyes and defying him to the uttermost—usually managing to snatch our charges from his clutches, though, occasionally, his unthinkable demands must be surrendered to and accepted after all.

A homebirth midwifery apprenticeship is something a woman does entirely on her own. Yes, God provides strength and wisdom and courage and heart. Yes, an amazing husband will often be the unflagging cheering section. Yes, the midwifery preceptor provides the opportunity to tag along and learn the art and science of the trade. But it's the homebirth midwifery apprentice who digs in and does the thing.

While wifing a cop and youth pastor, mothering and home-schooling our two home-born kids, arranging the details of four mission trips with groups of teenagers and ministering to the female teenagers within those groups of teenagers, renovating two homes, moving five times, entering paintings into art shows, enduring twelve throat surgeries, supporting my man through a career change, and—ever and always—cooking and cleaning, tidying and laundering, I attended the births of 123 babies, and singlehandedly created and executed my entire midwifery study curriculum. Then through the thirteen years since those accomplishments, we purchased and cleared a piece of property, began building our dream house, lost my husband's mother to cancer, lost our builder to—well—to issues, discovered my husband had cancer, lived outside while we and a host of faithful friends worked furiously to finish the house before winter, lost my husband to cancer, continued homeschooling our children, tried desperately to sell the home through four dismal selling seasons, saw my daughter graduate and off to the mission fields, welcomed her back again to finish her midwifery apprenticeship, sheltered two spectacular exchange students for one lovely year, moved with all four kids into a 1,000 square-foot rental, saw my son graduate and join the Army and deploy to Afghanistan, met and married my new husband, turned my practice over to my newly-married daughter and packed up for my move to Colorado, all while day-in and day-out tending to the care of 372 brand new babies and their mothers.

And that's it, folks. A homebirth midwifery apprenticeship is as homebirth midwifery is—a refining fire.

a LITTLE SOMETHING *to* GET YOU STARTED

THIS IS A LIST OF THE BOOKS I CUT MY TEETH ON AS an aspiring midwife. Most are now on the older side, and I suspect few would include them on a list of books earmarked for the homebirth midwife aspirant these days, but they're the stories of the first generation of women who sought to birth at home after half a century's worth of birthing in hospitals—they're the stories of our first-generation traditional, or direct-entry, midwives.

I feel it's important for the young girls to know the old girls' tales—the tales of those first-generation midwives, the far-seeing and formidable women who went so boldly before us and by their blood, sweat, and tears brought homebirth midwifery back to life. The training of many of these women was informal at best; they gained their knowledge and skill hardscrabble, sometimes from "friendly doctors," as Ina May says, other times with textbooks in one hand and medical dictionaries in the other. They always had the mothers and babies before them, the midwife's truest and most faithful teachers. These women had to scratch and claw their way to both proficiency and validity as midwives, with their relationship with the law and the medical system a tenuous one—often even a threatening one. They were continually forced to stretch the limits of resourcefulness in order to obtain the basic tools required to practice safely and effectively, but the gem hidden within that reality is it allowed them to sculpt their philosophies and expressions of practice to best suit the needs and desires of families they served.

I'm a second-generation midwife, and, as such, was spared the bulk of the grueling obstacles the old girls, those inimitably wise and brave girls, faced. By evading the worst of first-generation homebirth midwifery practice impediments, I was able to focus on and further the rich heritage gained and shared by those courageous women. And I went further indeed—going so far as to train my home-born daughter into a thriving midwifery career of her own! A third generation!

There are lots of other wonderful midwifery books out there, and I love and recommend most of them, but I choose to leave you with these. These I feel best recall and honor the roots of modern-day traditional midwifery. If you're contemplating a plunge into midwifery yourself, I urge you to unearth copies of these gems. Read them, absorb them, and allow them to lay the foundation you'll stand upon as a third or fourth generation midwife. Allow them to work their magic upon *you*.

1. *Heart and Hands: A Midwife's Guide to Pregnancy and Birth* by Elizabeth Davis
2. *Special Delivery* by Rahima Baldwin Dancy
3. *Spiritual Midwifery* by Ina May Gaskin
4. *The Birth Book* by Raven Lang

5. *Why Not Me? The Story of Gladys Milton, Midwife* by Wendy Bovard and Gladys Milton
6. *Motherwit: An Alabama Midwife's Story* by Onnie Lee Logan and Katherine Clark
7. *Silent Knife* by Lois J. Estner and Nancy Wainer Cohen
8. *Open Season* by Nancy Wainer Cohen
9. *Immaculate Deception* by Suzanne Arms
10. *Homebirth* by Sheila Kitzinger
11. *Becoming a Midwife* by Carolyn Steiger
12. *Into These Hands* by Geradine Simkins

Finally, join the Midwives Alliance of North America (MANA) and your state's midwifery group. There you'll meet a great many birth workers—midwives, doulas, apprentices, client advocates, photographers, and even mother-baby relevant retailers. Consider beginning with doula work.

Cultivate nourishing relationships as you attend classes, conferences, and events, and see where they lead you.

Blessings!

ACKNOWLEDGMENTS

I'M UNSPEAKABLY GRATEFUL FOR THE MIDWIVES, the wise women, who invested their knowledge, their skills, their wisdom, their time, and their hearts in me, especially Susan Rusk, Janice Marsh-Prelesnik, Laurie Zoyiopoulos, Patrice Bobier, Yolanda Visser, and, of course my preceptor and my own midwife, Jean Balm. Thank you, ladies, for showing me the way and for enveloping me in an environment of nourishment and inspiration as I learned and grew into my calling.

Jean Balm is, per her request, a pseudonym.

Within these pages, you've read about the births of one hundred twenty-nine babies. Some of the births are only briefly mentioned, while others are described in full. Every single one of them possesses a special place in my heart. I will never get over the fact I've been allowed within so many sacred and irreplaceable moments. It's impossible for me to adequately express my gratitude for the generosity and grace the families of those babies shared with me.

Most of the names of the families whose tales I tell in this book have been changed. A measure of the particulars surrounding the tellings of their tales has been mildly scrambled as well. Everything described within these pages occurred, however.

Within these pages, you read of my metamorphosis from babe to girl, from girl to woman, from woman to wife and mother and midwife. Numberless souls played a part in that transformation, but, naturally, there are those whose role was distinctive. I love and appreciate without bounds the Banfield and Hazlett families, especially my parents, Durrell and Mary Banfield; my sister, Kris Ratkos; my aunt, Kathy Shaw; my grandmother, Helen Banfield; my grandfather, John Hazlett; the Woodard and Van Camp families, my families "in-grace," as Larry liked to say, especially Larry and Patricia Woodard; Nan McCallum, the vivacious woman who fired my imagination with her songs and stories and stash of books; Ann Piper, sadly, gone now from this world, my far-seeing middle-school math tutor whose nonintrusive friendship provided a life raft for me to cling to amidst very troubled times; Liz (Warner) Bebeau, another life-raft-toting friend from middle school; Karen (Scherf) Sitts, the woman of infinitely tender heart who introduced me to the idea of homebirth and midwifery; Linda Carol Williams and Julianna Witte, a pair of sisters who colored my view of life with the beautiful ways they lived and loved their families; and Rod Reid, Dan Siedlecki, Dave Van Horn, and Ken Witte, the team of men who helped my folks take my education, my character, and my spiritual development in hand.

Every one of those vital souls entered my life just in the nick of time.

I would also like to acknowledge Fred McGlone, Harry Wilson, and Jim Ryckman, the trio who rose to help Larry Woodard call forth and let loose the man within the boy, Brent Woodard. A significant part in how far and how fast he flew is theirs.

Many thanks to Norma Yoder, my client and friend, who helped me with the southern Michigan/northern Indianan brand of "Pennsylvania *Deutsch*" I sprinkled throughout the text; Steven Osterholzer, my husband and first editor, for demanding my best efforts as I labored to write this story; Cindy Lambert, my second editor, for catching a whiff of its potential and promoting me to Wes Yoder; Wes Yoder, my agent, for bending his ear to Cindy and yielding to her insistence he take me on; Salem Books for catching Wes's enthusiasm and daring to take a chance on a brand-new author; and Gary Terashita, my third editor, for grasping the vision and spirit of this book and polishing it till it gleamed.

Thank you, God! I'm such an outrageously blessed woman!